Data Analytics for Business

T0300507

We are drowning in data but are starved for knowledge. Data Analytics is the discipline of extracting actionable insights by structuring, processing, analysing and visualising data using methods and software tools. Hence, we gain knowledge by understanding the data. A roadmap to achieve this is encapsulated in the knowledge discovery in databases (KDD) process. Databases help us store data in a structured way. The structure query language (SQL) allows us to gain first insights about business opportunities. Visualising the data using business intelligence tools and data science languages deepens our understanding of the key performance indicators and business characteristics. This can be used to create relevant classification and prediction models; for instance, to provide customers with the appropriate products or predict the eruption time of geysers. Machine learning algorithms help us in this endeavour. Moreover, we can create new classes using unsupervised learning methods, which can be used to define new market segments or group customers with similar characteristics. Finally, artificial intelligence allows us to reason under uncertainty and find optimal solutions for business challenges. All these topics are covered in this book with a hands-on process, which means we use numerous examples to introduce the concepts and several software tools to assist us. Several interactive exercises support us in deepening the understanding and keep us engaged with the material.

This book is appropriate for master students but can also be used for undergraduate students. Practitioners will also benefit from the readily available tools. The material was especially designed for Business Analytics degrees with a focus on Data Science and can also be used for machine learning or artificial intelligence classes. This entry-level book is ideally suited for a wide range of disciplines wishing to gain actionable data insights in a practical manner.

Wolfgang Garn is an Associate Professor at the University of Surrey. His research interests are in the areas of artificial intelligence, machine learning, operational research and business analytics. He is the CEO and founder of Smartana, which offers SMART analytics solutions and consulting services to businesses.

Data Analytics for Business

AI-ML-PBI-SQL-R

Wolfgang Garn

Routledge
Taylor & Francis Group

LONDON AND NEW YORK

Smartana

First published 2024
by Routledge
4 Park Square, Milton Park, Abingdon, Oxon OX14 4RN

and by Routledge
605 Third Avenue, New York, NY 10158

Routledge is an imprint of the Taylor & Francis Group, an informa business

British Library Cataloguing-in-Publication Data
A catalogue record for this book is available from the British Library

Library of Congress Cataloging-in-Publication Data
Names: Garn, Wolfgang, author.
Title: Data analytics for business : AI, ML, PBI, SQL, R / Wolfgang Garn.
Description: Abingdon, Oxon ; New York, NY : Routledge, 2024. |
   Includes bibliographical references and index.
Identifiers: LCCN 2023044907 | ISBN 9781032372631 (hardback) |
   ISBN 9781032372624 (paperback) | ISBN 9781003336099 (ebook)
Subjects: LCSH: Management—Statistical methods. | Management—Data processing. |
   Database management.
Classification: LCC HD30.215 .G37 2024 | DDC 658.4/033—dc23/eng/20230927
LC record available at https://lccn.loc.gov/2023044907

ISBN: 9781032372631 (hbk)
ISBN: 9781032372624 (pbk)
ISBN: 9781003336099 (ebk)

DOI: 10.4324/9781003336099

Typeset in Optima
by Apex CoVantage, LLC

Access the Support Material: www.routledge.com/9781032372631

Contents

Preface

P.R. Halmos stated, "Audience, level, and treatment – a description of such matters is what prefaces are supposed to be about".

This book has been initiated to support a module which is taught annually to about 120 students at the University of Surrey. *Data Analytics for Business* introduces essential tools and techniques. There are plenty of books about Data Analytics and Data Science available. This book differentiates itself by providing a practical introduction to databases and Business Intelligence tools. Furthermore, it includes a comprehensive chapter about artificial intelligence. Of course, it covers the important area of Machine Learning.

The prerequisites are minimal – GCSE maths and the wish to gain business insights analytically. Of course, a pre-existing computer science, mathematics or finance background may be helpful but it is not required.

This book is intended for PG students for a Business Analytics programme (course). However, the introductions plus a focus on essential applications allow it to be a supporting text for Master of Business Administration (MBA) classes. Yet, the material goes into depth, which makes it interesting to a more technically inclined audience. Thus, it should be of interest to Data Science programmes and more generally to Computer Science courses. For instance, modules (classes) such as Machine Learning, AI and Databases can benefit from this text. This material is tailored in such a way that it can be taught within one semester. However, it may be better to split the material into two or three semesters. The material is arranged so that parts of each chapter can be covered within nine lectures, each lasting two hours, with an additional two hours in the computer laboratory. If the module is taught over two semesters, then the first five chapters should be in the first semester and the remaining four in the second semester. The material could be split into three parts, allowing for more discussion and practice time. In this case, the first four chapters can be covered in Part One, followed by Chapters 5 to 7, and – as the final part – Chapters 8 and 9. A common understanding and overview of the theory, techniques and tools can be provided in the lectures. The laboratory sessions shall focus on solving business challenges and using software packages and coding languages. To be more specific, the lab sessions introduce MySQL, Power BI, RStudio and R.

I am confident that practitioners will find this book equally useful. I am always keen to improve the material and to answer any questions or provide feedback to the interested reader. So please feel free to contact me: w.garn@surey.ac.uk or wolfgang.garn@smartana.co.uk.

Wolfgang Garn
Surrey, August, 2023

Acknowledgements

The content of this book has grown over several years. Its origins go back to the founding of the Business Analytics programme. Hence, I would like to acknowledge Professor James Aitken for his continuous support in this process. The actual backbone for this book is the Data Analytics module, which I have been teaching with Dr Vikas Grover. Our discussions encouraged me to have a closer look at various topics such as the knowledge discovery process, regressions and many other topics. Professor Nick Ryman-Tubb is a true inspiration. We had endless detailed discussions about machine learning and artificial intelligence. I hope that I captured some aspects of it in this book. Dr Andy Hill opened my eyes to colour theory, story-telling and the importance of good visuals. There are many more people at my University who need to be thanked for creating such a stimulating environment.

I am grateful to my Data Analytics students for showing me which topics are enjoyable, challenging and beneficial. Many of them have secured jobs in the area of Data Analytics, and I am always glad when I hear back from them. Teaching – business analytics (including data analytics) – to MBA students produced many engaging conversations and motivated me to elaborate on the managers' views within the book. So, thanks to them, there are several interesting bit-sized challenges in the Business Intelligence chapter.

In the construction of this book, there were many supportive people. I would like to acknowledge Andre Cardoso and the Mix and Jam Channel for creating the Jammo character and permitting us to feature it on the title page. If you are into game development, the assets and channel are beneficial. I would like to acknowledge Paul Andlinger and DB-Engines (db-engines.com) from the Solid IT Consulting & Software Development GMBH for allowing us to use their figures and tables about the popularity of databases.

There are many authors of books, blogs and articles I would like to thank. They can easily be identified by looking into the reference section. Names, like Paul Wilmott, Chirag Shah, Gareth James, Trevor Hastie, Rob Tibshirani, Daniela Witten, Andy Field, Steven Brunton, Nathan Kutz, Peter Norvig, Stuart Russell, Jeremy Watt, Reza Borhani, Aggelos Katsaggelos, Andriy Burkov and many more will come up.

Finally, I want to offer my heartfelt thanks to my wife Marisol Garn and my children Dominic and Michael for their love, support and understanding while I wrote this book.

ONE

Fundamental Business Insights

Databases and Business Intelligence are tools needed to gain fundamental business insights. The Structured Query Language allows extracting useful business data from databases. Business Intelligence (BI) tools such Power BI offer interactive visualisations and analyses of business data.

1. Introduction

1.1 Data Analytics and Applications

What is Data Analytics?

What would you like to get out of Data Analytics? Data processing, data mining, tools, data structuring, data insights and data storage are typical first responses. So, we definitely want to analyse, manipulate, visualise and learn about tools to help us in this endeavour. We do not want to analyse the data for the sake of analysing it; the insights need to be actionable for businesses, organisations or governments. How do we achieve this? The process of discovering knowledge in databases and CRISP-DM helps us with this. Of course, we need to know about databases. There are tools such as Power BI which allow us to transform, analyse and visualise data. So we are "analysing" the data – analysing ranges from formulating a data challenge in words to writing a simple structured query and up to applying mathematical methods to extract knowledge. Of course, the "fun" part is reflected in state-of-the-art methods implemented in data mining tools. But in Data Analytics, your mind is set to ensure your findings are actionable and relevant to the business. For instance, can we: find trading opportunities, figure out the most important products, identify relevant quality aspects and many more so that

DOI: 10.4324/9781003336099-2

the management team can devise actions that benefit the business? This motivates the following definition:

Data Analytics is the discipline of extracting actionable insights by structuring, processing, analysing and visualising data using methods and software tools.

Where does Data Analytics "sit" in the area of Business Analytics? Often, Data Analytics is mentioned in conjunction with Business Analytics. Data Analytics can be seen as part of Business Analytics. Business Analytics also includes Operational Analytics. It has become fashionable to divide analytics into Descriptive, Predictive, and Prescriptive Analytics. Sometimes these terms are further refined by adding Diagnostic and Cognitive Analytics. What is what?

Descriptive Analytics – as the term suggests – is about describing the data. For instance, to show key performance indicators (KPIs) about the current state of a business, such as the sales volume, the production throughput or the customer satisfaction level. So it focuses on historical data, i.e. it answers the question "What has happened?".

Predictive Analytics is about learning from the data to derive a model that is able to predict and classify. This can be used for forecasting or evaluating new scenarios. Here are some examples: determining anticipated sales volume, forecasting the demand for products, predictive maintenance, foreseeing the likelihood of a customer churning, direct/targeted marketing, suggesting products for cross-selling, recommending a movie for a customer, credit card fraud detection and credit risk assessment. Predictive Analytics tells us what will happen.

Prescriptive Analytics provides optimal decisions given a challenge. Examples are the optimal production strategy, optimal supply quantities, minimising transportation costs, maximising sales profit and many more. Prescriptive Analytics states what shall happen.

Diagnostic Analytics aims to provide reasons for observed circumstances. It deals with identifying outliers and tries to detect anomalies. It also investigates the correlation of variables. Often, Diagnostic Analytics is seen as part of Descriptive Analytics.

Cognitive Analytics (CA) – in the year 2023 – is still in its infancy. One of the aims is to integrate AI and to be more humanlike. That means Cognitive Analytics may assume that all knowledge is known and available – not just the business data under study, which enables CA to know the likely context of data. The dictionary definition states that *cognitive* involves conscious intellectual activity such as thinking, reasoning or remembering. Explainable AI may become part of CA. Some authors state deep learning neural networks as CA. Natural Language Processing (NLP) is often associated with CA. Tools such as Apache Lucene Core (text search engine), GPText (statistical text analysis), SyntaxNet (NN framework for understanding natural language), Parsey McParseface (SyntaxNet for English), NuPIC (cognitive computing platform), OpenCV and ImageJ for visual recognition are associated with CA (Kaur, 2022).

The main focus of Data Analytics was Descriptive and Predictive Analytics but has begun to include Diagnostic and Cognitive Analytics. However, Prescriptive Analytics remains associated with Operational Analytics (aka Operational Research or Management Science).

The next paragraphs give several applications and examples of Data Analytics.

Applications

Organisations are typically divided into the functional units of operations, marketing, finance and administration. Administration may be further divided into customer services and human resources. These functional units can manifest themselves in departments. All these departments use (or could use) Data Analytics. Applications of Data Analytics for operations are forecasting demand, analysing inventory, machine utilisation, purchase recommendations and others. Examples of marketing utilising Data Analytics for marketing are targeted marketing, cross-selling and discovering shopping habits. Finance applications are profit (revenue, cost) insights, setting prices, credit scoring and fraud detection. Some applications of Data Analytics for administration are customer behaviour, workforce performance and employee turnover and retention. This motivates the benefits and shows the scope of Data Analytics.

The learning outcomes and prominent data mining techniques are mentioned in Section 1.2. This also gives an idea of how solutions are obtained for Data Analytics challenges. Section 1.3 gives an overview of essential software tools useful to data analysts. It also tells us "where to start from" and "where to go to by mentioning prominent data sources, data competitions, conferences, books and journals. Finally, we sketch out the remainder of the "journey" (book).

1.2 Learning Outcomes

The intended learning outcomes are:

- Analyse, evaluate and create databases;
- Visualise and evaluate data using a methodical analytical approach;
- Build customised data analytics solutions;
- Apply knowledge discovery processes to create data insights;
- Compare important data mining algorithms and techniques;
- Apply, analyse and evaluate state-of-the-art methods;
- Assess and propose classification and prediction models;
- Synthesis Artificial Intelligence to gain insights;
- Communicate and demonstrate Data Analytics to the management for decision-making.

Typically, businesses and organisations keep data in databases. It is important to know about them in general and to be able to extract relevant data. Therefore, it is necessary to learn how to translate business questions into the structure query language. This enables us to extract and analyse data. Often, the analysis of data continues using Business Intelligence tools and Data Science languages. The corresponding tools integrate several useful methods. For instance, we will learn about trend lines, forecasts and key influencers. There are well-established guidelines on how to approach Data Analytics projects. In this book, the knowledge discovery process in databases and the cross-industry standard process for data mining are discussed. Classifications and predictions are key to machine learning. Prediction techniques such as regression trees, random forest and linear regression will be introduced. Examples of classification methods covered in this text are logistic regression, classification trees and nearest neighbours. State-of-the-art methods include neural networks, self-organising maps and support vector machines. We will introduce the machine learning process to embed the above in an overarching framework. On top of all these essential techniques, we will learn about Artificial Intelligence and its applications and even show how to create a chess program.

1.3 Tools and Data

We will focus on using the following:

- MySQL for dealing with databases;
- Power BI for gaining data insights;
- R (with RStudio) as a Data Science language for all kinds of Data Analytics challenges.

MySQL is the most prominent open-source database system. Hence, it is used in many industries and serves them as a primary tool for data storage. The affiliated Structured Query Language allows us to analyse the data to gain actionable data insights. Here, we are mainly in the diagnostic and descriptive analytics domain. Business Intelligence tools such as Power BI allow us to link to MySQL and visualise and evaluate the data to solve business challenges. Power BI is suitable for presenting Data Analytics insights to a wider audience including management. These insights can be tailored to support decision-making in a business context. In addition to the diagnostic and analytics domain, we are covering the predictive analytics domain. In theory, we could integrate prescriptive and cognitive analytics into this tool using Data Science languages such as R. R allows us to apply, evaluate and compare state-of-the-art data mining algorithms. R covers all analytics domains. We can design, develop and create software, analyses and reports for any purpose.

Data and tutorials

Here is a non-exhaustive list showing several websites, which provide datasets and tutorials relevant to Data Analytics.

- **W3schools** (w3schools.com/sql) – includes a thorough introduction to SQL with many examples and an interactive environment.
- **Kaggle** (kaggle.com) – has a huge repository of data and code and hosts competitions for data scientists.
- **KDnuggets** (kdnuggets.com) – Knowledge Discovery Nuggets (KDnuggets) covers Business Analytics, data mining and Data Science, providing many resources.
- **Smartana** (smartana.org) – Smart Analytics (Smartana) provides tools, data and tutorials relevant to Business, Operational and Data Analytics. It has an interactive tutorial tailored for this book.
- **An Introduction to Statistical Learning** (statlearning.com) – The authors provide free comprehensive books and various related videos.

Within the individual chapters, we will provide more references and links to data sources and complementing tutorials.

Structure

This book is structured into four parts. In the first part, fundamental business insights are obtained by extracting relevant data from databases and visualising it with business intelligence tools. The second part provides the background to take data analyses to the next level. It introduces coding to develop customised Data Analytics tools. Furthermore, frameworks are discussed to guide through the process of Data Analytics projects. This includes a detailed machine learning roadmap, which can be used when coding in the data science language R. The third part is all about the details of learning. Here, we consider supervised and unsupervised learning. Predictions and classification models are learned and applied to various business challenges. Finally, artificial intelligence is introduced, which provides a new dimension to Data Analytics. Here, we look at neural networks to complement the learning aspects. We even offer problem-solving approaches such as genetic algorithms, which can be used for all kinds of challenges.

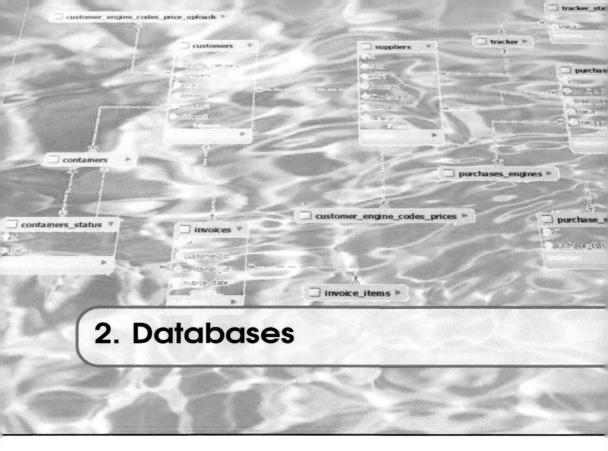

2. Databases

2.1 Introduction

2.1.1 Overview

This chapter introduces databases and the Structured Query Language (SQL). Most of today's data is stored in databases within tables. In order to gain knowledge and make valuable business decisions, it is necessary to extract information efficiently. This is achieved using the *Structured Query Language*. Good relational databases avoid repetitive data using standard normalisation approaches: for instance, by splitting raw data into multiple tables. These tables (=entities) are linked (=related) using business rules. Structured queries make use of entity relationships to obtain data. This is one of the fundamental concepts of data mining of structured data.

We work towards the following learning outcomes:

- Being able to analyse data using a methodical analytical approach;
- Having familiarity with important data mining techniques.

Section 2.2 mentions popular database systems and businesses using them. The setup and practicalities of database systems are also explained in this section. Section 2.3

DOI: 10.4324/9781003336099-3

shows how to create tables using SQL. Section 2.4. shows how to write SQL queries and provide views on tables. Entity relationships between tables are discussed in Section 2.5.

2.1.2 Motivation and Managers

Here, we will discuss databases and their relevance to the management level. Typically, data analysts report to managers. Hence, this section may help data analysts communicate insights to their managers. It may also help managers better understand data analysts. Further, this section motivates the importance of database systems.

Can Managers Use SQL for Decision Making?

My guess is that 95% of managers do not have the "luxury" of using SQL because of the time required to get to know the database. On one hand, we are stating that managers and businesses should make data-driven decisions. On the other hand, most managers and businesses may lack the time or capability to do this within databases. In most situations, managers will not be able to set aside the time to familiarise themselves with the available and needed raw data. So, they rely on analysts to prepare the data in graphs and the analysts' suggestions. That means analysts are preparing and visualising data and guiding the decisions on behalf of managers. However, the gap is closing between analysts and managers due to Business Intelligence tools. In summary, I would recommend that a manager of a large or medium-size company not use SQL for decision making directly, but rather indirectly, via analysts and Business Intelligence (BI) reports.

How Does SQL Help in Preparing Decisions?

Descriptive Analytics can be achieved with databases. That means the earlier examples concerning key performance indicators (KPIs) of the current state of a business, such as sales volume, production throughput and the customer satisfaction level, can be answered by querying the database using SQL. A manager does not have to specify details, but once the analyst is querying the data, he needs to add precision to the manager's statement. For instance, if the manager asks, "What is the sales volume?" the analyst will immediately ask, "Why do you want to know?" Because, without further specification, millions of sales records over time will be needed to provide the answer. However, most likely the reasons for the sales volume request are:

- To see which products have done better in the last quarter (month, week);
- To get an idea of whether the demand is rising or falling;
- To trigger actions such as market analysis, marketing campaign, etc.;

9

- To restock the inventory;
- To start/stop/plan production;
- To invest and employ people.

Hence, the SQL statements can extract and prepare relevant business data, which can be used for decision making (often after visualisation).

Why Do I need to Know about Databases?

Why are databases important for businesses?

We are living in an age in which we drown in data and starve for knowledge. The data volume puts managers and analysts in the position of doing data-driven decision making (DDDM), which means making organisational decisions based on actual data, rather than intuition or observations. As a manager, it is important to know the extent to which data availability can help the decision-making process. As an analyst, the data's limitations for providing business insights are important to acknowledge.

The huge amount of data stems from corporations' dependency on it for their daily business activities. Hence, database systems were established to assist with this endeavour. These activities are often placed in one of four categories: (1) operations, (2) marketing (sales), (3) finance and (4) human resources. These are supported by information systems accessing operations data, customer (sales, marketing) data, financial data and human resource data.

One needs to be careful that data is recorded correctly. "Bad" data lead to wrong decisions. Here, "bad" can mean incorrect, faulty, insufficient, wrong or non-existent. A phrase commonly used by analysts is "Rubbish in, rubbish out".

Unbelievably, cleaning and organising data can take up to 80% of the time of an analyst. Surveys from Kaggle and Figure Eight (Crowd-flower) give a more detailed breakdown – varying from year to year and becoming less, but still in the range of 25%. The point is that if data is prepared well already, the time for analyses can be reduced significantly. This, in turn, means managers' data-driven decision making can be accelerated by improving data quality in the organisation.

If you are a CTO, COO or manager or you are in a management role depending on a strategic unit such as Business Intelligence, then you could state that an organisation can thrive on data by employing the right people. Which roles deal with the databases? Data engineer, data manager, data analyst and data scientist.

Who Needs Databases?

Indirectly, via a frontend, customers may do their shopping online, which generates customer records and transactions. These are saved in databases. Another example is a purchase manager storing supplier data. Achievements of a sales agent can be recorded in a database, as well as marketing records such as surveys. The finance department needs a database to record and analyse its accounting information. Operations needs to know the demand for production, which is based on historic data stored in databases. Human resources needs to store employee information and records. In summary, people across the entire business rely on a database (or several databases) in the background. Often, these database users are unaware of the database's existence because another system (e.g. an ERP system) is in between.

Strategic analyses – are they based on live data or historic data? Should they be? Live is current but may affect daily operations. Hence, I would recommend doing strategic analysis on an offline database (e.g. a snapshot/extract of the live database) using historic data. Business Intelligence tools offer this opportunity but also allow direct queries. We will discuss this further in the Business Intelligence chapter.

Most people use Excel Maps: for instance, HR to manage the employees and operations to do their planning. Should you encourage them to use databases? Advantages of using databases are consistency with regard to a predefined data structure and durability (e.g. when people leave the organisation) and recording the history. Disadvantages of databases are that IT is usually required for creation and adaption. There will be the need for a frontend. Furthermore, the data structure will be predetermined and, hence, will become inflexible to small changes. Using different data sources gives you more "flexibility".

What are the advantages/disadvantages of an SQL database instead? The advantage are well-defined data, ease of query, the fact that changes can be recorded and the independence of "individuals". The disadvantage is that updating may require interface, which will cost the company additional resources. The decision to switch to a relation database or stay with heterogeneous data sources needs to consider the trade-off between data flexibility and consistency.

Why do managers get inconsistent reports? Sometimes, different departments use different data sources. It can be as simple as an inconsistent date range being used. Even using the same data range, retrospective or delayed data updates can cause inconsistencies, which I observed during my time at Telekom Austria. Let us summarise some issues of not having a database:

- Data silos for each department, such as operations, sales, finance and others;
- Each department has its own set of data – sharing;
- Heterogeneous data sources – data cannot be linked;
- Excel maps – many different versions, many different people, inconsistency through sharing;
- Data may fall into the wrong "hands" – data security;
- Data gets lost.

Hence, databases may be the answer to resolve these issues.

2.1.3 Database Integration and Cloud Solutions

Does a database "integrate" with other systems such as enterprise resource planning (ERP), customer relationship management (CRM) and website? With hardly any exception, those systems rely on a database in the background. In fact, most systems, including manufacturing execution system (MES), warehouse management systems (WMS) and transportation management systems (TMS) are based on databases. Let me mention a few popular systems and their databases. JD Edwards (ERP) uses the Oracle database. *Enterprise resource planning* integrates business activities such as marketing, operations, human resources and finance into a single system (software) with a common database. JD Edwards was bought by People Soft in 2003 for $1.8bn and was then taken over by Oracle in 2005. Microsoft Dynamics (ERP and CRM) is often used in conjunction with the SQL Server but offers a common data service (CDS) "MS Dataverse". The CDS can include other databases. On 11 June 2002, Navision (part of MS Dynamics) was acquired by Microsoft for $1.45bn. SAP has its HANA database but allows other databases; again, Oracle is prominent here. SAP is the most classic – historically important – example. The previous examples illustrate that frontend database solutions are extremely valued by organisations. However, they live and breathe because of their databases.

Should a database be inside the company building? If there might be fire or water damage, then an external location is beneficial. It is best to have backup servers in at least two different geographic locations.

Cloud-based databases are becoming more and more "fashionable". Here are five prominent ones:

1. Microsoft Azure SQL Database
2. Amazon Relational Database Service
3. Google Cloud SQL
4. IBM Db2 on Cloud
5. Oracle Database

Personally, I like using Digital Ocean for small enterprises which allows the installation and usage of various database systems. It is well suited for small enterprises because it is inexpensive and easy to administer and offers sufficient resources.

2.1.4 Security, Ethics and Law

Often, databases contain confidential information about customers, staff, account holders and suppliers. They also contain vital data about the business or corporation, including finance, services, marketing and others.

What are the legal responsibilities of a company (corporation etc.) to protect their database? This depends on where the company is situated. We will focus on the UK. In a nutshell, the company has to protect the data (database). The *General Data Protection Regulation* (GDPR) has seven key principles: lawfulness, fairness and transparency; purpose limitation; data minimisation; accuracy; storage limitation; integrity and confidentiality (security); and accountability. The bare minimum for the GDPR are files that detail data breach policy (including a log file), data protection compliance, data subject access requests, password policy and any non-compliance issues.

Your business *"must make sure the information is kept secure, accurate and up to date"* (https://www.gov.uk/data-protection-your-business). If someone's personal data is recorded, the business must inform them how the personal information is used and whether the data is shared. Furthermore, each person has the right to see the information that is held about them, request the data deletion and request that the data not be used for certain purposes. A company can appoint data protection officers (DPOs), who are independent data protection experts, to ensure their data protection obligation. There is detailed information in the UK GDPR guide, hosted by the Information Commissioner's Office organisation.

2.2 Systems

2.2.1 Concept

A typical database system consists of a server, service, databases and a client.

database system = server + service + databases + client access
Database Management System (DBMS)   Database Engine

FIGURE 2.1 Database system.

The server is a computer, which is usually connected to the inter- or intranet. The server runs a software which handles the access to stored data. Here, the software is called database service, and the stored data are known as databases. Usually, a client connects to the server, which runs the database service to query data. A *database* is a structured collection of data – often with an underlying relational model. The database service offers a simplified language to query data, which is known as *Structured Query Language* (SQL). It also manages access and synchronisation issues for multiple clients. A client allows one user to "communicate" with the server to control one or several databases.

The term database is often used for any component of the database system, and context is used to identify whether it is the server, service, the "actual" database or the client. This will be adapted in this text occasionally.

2.2.2 Database Engines

Some of the most popular commercial database services are Microsoft SQL Server, Oracle, and IBM's DB2. These are often used by large companies. Two non-commercial database services are PostgreSQL and MySQL, which are widespread.

Figure 2.2 shows the development of commercial and open-source database services over a period of ten years.

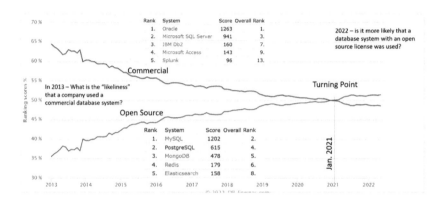

FIGURE 2.2 Commercial versus open-source license database services.
Source: Adapted from DB-Engines.

We can see that in 2013, it was more likely for a commercial database to be used. Commercial database services had a ranking score of 65% whilst open-source companies had 35%. The ranking scores were adapted from db-engines.com (*DB-Engines Ranking*, 2023), where the score definitions can be found. January 2021 was the turning point, where the ranking score changed in favour of the open-source database services. That means in 2022–2023, it was more likely for a company to use a service with an open-source licence. These figures also show the top five commercial and open-source databases. Figure 2.3 is a snapshot from db-engines.com of the top ten database systems.

PostgreSQL* is used by numerous famous organisations, such as:

- Uber, Netflix, Instagram, Spotify;
- Twitch, Reddit, IMDb, TripAdvisor;
- Yahoo, Myspace, Skype, Apple;
- OpenStreetMap, Sony Online, Sun;
- The International Space Station.

MySQL has also several prominent organisations behind it, such as Facebook, YouTube, Wikipedia, X (formerly known as Twitter) and many more.

Rank			DBMS	Database Model	Score		
May 2022	Apr 2022	May 2021			May 2022	Apr 2022	May 2021
1.	1.	1.	Oracle	Relational, Multi-model	1262.82	+8.90	-7.12
2.	2.	2.	MySQL	Relational, Multi-model	1202.10	-2.06	-34.28
3.	3.	3.	Microsoft SQL Server	Relational, Multi-model	941.20	+2.74	-51.46
4.	4.	4.	PostgreSQL	Relational, Multi-model	615.29	+0.83	+56.04
5.	5.	5.	MongoDB	Document, Multi-model	478.24	-5.14	-2.78
6.	6.	↑7.	Redis	Key-value, Multi-model	179.02	+1.41	+16.85
7.	↑8.	↓6.	IBM Db2	Relational, Multi-model	160.32	-0.13	-6.34
8.	↓7.	8.	Elasticsearch	Search engine, Multi-model	157.69	-3.14	+2.34
9.	9.	↑10.	Microsoft Access	Relational	143.44	+0.66	+28.04
10.	10.	↓9.	SQLite	Relational	134.73	+1.94	+8.04

FIGURE 2.3 DB-engines.com – database systems ranking.
Source: DB-Engines

Both PostgreSQL and MySQL have also been widely adapted by the industry because of their ease of setup. MySQL in particular has a reputation for being useful in conjunction with websites.

NoSQL (not only SQL) database systems such as Neo4J and Mon-goDB are gaining more attention; one prominent user is Google.

We will focus on MySQL and PostgreSQL because of their widespread use.

2.2.3 Setup and Configuration

Figure 2.4 illustrates the usual setup of database systems.

Let us look at the PostgreSQL database system. A server identified by its IP address or hostname runs an operating system based on Unix (Ubuntu, AIX, Linux) or Windows. The OS runs the PostgreSQL service. A client computer can connect via the internet (or intranet) to the server. In order to achieve this, the server's and client's firewalls need to allow communication via port 5432. A port can be imagined as a "door" which allows the data to flow in and out to the registered service. The client runs a program known

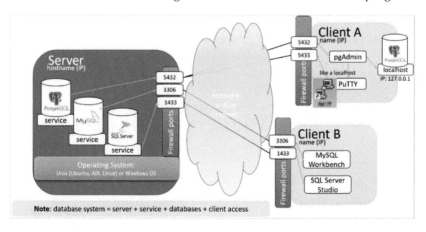

FIGURE 2.4 Setup of database systems.

as pgAdmin to connect to the server. Developers, researchers or micro businesses may choose to run the client and server software on one computer. For instance, client A may have a local installation of the database service. Here, the server's IP address is identified as 127.0.0.1 and localhost as hostname. In case client A requires multiple PostgreSQL service connections (e.g. remote and local or several remote severs), you can use PuTTY to redirect via multiple receiving ports.

A MySQL system can be set up similarly to the Postgres system. That means you install and start a MySQL service on a server. Next, you need to ensure the firewall allows connections on port 1433. Then install the software MySQL Workbench on the client computer, again ensuring that the firewall allows connections.

Figure 2.5 demonstrates the essential steps for an actual database system setup.

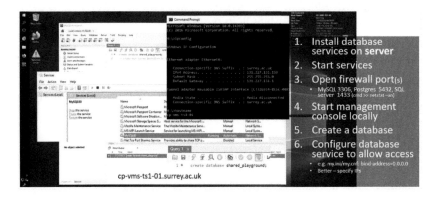

FIGURE 2.5 Database system setup in reality.

It gives a snapshot of the database server running on a Windows OS. The command prompt window shows the hostname, cp-vms-ts1–01.surrey.ac.uk, and the IP address, 131.227.131.159, displayed by the commands `hostname` and `ipconfig` respectively. The services app shows that the MySQL service (MySQL80) is running. In the background, we see the client software MySQL Workbench, including a query ready to create a database called "shared_playground".

MySQL Service Installation

Here are the steps to install, start and test a MySQL service for the first time on your computer.

1. Download MySQL server: `https://dev.mysql.com/downloads/mysql/`;
2. Extract zip file to a folder of your choice [usually `C:/mysql`];
3. `Start » cmd » cd C:/mysql » mysqld` – initialize (note password for root or recover it from *.err file in `C:\mysql\data`);

4. ALTER USER `'root'@'localhost'` IDENTIFIED BY `'your root password'`;

5. Start MySQL service » mysqld – console;

6. Connect via MySQL Workbench to test the connection.

Connecting via MySQL Workbench

First, log in to a client computer. Next, start the MySQL Workbench and add a connection via Windows Start » MySQL Workbench and click + ⊕, which is next to MySQL Connections text (Figure 2.6). Now, set up a new connection. We will use the following five input fields to connect via the MySQL Workbench to the MySQL Server.

- Connection name: [your username];
- Hostname: localhost;
- Username: [your username];
- Password: [your username] and a dot;
- Default Schema*: [your database].

Test the new connection. You should get a message such as the one displayed in Figure 2.7. Once the OK button is pressed, the MySQL Workbench working environment appears (Figure 2.8).

FIGURE 2.6 MySQL Workbench start-up window.

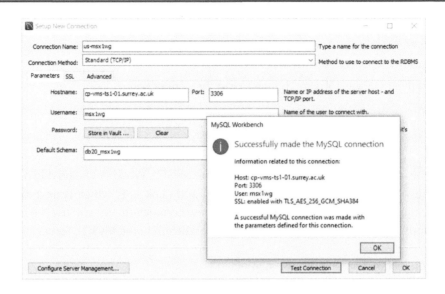

FIGURE 2.7 MySQL Workbench – set up new connection.

FIGURE 2.8 MySQL Workbench – work environment.

2.2.4 *Databases*

Database Examples

Several MySQL sample databases are available, such as world, sakila and others (see Table 2.1). You can find most of them as zip files at: `https://dev.mysql.com/doc/index-other.html`. After downloading and extracting the zip file, you can find an

SQL file, which can be opened with any text editor. `Wiki.postgresql.org/wiki/Sample_Databases` lists several PostgreSQL databases.

Database Export and Import

Existing databases can be exported (e.g. as database backup) and imported via the MySQL Workbench via Server » Data Export and Server » Data Import. Note that the MySQL administrator has to grant this privilege to the users (e.g., xy) by running **GRANT** `PROCESS`**, SELECT ON** `*.*` **TO** `'xy'@'%'` in the MySQL Workbench.

Example 2.2.1 (World database). In this example, we will download the data, create a database and import the data. Begin by downloading the world database (i.e. world-db.zip), which contains the file `world.sql` using the link from the beginning of this subsection. Next, run the MySQL Workbench (see Section 2.2.3 for installation instructions) and open a connection (see Section 2.2.2). Now, a database can be created. Next, the world.sql needs to be opened and executed. This will create the `world` database.

TABLE 2.1 MySQL sample databases.

Database	Origin & Zip file	Size	Content	Origin
World	dev.mysql.com, world-db.zip	91kB	Countries, cities, etc.	Statistics Finland
Sakila	dev.mysql.com, sakila-db.zip	713kB	DVD rental store	Dell sample database, and D. Jaffe, R. Bradford and many more. (New BSD license)
Airport	dev.mysql.com, Airport-db.zip	625MB	Airports, flights, bookings, passengers, weather	Flughafen DB developed by Stefan Proell, Eva Zangerle, Wolfgang Gassler (CC license)
Menagerie	dev.mysql.com, menagerie-db.zip	4kB	Animals, pets	-
Employee	dev.mysql.com, Several files	168MB	Employees, salaries, departments	Fusheng Wang and Carlo Zaniolo at Siemens Corporate Research (CC license)
Classicmodels	www.mysqltutorial.org, mysqlsampledatabase.zip	54kB	Retailer of classic cars scale models	MySQL tutorial

SQL – Databases and Users

In this section, we will introduce fundamental SQL statements to create (drop) databases, schemas and users and show how to associate users with databases.

A database service administers one or several databases. A database is created with the following command, which can be undone by using the drop statement.

```
CREATE DATABASE db_name;
DROP DATABASE db_name;
```

A database has one or several schemas. A schema is like a subfolder. The following shows how to create and drop one.

```
CREATE SCHEMA schema_name;
DROP SCHEMA schema_name;
```

In MySQL, *schema* is a synonym for *database*. That means there is no need to create a schema. In PostgreSQL, a database can have several schemas in which "public" is the default schema.

A database needs to be associated with a database user. The database user is usually different from a Windows user. A database user needs to be identified by a password. A database user can stand for an individual (e.g. Wolfgang), a group (e.g. ITDepartment) or a function (e.g. ReadBI).

A user is created (dropped) via:

```
CREATE USER a_user IDENTIFIED BY 'your password';
DROP USER a_user;
```

The user is associated with a database including their rights (privileges) using:

```
GRANT ALL PRIVILEGES ON db_name.* TO username
GRANT SELECT ON db_name.* TO a_user;
REVOKE ALL PRIVILEGES ON db_name.* FROM a_user
```

You can change your password:

```
ALTER USER your_username IDENTIFIED BY 'new-password';
```

In PostgreSQL, replace IDENTIFIED **BY** with **WITH PASSWORD**.

Tip: once you have changed your password, disconnect from the server and log in again using the new password. This ensures that the client's workbench works as expected.

Exercise 2.1 (Set up a new database). We will create the database "movme" (short for movies for me), which can be accessed (for queries only) by all people.

```
create database movme; -- "movies for me"
create user mm4all identified by 'mm4all.'; -- for all
grant select on movme.* to mm4all; -- allow queries
```

A useful command to see all users is: **select** * **from** mysql.**user;** in MySQL and use: **SELECT** usename **FROM** pg_catalog.pg_user;

2.3 SQL – Tables

2.3.1 Definition

In this section, we will show table structure creation and changes to it. We will show several ways to insert records and remove them. We will also introduce normal forms of tables.

Roughly speaking, a table consists of rows and columns. A *table* is a named data structure defined by fields (i.e. columns). A *field* is defined by a name, its data type. Additionally, a field may contain a constraints or clauses. Typical data types are numeric (e.g. integer or double), date (e.g. datetime or time) and string (e.g. varchar or text). Often-used *constraints* are not-null, unique and primary key. A typical example of a field-clause is the specification of a default value.

Let us *create* an empty film table that will contain information about movies.

```
CREATE TABLE film
(id int primary key, -- unique identifier
     movie_name text not null, -- e.g. Avatar
     produced_by text,
     year_released int,
     production_company text,
     image_file text default 'placeholder.jpg');
```

This statement is easy to read. The first column is called id, which is commonly used as an abbreviation for identifier. In our table, the id is an integer (i.e. whole number) – abbreviated as **int**. It is almost always a good idea to introduce a primary key; this is

21

achieved by adding the attribute **primary key**. Generally, a primary key uniquely identifies the row. That means the *primary key* (PK) column is not null and unique; moreover, only one PK is allowed per table. It may be helpful to provide comments and examples for the columns. In the SQL code, a comment can be added using two dashes and a space (`-- my comment`). Our table also contains columns that specify the name of the movie, who produced it, the year it was released, the production company and the file name of the image. Here, we specified a default clause for the image file name. Images are often saved on the hard disk's file systems rather than within the database. (By the way, a table is also called *relation*, and a column is also known as an *attribute*.)

A table is removed (deleted) using the *drop* command: e.g., **drop table** `film;`

We can add a column or drop it using the *alter* command:

```
alter table film add trailer text;
alter table film drop trailer;
```

2.3.2 Inserting Records

The *insert* command adds records (rows) to an existing table. There are several ways to add data to tables using the insert command.

We begin by adding a single complete record to a table.

```
insert into film values
(1, 'Avatar: The Way of Water', 'James Cameron', '2022',
'Lightstorm Entertainment', 'Avatar_Water.jpg');
```

This kind of command is often triggered by frontends such as websites to add data.

We can insert multiple records as well:

```
insert into film (id, movie_name, year_released)
values
(2,'Indiana Jones and the Dial of Destiny',2023),
(3,'Oppenheimer',2023),
(4,'Guardians of the Galaxy Vol. 3',2023),
(5,'Ant-Man and the Wasp: Quantumania',2023);
```

This SQL statement inserts four records. Here, we had to specify the id and movie_name because of the primary key and not null constraints. Additionally, we provided the year released field. The unspecified fields will be assigned the default value.

Often, you will insert data from a query:

```
insert into my_table(my_col)
select my_col from another_table;
```

We will discuss queries in Section 2.4.

2.3.3 Deleting Records

A record can be removed from a table using the *delete* command.
Let us remove the record with identifier three:

```
delete from film where id = 3;
```

Next, the records with identifiers two and four are deleted from the film table:

```
delete from film where id in (2,4);
```

Now, we demonstrate how to remove an entire set of records using a logical condition.

```
delete from film where year_released = 2023;
```

Here, all records with release year 2023 are removed.

2.3.4 Normal Forms

Typically, a database has many tables which are related to each other. That means the tables are linked. Hence, we call them relational databases, which are most widely used, as we observed in Section 2.2. That means that rather than having one "large" table – common for machine learning – there are several "small" tables. The advantage of having several small tables is reduced storage space, consistent data and efficient modification (e.g. updating) of data. The "small" tables are achieved using normalisations. *Normalisation* is the process of structuring data and removing redundancy. Figure 2.8 shows various normal forms, which are stages of normalisation.

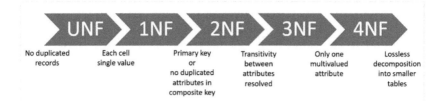

FIGURE 2.9 Normal forms – normalisation process.

UNF to 1NF

We begin the normalisation process with the *unnormalised form* (UNF). This represents a "large" table with potentially duplicated data and structural issues. However, even this table has been already processed such that no two rows are identical. The UNF is transformed into the *first normal form* (1NF) by ensuring that each cell in the table contains only a single value. Obviously, in the 1NF, each record (row) is unique.

Example 2.3.1 (UNF to 1NF). In Table 2.3, we have records of people who have watched certain movies. This table is in UNF because the movie column contains multiple films in a single cell.

Table 2.2 is transformed into 1NF by "repeating" rows (see Table 2.3). That means, at the moment, we are expanding the table size, which is contrary to our objective of creating several small tables. However, we achieve a better structure.

TABLE 2.2 Unnormalised form (UNF).

Name	Address	Movies	Title
Wolfgang Garn	27 Harmony Road	Guardians of the Galaxy, The Saint, Indiana Jones	Prof.
David James	31 Talma Garden	Oppenheimer, Ant-Man and the Wasp	Mr.
David James	11 Oxford Street	Avatar, Guardians of the Galaxy	Dr.
Emma Watson	193 Hermitage Road	Avatar, Harry Potter	Ms.

TABLE 2.3 First normal form (1NF).

Name	Address	Movie	Title
Wolfgang Garn	27 Harmony Road	Guardians of the Galaxy	Prof.
Wolfgang Garn	27 Harmony Road	The Saint	Prof.
Wolfgang Garn	27 Harmony Road	Indiana Jones	Prof.
David James	31 Talma Garden	Oppenheimer	Mr.
David James	31 Talma Garden	Ant-Man and the Wasp	Mr.
David James	11 Oxford Street	Avatar	Dr.
David James	11 Oxford Street	Guardians of the Galaxy	Dr.

Name	Address	Movie	Title
Emma Watson	193 Hermitage Road	Avatar	Ms.
Emma Watson	193 Hermitage Road	Harry Potter	Ms.

1NF to 2NF

If the primary key (PK) is determined by one column (single PK), then the 1NF is already in *second normal form* (2NF). However, if the PK is defined as a composite key (i.e., made up of multiple attributes), then duplicates have to be removed. Often, there is a discussion about natural keys (understandable ones) versus short ones (integers). Since this is not a database design text. I will point to Codd's seminal paper written in 1970 (Codd, 1970).

Example 2.3.2 (1NF to 2NF). In the previous example, the 1NF was derived and displayed in Table 2.3. A compound key defined by name and address, which resembles an account identifier, could be used. By splitting Table 2.3 into two tables, account identifier and watched movies data reduction can be achieved. However, we need to introduce a new PK for the accounts and use it in the watched movies table as a foreign key (see Table 2.4).

The compound key should be a minimal combination of columns resulting in a unique identifier. We have also assumed that there are two different people called David James, but there would have been the possibility that David James had an historic account in Talma Gardens.

2NF to 3NF

We have tables in 2NF, which are converted to the *third normal form* (3NF) by removing transitive functionality. That means, there is no dependencies on non-key (i.e., normal) attributes.

TABLE 2.4 Second normal form.

id	Name	Address	Title
1	Wolfgang Garn	27 Harmony Road	Prof.
2	David James	31 Talma Garden	Mr.
3	David James	11 Oxford Street	Dr.
4	Emma Watson	193 Hermitage Road	Ms.

(a)

MOVIE	ID
Guardians of the Galaxy	1
The Saint	1
Indiana Jones	1
Oppenheimer	2
Ant-Man and the Wasp	2
Avatar	3
Guardians of the Galaxy	3
Avatar	4
Harry Potter	4

(b)

Example 2.3.3 (2NF to 3NF). We continue the previous example. There is a functional dependency (title » first name » sure name » road name » road number). However, we can assume that Name implies Address and Address implies Title; additionally, Name implies Title in this case; there is a transitive relationship. So, we create another table (Table 2.5) with the title identifier.

TABLE 2.5 3NF transitive split.

id	Name	Address	title id		Title	id
1	Wolfgang Garn	27 Harmony Road	1		Prof.	1
2	David James	31 Talma Garden	2		Mr.	2
3	David James	11 Oxford Street	3		Dr.	3
4	Emma Watson	193 Hermitage Road	4		Ms.	4

(a)   (b)

The 3NF is usually a good state to find a database in. Note that this can be further refined to the 4NF by allowing only one multivalued attribute. It may be possible to achieve an even higher normal form through lossless decomposition into smaller tables.

2.3.5 Data Access and R

How to Import a Local Text File Using MySQL

In MySQL Workbench, issue the following two commands:

```
Set global local_infile=true;
SELECT @@GLOBAL.secure_file_priv;
```

This command returns a path, e.g. **C:\ProgramData\MySQL\MySQL Server 8.0\ Uploads\;** if needed, adapt the path in the import command. Copy the text files you want to import into this folder. Next, execute the following line.

```
load data infile 'C:/ProgramData/MySQL/MySQL Server 8.0/
Uploads/my_text_file.txt' into table TABLE_NAME fields
terminated by '\t' lines terminated by '\n';
```

Here, change the path, file name and table name as needed.

If the following error message is received instead of a success message: **ERROR 3950 (42000): Loading local data is disabled;** then the loading needs to be enabled on both the client and server side. On a Windows server, click: **Start » MySQL command line client** and in the MySQL command window, run **SET GLOBAL local_infile = 1;** Check whether the **local_infile** is on via **show global variables like 'local_infile';** This should resolve the issue on the server side.

How Do I Add Images within a Database?

Images must be uploaded on the server. The configuration file might need a bit of "massaging". That means, in my.ini, set secure-file-priv (for path) and allow uploading (similar to the previous answer). Furthermore, in my.ini, remove STRICT_TRANS_TABLES from sql-mode. Decide about the image size, type "blob" truncates images (choose medium or long).

```
create table image (id int primary key, image mediumblob);
insert into image(id,image) values (1, LOAD_FILE(
'D:/MySQL/Uploads/images/Avatar_poster.jpg'));
```

This example creates a table and inserts an image. The insertion is achieved via the load_file function. In the MySQL configuration file (my.ini) modify the line: secure-file-priv="my_upload_path" as needed. By the way, you can find the currently set path using

```
select @@GLOBAL.secure_file_priv;
```

The images can be displayed within the database. First, run **select * from** image; followed by right-clicking on blob » Open Value Editor (see Figure 2.10).

FIGURE 2.10 Displaying an image within MySQL.

When similar operations have to be done repeatedly, then procedures are appropriate. For instance, assume you need to update many image names. A single update is achieved with the following SQL:

```
update film
set image_file='Uncharted_Official_Poster.jpg'
where id =7;
```

We would like to have a procedure which takes the image file and id as input. The following defines this procedure:

```
DELIMITER $$
CREATE PROCEDURE update_image (IN fn text, IN fid int)
  BEGIN
  update film
  set image_file=fn
  where id =fid;
  END$$
DELIMITER;
```

This procedure can now be used multiple times.

```
call update_image('Indy_5_-_Teaser_Poster.jpeg', 2);
call update_image('Oppenheimer_(film).jpg', 3);
call update_image('Guardians_of_Galaxy_poster.jpg', 4);
```

This will make the SQL script more readable. All defined procedures in the database movme can be displayed with:

```
show procedure status
where db = "movme";
```

How Do I Create a MySQL Connection in RStudio?

First, check existing drivers in Windows » Start » ODBC Data Source Administrator (64bit) » Drivers; if you see a MySQL driver, then you are in luck (see Figure 2.11); otherwise, install ODBC drivers. Use the following link: https://dev.mysql.com/downloads/connector/odbc/. (This will require administrator rights.)

Next, we create a MySQL connection in RStudio. First, ensure that you can connect to a database using MySQL Workbench, then execute the following command in RStudio (your server, uid and pwd may vary):

```
con <- DBI::dbConnect(odbc::odbc(),
Driver = "MySQL ODBC 8.0 Unicode Driver",
Server = "localhost",Port = 3306,
UID = 'various',PWD = 'various.')
```

This creates a connection in RStudio. Now, you can create a SQL query (see SQL script – do not forget to adapt the first line). All available databases can be explored within the Connections tab (see Figure 2.12).

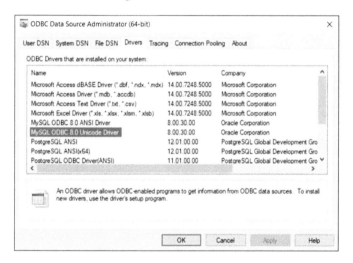

FIGURE 2.11 ODBC Datasources system dialogue.

FIGURE 2.12 RStudio and SQL connection.

If you want the tables in the world database available by default, add database = 'world' to the dbConnect function.

How Do I Use the RStudio Connection Directly in the R Code?

In this example, we connect to the previously created database movme. Then, we demonstrate how to read a table and execute a query.

```
library(pacman) # install this library first
p_load(DBI,odbc) # database connection libraries
con <- dbConnect(
odbc::odbc(), Driver = "MySQL ODBC 8.0 Unicode Driver",
database = "movme",
Server = "localhost",
UID = "mm4all", PWD = "mm4all.",
Port = 3306)
F <- dbReadTable(con,"film")
S <- dbGetQuery(con, "select * from film where id in (1,2,3)")
dbDisconnect(con) # always disconnect
```

How Do I Display Blobs from Databases in R?

Use the previous code to connect to the database and add

```
images <- dbReadTable(con,"image") # fetch all images
```

Next, we need to load visualisations libraries. Then, we extract the first image and convert the binary blob into a jpeg. Now, the image can be visualised.

```
p_load(ggplot2, jpeg, grid) # load visualisation and
        image libraries
f1 = unlist(images$image[1]) # get first image
r1 = jpeg::readJPEG(f1, native = TRUE) # convert raw
        (blob) to jpeg
# display image
ggplot()+inset_element(p=r1,left=0,bottom=0,right=1,top=1)
```

Miscellaneous Commands

MySQL collects large numbers of log files, which may consume needed hard disk space. The following command deletes those files.

```
PURGE BINARY LOGS BEFORE NOW();
```

How can I allow someone to upload files? The following will be part of it:

```
GRANT PROCESS, select ON *.* TO 'myUser'@'%';
```

How can I find a particular table within lots of databases in MySQL?

```
select table_schema as database_name, table_name
from information_schema.tables
where table_type = 'BASE TABLE'
and table_name like '%search string%'
order by table_schema;
```

2.4 SQL – Queries

A *query* retrieves information from one or several tables. Later, we will see that we can "nest" queries: i.e., retrieve data from another query or view. We will introduce select queries by mentioning several examples. Most of them are based on the table created in the previous section.

2.4.1 Unconditional Query

The following SQL displays all records from the film table, which is in the moveme database.

```
select * from film;
```

	id	movie_name	produced_by	year_rele	production_company	image_file	directed_by
▸	1	Avatar: The Way o...	James Cameron	2022	Lightstorm Entertai...	Avatar_The_Way_of_...	James Cameron
	2	Indiana Jones and ...	Kathleen Kenn...	2023	Lucasfilm Ltd.	Indy_5_-_Teaser_Po...	James Mangold
	3	Oppenheimer	Emma Thomas	2023	Universal Pictures	Oppenheimer_(film).j...	Christopher Nolan
	4	Guardians of the G...	Kevin Feige	2023	Marvel Studios	Guardians_of_the_Ga...	James Gunn
	5	Ant-Man and the ...	Kevin Feige	2023	Marvel Studios	Ant-Man_and_the_W...	Peyton Reed
	6	The 355	Jessica Chastain	2022	Kinberg Genre Films	The_355_poster.jpeg	Simon Kinberg
	7	Uncharted	Charles Roven	2022	Columbia Pictures	Uncharted_Official_P...	Ruben Fleischer
	8	Five Eyes	Jason Statham	2022	Miramax	Operation_Fortune.jpg	Guy Ritchie
	9	The Lost City	Sandra Bullock	2022	Fortis Films	TheLostCityPoster.jpg	Adam Nee
	10	Morbius	Avi Arad	2022	Columbia Pictures	Morbius_(film)_poste...	Daniel Espinosa
	11	Top Gun: Maverick	Jerry Bruckhei...	2022	Skydance	Top_Gun_Maverick_P...	Joseph Kosinski
	12	Jurassic World: Do...	Frank Marshall	2022	Amblin Entertainm...	JurassicWorldDomini...	Colin Trevorrow
	13	Elvis	Baz Luhrmann	2022	Warner Bros. Pictures	Elvis_2022_poster.jpg	Baz Luhrmann
	14	Secret Headquarters	Jerry Bruckhei...	2022	Paramount Pictures	Secret_Headquarters...	Henry Joost;
	NULL	NULL	NULL	NULL	NULL	NULL	NULL

SQL OUTPUT 2.1 Film query returning all columns and rows.

The query is pretty self-explanatory. We say: "select star from film". The star symbol means to return all columns. The star is also known as wildcard, asterisk or joker.

The data can be sorted using `order by` by a specified field: here, the release year.

```
select * from film order by year_released;
```

Alternatively, we could have sorted by the movie's name. The direction, descending or ascending, can be specified using the keywords `DESC` or `ASC`.

```
select * from film order by movie_name desc;
```

If we are interested only in specific columns, then we can specify them instead of the star symbol.

```
select movie_name, year_released, production_company
from film order by movie_name desc;
```

Note: The columns can be added to the query from the Navigator window without writing via a double click or drag and drop.

2.4.2 View

A query we intend to use multiple times or which is of general interest/importance can be saved within the database as a *view*. For instance,

```
create view sorted_film as
select * from film order by movie_name;
```

Another example could be to provide a view of the produced films.

```
create view produced_movies as
select production_company, year_released, movie_name
from film order by production_company;
```

The view can be displayed using a simple select query.

```
select * from produced_movies;
```

A view can be deleted using the drop command.

```
drop view produced_movies;
```

2.4.3 Conditional Query

Let us now introduce filtering mechanisms. The filtering (aka slicing) of data is achieved with the *where clause*.

```
select * from film
where movie_name="Oppenheimer";
```

This returns all records for the movie named *Oppenheimer*. Often, the exact name or only a part of the search string is known. For instance, we know there is a movie that contains the word *Avatar*.

```
select * from film
where movie_name like "%Avatar%";
```

This returns all films which contain the word *Avatar*. The wildcard (%) allows any string before the word *Avatar* and any string afterwards. These wild cards could be placed anywhere: e.g. A%tar%. (Note: in Access, the wildcard is *.)

There are also numerical filters. All films produced after the year 2022 are obtained via:

```
select * from film
where year_released>2022;
```

We can also create more complex where clauses by using a Boolean expression. For instances, let us get all movies which contain the string *qu* and were released after 2022.

```
select * from film
where movie_name like "%qu%" and year_released>2022;
```

2.4.4 Group and Aggregate

Grouping and aggregation are among the most useful SQL features, often used by data and business analysts. *Grouping data* via the group command extracts a subset from the given data. *Aggregated fields* are obtained by grouping one or several fields and using aggregation functions such as count, sum and min on some of the other fields.

The following example will clarify these definitions. Let us have a look at how many films for each year are recorded.

```
select year_released, count(id) as nb
from film group by year_released;
```

Note that count is an aggregate function. The keyword AS defines a new column header. Generally, the as command is used for *renaming fields* from a query. This concept is also known as pivoting and is also used in Excel to create pivot tables.

Let us use the example of house prices. This table is located in the various database (see Section 2.2.4).

```
select Neighborhood, count(Home) as nb,
sum(Price) as total_value, avg(Price) as avg_value
from houseprices
group by Neighborhood;
```

Neighborhood	nb	total_value	avg_value
▸ East	45	5635400	125231.11111111111
North	44	4846800	110154.54545454546
West	39	6212500	159294.87179487178

SQL OUTPUT 2.2 Query with aggregates.

Here, we group by neighbourhood and provide the number of observed properties, the total value (sum) and the average value per property. That means in the West neighbourhood, properties are most expensive (on average, $159,300).

2.4.5 Join Query

Often data comes from multiple tables which need to be joined together.

Figure 2.13 shows the most essential joins. For simplicity – to demonstrate the concept – we create two tables, A and B, and insert a few records.

```
create table A (id int);
create table B (id int);
insert into A values (1),(2),(3),(4),(5);
insert into B values (4),(5),(6),(7),(8);
```

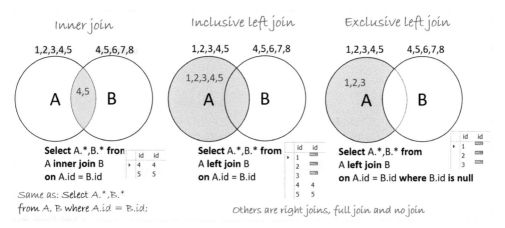

FIGURE 2.13 Essential joins of tables.

Probably the most frequently used join is the *inner join*, in which two tables with the same identifier are linked (related) with each other.

```
select A.*,B.* from A inner join B on A.id = B.id;
```

This returns joint rows in which the identifiers agree. Many people prefer to write this join using the where clause instead.

```
select A.*,B.* from A, B where A.id = B.id;
```

The *inclusive left join* keeps all records from the left table (A) and adds those records from B in which the on clause is true. Whenever the on clause is false, null values are inserted for the missing records from B.

```
select A.*,B.* from A left join B on A.id = B.id;
```

The *exclusive left join* subtracts the common identifiers (or true on clauses) from the left table (A).

```
select A.*,B.* from A left join B on A.id = B.id where
B.id is null;
```

It is possible to join more than two tables at once. For instance, let us join three tables: film, film_actor and actor. These tables are from the database sakila (Section 2.2.4).

```
select title, first_name, last_name
from film as f, film_actor as fa, actor as a
where f.film_id = fa.film_id and fa.actor_id = a.actor_id
order by last_name;
```

title	first_name	last_name
▸ BACKLASH UNDEFEATED	CHRISTIAN	AKROYD
BETRAYED REAR	CHRISTIAN	AKROYD
CAPER MOTIONS	CHRISTIAN	AKROYD

SQL OUTPUT 2.3 Derived from join query with three tables.

This query used two inner joins on three tables. For convenience, we abbreviated the tables with letters to access the identifiers efficiently. That means the tables film and actor were linked via the "link"-table film_actor, where table film has the PK film_id and actor has the PK actor_id. The link-table contained the mentioned PKs as identifiers and even used foreign keys (see Figure 2.14).

FIGURE 2.14 Foreign keys in MySQL Navigator.

Generally, *foreign keys* allow us to relate tables with each other and add functionality. In the previous example, `film_actor` references the actor table using the column `actor_id`. Moreover, a foreign key definition was provided that cascades any updates and delete operations between the tables. Here are details of the `film_actor` table.

```
CREATE TABLE film_actor (
actor_id smallint unsigned NOT NULL,

PRIMARY KEY (actor_id,film_id),
KEY idx_fk_film_id (film_id),

CONSTRAINT fk_film_actor_actor FOREIGN KEY (actor_id)
REFERENCES actor(actor_id) ON DELETE RESTRICT ON UPDATE CASCADE,
CONSTRAINT fk_film_actor_film FOREIGN KEY (film_id)
REFERENCES film(film_id) ON DELETE RESTRICT ON UPDATE CASCADE
)
```

Note: In Microsoft Access, foreign keys are created via Tools » Relationships. In SQLite and PostgreSQL, the same approach as in MySQL works.

Further examples can be found in the book's supporting online material (https://smartana.org/tutorials).

2.5 Entity Relationships

Tables are also known as *entities*. At the end of the previous section, we showed ways to join tables via identifiers (e.g. primary and foreign keys). We will abbreviate *entity relationships* as ER for the remainder of this chapter.

2.5.1 Directional ER

There are four possible resulting directional relationships:

1. Must have one;
2. Can have one;
3. Must have one or more; and
4. Can have one or more.

These relationships are also known as *business rules*. Practically, they are created using foreign keys.

Each record in table A must have exactly one associated record in B. Figure 2.15 displays this relationship using the visual ―╫. Table B contains A's primary key as foreign key. That means each record from A is linked to exactly one corresponding record in B. Let's say there are three records in A identified with 1, 2 and 3. Then B must have exactly three records with the foreign keys 1, 2 and 3. Note that B cannot include an A.id such as 4, which is not in A nor a null entry.

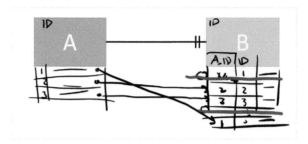

FIGURE 2.15 Relationship in which each record from A must have exactly one record in B associated.

Each record in table A has one or no associated record in B. Figure 2.16 shows this relationship using the notation (visual) ─○├.

This is very similar to the previous relationship, but not every identifier from A has occur in B as foreign key. Again, assume A has records 1, 2 and 3; then it is fine that B only has 2 and 3. However, it cannot have the identifier 3 occurring twice.

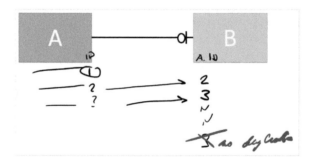

FIGURE 2.16 Each record in table A has one or no associated record in B.

Each record in table A must have one or more records in B. Figure 2.17 shows this one-to-many relationship.

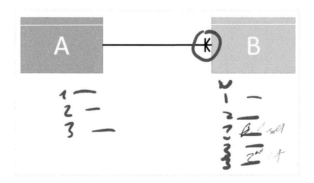

FIGURE 2.17 Each record in table A must have one or more records in B.

By the way, this inspired the name of what's known as crow's foot notation because of its resemblance to a bird's foot. This business rule is a bit more relaxed, allowing the foreign key to occur multiple times in B. For instance, identifier 3 occurs three times in B.

Each record in table A can have one or several records in B. Figure 2.18 presents this relationship visually.

FIGURE 2.18 Each record in table A can have one or several records in B.

Example 2.5.1 (Room booking). Let us consider and read the entity relationship diagram in Figure 2.19. A customer can book one or several rooms. A room can have one or more reservations. This makes sense since a room can be allocated over time to several customers. Now, let us reverse the direction. A reservation must have a room. A room can have a customer, which makes sense because not all rooms may be occupied. Generally, it makes sense to be more restrictive with business rules and relax them later. For instance, we could have demanded that a customer record appear in the database only if the customer booked a room: i.e. a must-have relationship.

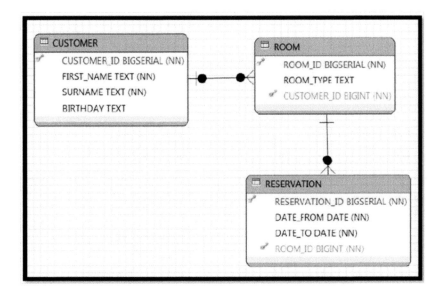

FIGURE 2.19 Entity relationship diagram for a room booking system.

2.5.2 Combining Entities

How to Combine Tables

Tables can be merged (bound) via columns or rows. Assume we have three tables X, Y and Z. In order to combine these tables, they must be in a certain format. In order to merge the columns from X and Y, the number of rows in both tables must be identical, and they must have a common identifier. The merging is achieved via a natural inner join (see Figure 2.20). The inner join used is:

```
select X.*, Y.f3 from X, Y where X.id = Y.id;
```

To merge the rows of two tables, both tables must have the same number of columns. The union operator accomplishes the binding of the rows (see Figure 2.20 for an example), which uses:

```
select * from X union select * from Z;
```

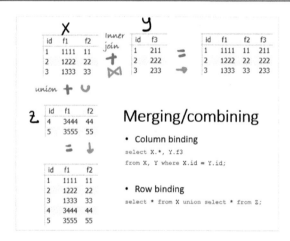

FIGURE 2.20 Merging tables.

The following SQL statements were used to define the tables.

```
create table X (id int, f1 int, f2 int);
create table Y (id int, f3 int);
create table Z (id int, f1 int, f2 int);
insert into X values
      (1,1111,11),(2,1222,22),(3,1333,33);
insert into Y values (1,211),(2,222),(3,233);
insert into Z values (4,3444,44),(5,3555,55);
```

Sometimes, the tables do not have identifiers, but we know the order is fixed. We can add an identifier with the following query:

```
select @row_number:=@row_number+1 AS nb, X2.*
from X2, (select @row_number:=0) as t1;
```

where the table X2 is defined via:

```
create table X2 (f1 int, f2 int);
insert into X2 values (1111,11),(1222,22),(1333,33);
```

Alternatively, we could use the auto-increment feature, but then we need to create a new table and insert the data:

```
create table X3 (
id int auto_increment primary key,
f1 int, f2 int);
insert into X3(f1, f2) select * from X2;
```

In *relational algebra*, the following operations and symbols are standard: select σ, projection π, union ∪, intersect ∩, set difference \, Cartesian product ×, inner join ⋈, outer join and others. We have used these operations before.

2.6 Summary

This chapter introduced database systems and the Structured Query Language (SQL). We motivated the need for database systems for managers, analysts and database users. We looked at popular commercial and open-source database systems and gave a detailed description of them. We showed the creation of databases and its tables. We discussed normal forms of tables and how to relate them with each other. SQL queries were introduced to extract information efficiently from tables. This allows us to analyse data using a methodical analytical approach and is part of data mining.

Annotated Bibliography

Introduces SQL but goes further, covering Big Data and analytics:

1. Beaulieu, A. (2020). *Learning SQL: Generate, Manipulate, and Retrieve Data*. Farnham: O'Reilly (3rd ed.).

An historic and influential work:

2. Codd, E. F. (1970). A relational model of data for large shared data banks. *Communications of the ACM* 13 (6), 377–387.

Storytelling with SQL based on real-world examples for PostgreSQL and MySQL:

3. Debarros, A. (2022). *Practical SQL: A Beginner's Guide to Storytelling with Data.* San Francisco, CA: No Starch Press (2nd ed.).

Includes a MySQL chapter:

4. Shah, C. (2020). *A Hands-on Introduction to Data Science.* Cambridge, England: Cambridge University Press.

Introduces all SQL fundamentals using SQLite:

5. Shields, W. (2019). *SQL QuickStart Guide: The Simplified Beginner's Guide to Managing, Analyzing, and Manipulating Data with SQL.* ClydeBank Media LLC.

w3schools.com is a great systematic introduction into SQL:

6. *SQL Tutorial* (2023). [Online] https://www.w3schools.com/sql (Accessed 16 June 2023).

3. Business Intelligence

3.1 Introduction

Business Intelligence (BI) uses Data Analytics to provide insights to make business decisions. Tools like Power Business Intelligence (PBI) and Tableau allow us to gain an understanding of a business scenario rapidly. This is achieved by first allowing easy access to all kinds of data sources (e.g. databases, text files, Web). Next, the data can be visualised via graphs and tables, which are connected and interactive. Then, analytical components such as forecasts, key influencers and descriptive statistics are built in, and access to the most essential Data Science languages (R and Python) is integrated.

3.1.1 Definitions

There are several definitions of Business Intelligence. Let us begin with a definition which is generic but emphasises that found insights are useable for decision making.

Business Intelligence (BI) transforms data into actionable insights that inform an organisation's strategic and tactical business decisions.

DOI: 10.4324/9781003336099-4

Business Intelligence systems combine data gathering, data storage and knowledge management with analytical tools to present complex internal and competitive information to planners and decision makers (Adam and Pomerol, 2008).

These systems set out to improve or optimise organisations by providing employees and managers with business insights that lead to faster, better and more relevant decisions.

Webster's Dictionary (1958) defines *intelligence* as "the ability to apprehend the interrelationships of presented facts in such a way as to guide action towards a desired goal". The *Oxford Dictionary* (2021) provides two definitions for *intelligence*: "the ability to learn, understand and think in a logical way about things" and "secret information that is collected, for example about a foreign country, especially one that is an enemy". The *Oxford Dictionary* (2021) defines *business* as "the activity of making, buying, selling or supplying goods or services for money".

We will propose the following definition: *Business Intelligence (BI)* is the ability to collate facts and data to derive activities in a logical way to improve the competitiveness of an entity. Here, an entity could be a company, an organisation or an individual. Competitiveness refers to financial aspects directly or indirectly. Activities may refer to making, buying or selling goods.

It should be noted that sometimes Business Intelligence is seen as a discipline within the area of Computer Science and Applied Mathematics. Occasionally, Business Intelligence is used synonymously with Business Analytics. Generally, Business Analytics focuses on Descriptive, Predictive and Prescriptive Analytics. *Data Analytics* is the discipline of extracting actionable insights by structuring, processing, analysing and visualising data using methods and software tools. Consequently, it is an essential part of Business Intelligence. However, BI usually includes Prescriptive Analytics as well. The discipline of Operational Research provides the methods for Prescriptive Analytics and Management Science offers the business applications.

So, in a nutshell, BI supersedes Data Analytics. That means, since we are treating BI as a chapter in this Data Analytics text, that we will have to limit ourselves to certain aspects. We will show the data gathering, modelling and manipulation traits. This can be nicely linked to the previous database chapter. Then we will discuss visuals with storytelling facets. Descriptive and Predictive Analytics are discussed briefly; we will expand on them in the remainder of the book. Finally, we will check out a few example applications.

We work towards the following learning outcomes:

- Being able to analyse and visualise data using a methodical analytical approach;
- Having familiarity with important data mining techniques;
- Knowing how to apply state-of-the-art tools to build and predict models;
- Communicating and providing resulting information to the management for decision making.

Section 3.2 gives an overview of BI tools. Designing BI reports and essential visualisations are discussed in Section 3.3. Typical analytics features such as descriptive statistics, timeseries and forecasts within BI tools are explained in Section 3.4. Section 3.5 gives an idea of how to integrate Data Science languages. The last section provides miscellaneous topics such as best practices, bit-sized challenges (i.e. various examples) and the creation of custom R visuals for PBI.

3.2 Tools

A *Business Intelligence tool* is a software that curates, analyses and visualises data to gain actionable insights.

Data curation is defined as the process of obtaining, organising, describing, cleaning, enhancing and preserving data (see Section 5.3, Stage 1). Data modelling refers primarily to entity relationships (see Section 2.5) and is part of the data curation definition as organising data.

Analysing data allows the usage of descriptive statistics (such as average, min, max, count etc.), forecasting methods and machine learning (e.g. via Data Science languages). At the time of writing, Operational Analytics have not been integrated in the analysis yet. Technically this can be achieved easily (e.g. using R or Python in conjunction with LP Solve, SciPy, PuLP).

Visualising data refers to displaying tables, figures and filters. Tables automatically aggregate fields. Typical figures include bar charts, line charts, scatter plots and pie charts. They also include tree maps, funnel graphs and ribbon charts. Moreover, maps (GIS), gauges and key influencers can be found as visuals. Technically, a key influencer visual analyses the data. It is common to integrate the analysis of the data using machine learning techniques within a visual. Filters allow the slicing of the data (e.g. focusing on a certain time period or a set of items). The built-in visuals often have filtering mechanisms integrated. For instance, selecting a specific bar within the bar chart updates related figures and tables.

Typical users of Power BI are managers, analysts, database users, data scientists and end customers. They help analysts prepare, visualise and quickly gain insights from data. BI analysts access and analyse datasets and present analytical findings in reports, dashboards, graphs, charts and maps to provide users with detailed intelligence about the state of the business. BI tools allow managers to make decisions based on Business Analytics.

Some of the most popular BI tools are Power Business Intelligence (PBI), Tableau and Qlik. Figure 3.1 shows their popularity as a Google search term over the past few years. It can be seen that at the time of writing, PBI has the highest Google Search score. Power BI was initially released in 2011. Tableau was founded in 2003 and acquired by Salesforce in 2019 for $15.7bn. There are a few classic BI tools such as Cognos Analytics from IBM, Oracle BI and SAP BI which have been around for several years. There are many more BI tools: Domo, Dundas, Geckoboard, Sisense, MicroStrategy, Datapine, Yellowfin BI, Zoho Analytics, Sisense, Looker, Clear Analytics and others.

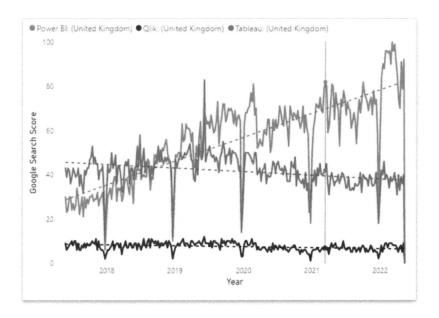

FIGURE 3.1 Popularity of BI tools.

Most BI tools allow importing from heterogeneous data sources such as csv files, databases, webpages and many more. Once the data is accessible within the tool, it can be structured and linked, similarly to entity relationship models. Tabular views and some functionality found in spreadsheet programs are typically supported. Furthermore, they provide functionality to aggregate, filter and join the data to gain data insights in tabular and visual form. Hence, BI tools are used as database "visualisers". Further, BI tools provide visual interactivity such as selecting a fraction of a pie chart filters and update related graphs. Besides offering standard graphs such as bar plots, timeseries and tree maps, custom visuals can be created. In Power BI, the Data Science languages R and Python are supported to allow self-made visualisations. Moreover, BI tools include a variety of analytics tools, ranging from basic statistics (mean, standard deviation) to forecasts and key influencer identifiers. Many BI tools allow access to the interactive visualisation on websites and mobile devices.

So, overall, an infrastructure is provided that allows the user to gain actionable data insights. The effort is minimal for typical business challenges, but the integration of custom add-ins allows addressing any kind of complexity.

3.2.1 PBI Overview

The focus in this chapter will be on PBI, but other BI tools are similar. The first step is to obtain data, and PBI provides a convenient interface to achieve this. Data can be imported either from a single data source or from various heterogeneous data sources into the BI tool. For instance, we could import data from an Excel map, a CSV text file or various different databases such as PostgreSQL, MySQL and SQL Server. Figure 3.2 shows an overview of import options and functionality for the Power BI tool. Moreover, we can extract data from websites via the BI tool and integrate it. The BI tool can store data locally. That means the live data source will not be affected for subsequent analytical processing. The BI tool offers a convenient mechanism to update data. These updates can be scheduled periodically. However, BI tools also offer the possibility to link to the data rather than importing it. In summary, this is known as *data integration*, in which various formats from numerous data sources are converted to one standard format.

PBI's functionality can be seen as a mixture of Access and Excel.

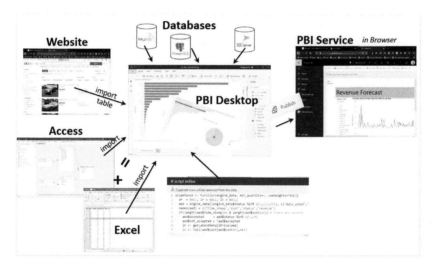

FIGURE 3.2 Power BI overview of import and functionality.

After the data import, individual sheets/tables are transformed. This is achieved with the Power Query Editor, a tool called from within PBI. (By the way, this tool can also be called from within Excel.) Usually, data types are changed, new columns are introduced, identifiers are created and duplicates are removed. Sometimes data needs to be merged or appended. Pivoting and unpivoting are additional often-used features. PBI even has the ability to normalise data (see Section 2.3). Once the data preprocessing is completed, the various tables need to be linked. This is achieved in the (Data) Model view. For instance, a customer table (with name and address) needs to be linked with an order table (including items, quantity, price and order date). This step is a reflection of the entity relationship model (see Section 2.5; entity = table, relationship = link via identifiers). Entity relationships are also known as business rules. For instance, an order must have exactly one customer, or an order can have one or many items. All this can be summarised as *data curation*.

After the "modelling", we switch to the Report view, where the data presentation, visualising, and analytical processing take place. Hence, this can be seen as a good graphical extension for databases by delivering visualisation capabilities. Generally, BI tools offer a fast and easy way to create visualisations. Particularly impressive is the capability to visualise and analyse across tables due to the implicit usage of the underlying model. Continuing the previous example, we can join the customers and orders in a single visualisation. Often, we want to filter, focus on or investigate certain parts of the data (e.g. focus on the last quartal or a certain product segment). This can be easily achieved with the Filter Pane or Slicer and propagates through all relevant graphs and tables. The interactivity of the graphs is another feature typical of BI tools. For instance, you click on a pie chart which displays a supplier's contribution, and the timeseries adjusts to show their activities. PBI has a great range of visualisations. They include typical charts such as bar charts, line charts, pie charts and tree maps. Some of them can be augmented with analytics, such as forecasts, trends and summary statistics. But PBI also offers more advanced visuals such as GIS maps, key influencer diagrams and smart narratives. Moreover, it is possible to add customised visuals using the two popular Data Science languages, R and Python. Sharing and collaboration of PBI reports and components can be easily done via the PBI service, which is a web service. Moreover, PBI can also be used on mobile devices.

3.3 Design and Visualisations

3.3.1 Visualisations

Principles for good data visualisations include understanding the context, choosing an appropriate visual display, removing clutter, drawing the attention to relevant parts, thinking like a designer and telling a story (Knaflic, 2015). In this section, we will contrast "good" and "bad" visualisations.

Bar and Line Charts

Figure 3.3 shows (a) a 3D bar chart, (b) a 3D shape chart and (c) a line chart. The first two charts reveal some perspective issues: e.g. some data points are visually blocked. Overall, the first two graphs seem aesthetic but are difficult to read. Hence, never ever use 3D bar charts, no matter how "cool" they look. The third chart (c) provides an appropriate visualisation. The x-axis represents years; hence, it is a time axis. Time is continuous, so a line chart is appropriate. It is easy to read and interpret the chart. For instance, Tableau was the most popular BI tool in 2018, but from 2020 onwards, Power BI had the highest popularity score.

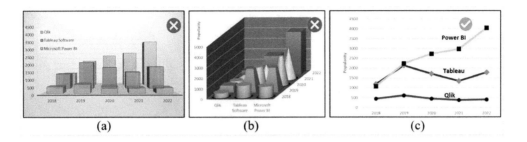

FIGURE 3.3 3D bar charts versus line chart: (a) 3D bar chart, (b) 3D shape chart and (c) line chart.

Figure 3.4 (a) has several issues, which were sorted out on the right side. The following issues can be observed on the right: 3D layering with drop shadows, wrong colour scheme and the wrong format. Furthermore, discrete categorical data can be visualised with a bar chart but not with a line chart. The axis should start at zero, and the chart needs to be sorted. Colours need to be used for focus. A reference line can add further value. Figure 3.4 (b) has addressed these issues. However, even this figure can be further improved by adding a "story": i.e. explaining its purpose. In cases in which differences have to be emphasised, a higher starting value is appropriate.

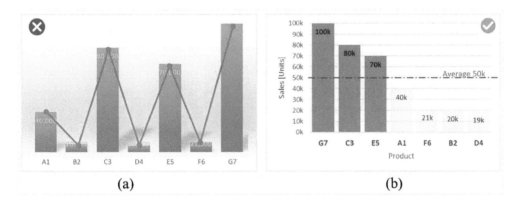

FIGURE 3.4 Bar chart visual (a) illustrates issues; (b) is the improved version.

Pie Charts

Pie charts are meant for sum percentages or relative measures. They are suitable for comparisons of relative values from categories in the form of percentages. Figure 3.5 shows an incorrect and a correct pie chart, which compare the operating system (OS) usage. Figure 3.5 (a) is incorrect as it distorts the percentage. It makes the Windows OS usage appear to be more than its actual value. One fundamental check for percentages on pie charts is to add them up and ensure the sum is 100%. In Figure 3.4, we notice that there are only five categories, which indicates that several operating systems were

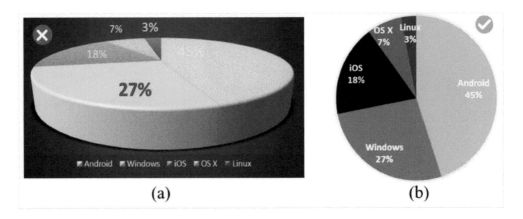

(a)   (b)

FIGURE 3.5 Charts: (a) 3D distorted, (b) acceptable.

omitted – this could constitute an issue. In general, there should never be more than seven categories. (Some even recommend only five categories.)

Figure 3.6 shows an unsuitable donut graph. It contains eight categories. Most likely, the sum does not represent 100% of the company's salaries. For these two reasons, a bar chart is more appropriate.

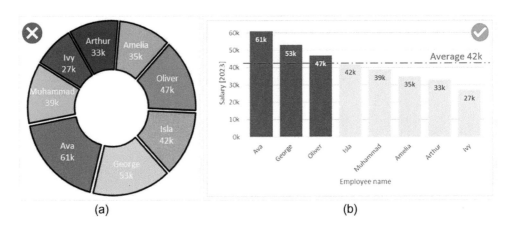

(a)   (b)

FIGURE 3.6 (a) Incorrect donut graph, (b) appropriate bar chart.

Tables

Table 3.1 contrasts two tables. The first table has several flaws: wrong unit, truncated column names, no neutral background colour and others. Figure 3.7 (b) resolves these issues: the units are in the table header, the percentages are more readable, the year-by-year sales drop in West Europe is highlighted and the meaningless change percentage sum has been removed. Lastly, the table is sorted by sales volume.

Area	Pieces	Sales in P	Percentag	Change
North Europe	£12,000.00	147000	12.50%	11.0%
South Europe	£31,000.00	379750	32.29%	7.00%
East Europe	£27,000.00	330750	28.13%	14.30%
West Europe	£ 7,000.00	85750	7.29%	-6.30%
Central Europe	£19,000.00	232750	19.79%	3.20%
Total	£96,000.00	1176000	100.00%	29.20%

(a)

Area	Units	Sales [£]	Sales [%]	Change
South Europe	31,000	379,750	32.3%	7.0%
East Europe	27,000	330,750	28.1%	14.3%
Central Europe	19,000	232,750	19.8%	3.2%
North Europe	12,000	147,000	12.5%	11.0%
West Europe	7,000	85,750	7.3% ▼	-6.3%
Total	96,000	1,176,000		

(b)

FIGURE 3.7 Formatting and design of tables: (a) table with issues, (b) proper table.

Transforming a Bad Visual into a Good Visual

Let us look at the following business scenario. Alarm systems are installed by technicians. The jobs are logged. Recently, two employees left the company, and the team is struggling to keep up with the workload. The aim of the team manager is to persuade his line manager to hire two more staff.

The team manager has logged all the tasks in a spreadsheet for the past year. The two employees left at the end of November. Figure 3.8 (a) shows an initial attempt. However, it is unlikely that this graph will trigger the leadership to even consider the manager's wish. Figure 3.8 (b) is much improved. It provided axes labels. It shows the "development" of the number of orders versus the number of jobs. It indicates the event that two employees left. It illustrates that there is a gap between #jobs and #orders. Strictly speaking, the gap will remain the same. Hence, another visual highlighting the increasing backlog of jobs and stating the objective will be even more effective in convincing the leadership to employ another two technicians. Figure 3.9 gives a simple story about the past, the current state and the future. It clearly shows the effect of the event (employees leaving). It draws attention to the increasing backlog of orders and conveys a clear message that two new employees are needed. This figure should convince sensible leadership to address the business challenge.

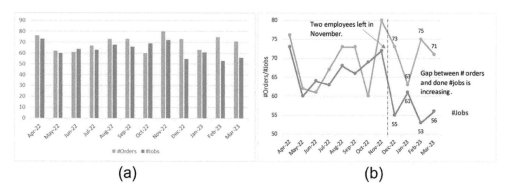

(a)

(b)

FIGURE 3.8 Making a business case using story in a visual: (a) unconvincing attempt, (b) getting there.

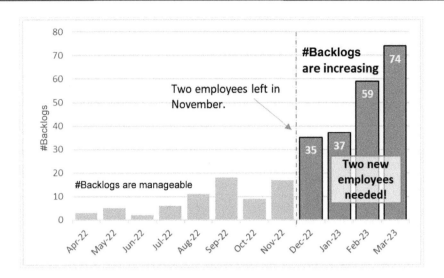

FIGURE 3.9 Telling a story about the past changes and states the objective.

Colour Theory

Sir Isaac Newton invented the colour wheel in 1666 based on the human perception of the wavelengths of light. He divided them into primary colours (red, blue, yellow), secondary colours (mixtures of primary colours) and tertiary colours (mixtures of primary and secondary colours). These days, colour is also known by the term *hue*. However, there are two more properties used: saturation and value. *Saturation* is also known as *lighting* and defines how bright a colour appears. The *value* (*chroma*) defines the colour's shades (black to white). Figure 3.10 (a) visualises the three colour properties and (b) shows the colour wheel.

Figure 3.10 shows a colour wheel with three different schemes. The schemes are based on a fixed saturation and fixed value but a varying hue. Figure 3.11 (a) shows an example of a complementary colour combination (orange and blue). In previous examples (e.g. Figure 3.4 (b) and Figure 3.8 (b)), we used these complementary colours to achieve a maximum contrast. By the way, these two colours are appropriate to use for colour-blind people. Other complementary colours are: purple versus yellow and green versus red. Generally, they are used to contrast two groups. The visual in the middle shows an analogous scheme (using three colours). This can be used to emphasise the harmony or relatedness of categories. The triadic (Figure 3.11 (c)) is used for contrasting three groups. It provides a "vivid" impression. This can be used for presentation slides. There are a few more well-known schemes, such as *split-complimentary*, in which one colour is contrasted against two almost neighbouring colours. The *tetradic* scheme uses four hue values, with two of them being contrasting and two almost analogous. Other famous schemes are monochromatic schemes in which one hue is taken, and the others are obtained by changing saturation and value.

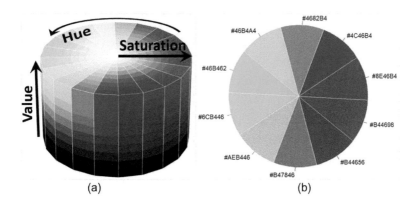

FIGURE 3.10 Colour: (a) HSV cylinder, (b) wheel.

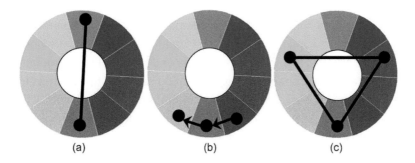

FIGURE 3.11 Colour wheel schemes: (a) complementary, (b) analogous and (c) triadic.

3.3.2 PBI Crash Course

In order to demonstrate the creation of PBI maps and their business use, we need a company. The primary objective of a successful business is to make a profit (before reinvestment). Even if there are secondary objectives such as sustainability, charity or sociality, the higher profit allows growth and greater achievement of the secondary objectives. We will look at a fictional manufacturing business. Other industry sectors, such as tourism, telecommunication and others, will follow a similar approach to the one explained later. The business objective is to manufacture and sell products to individuals (e.g. beverages, bikes, food, technology etc.). We will keep the system simple and universal. However, to create some data, we need something a bit more specific. Let us say that we will enter the market with a business called Healthy Crisps, which sells dried crisp slices of fruits and vegetables. We begin with the product family "Apple" and several product variants. Each product has components (or, in our case, ingredients). For instance, we will create products such as Apple Honey, Apple Cinamon, Apple Blue etc. with the ingredients apples, honey, cinnamon and blueberries. The products are produced in batches and placed in cardboard boxes. The cardboard boxes are sold to supermarkets (i.e. customers of Healthy Crisps). That means customers have a certain demand for products, and sales prices may differ among customers. However, the production costs are fixed during certain periods.

We have the following objectives:

1. Provide a financial overview;
2. Show the overall quarterly revenue, cost and profit and their trends;
3. Forecast the anticipated profit;
4. Analyse and compare products (by profit and demand);
5. Compare the customers (demand, profit, geography);
6. Predict the weekly demand for the next two weeks.

The first two objectives check whether the company is doing well financially. If it is, the company can be scaled up (e.g. targeting new areas and internationalisation). The product analysis can give insights into the popularity and profitability of products. Unprofitable products can be discontinued. High demand may force the business to outsource or invest in new machinery. Insights into the customers may identify issues such as demand growth. A practical issue is scheduling the work for the upcoming weeks, which requires a forecast of the weekly demand.

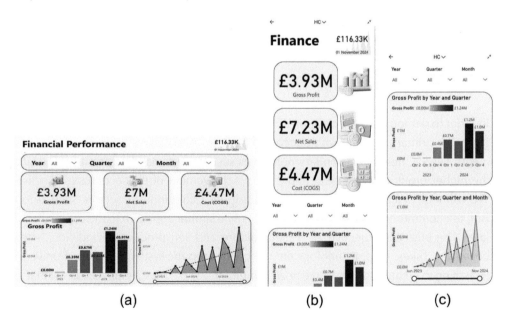

FIGURE 3.12 Power BI finance dashboard for (a) desktop and (b), (c) mobile device.

We begin our tutorial by creating the dashboard displayed in Figure 3.12. It will cover data import, modelling, visualisations and publishing. The goal is to give a quick overall understanding of how to create a Power BI map and share it. The intended financial performance dashboard is all about the gross profit. Hence, it would be good to have a basic understanding of this metric. *Gross profit* is defined as the difference between net sales (revenues) and cost of goods sold (COGS).

$$\text{Gross Profit} = \text{Net Sales} - \text{COGS} \tag{3.1}$$

Net sales are the sales after discounts, returns and allowances. *COGS* may include labour cost, product cost, cost of raw materials and inventory cost. Obviously, a company will attempt to maximise sales and minimise costs. We will create two more dashboards providing details about net sales and COGS.

Data Import

We begin by considering the existing data. The data is provided to us as an Excel map called `BusinessData.xlsx`, which can be found on `smartana.org`. The map contains some sheets related to the product, a few related to orders and some others. One of the first steps of a data analyst is to explore those tables (sheets) and gain a basic understanding. The product table reveals five items (AC, AH, AL, AO and ABB), which are all based on apples and a flavour. You should continue looking through the sheets and make notes of which information may be relevant for creating the gross profit. You will discover that the OrderCost sheet includes the COGS, and the OrderRevenue sheet includes revenue and gross profit columns.

Now that we have identified what we need, we are ready to create a PBI map. I recommend creating a folder called HealthyCrisps, with subfolders for data and images (Explorer » New » Folder . . .). The BusinessData.xlsx is saved in the data folder.

Next, we start Power BI Desktop (and close the splash-up screen; registering can be done later) and save the pbix file. You should see a PBI desktop similar to the 2023 version in Figure 3.13. I have highlighted frequently used elements. We start with (1) getting data and (2) transforming it. Then, we check (3a) the relationships (links) and (3b) the data tables (which may cause a return to step 2) and end up in (3c) the report view. In the report view, we will add text boxes (4) and visuals (5) based on data (6).

We will now import our business data. This is achieved using the "Get Data" option or by selecting "Import data from Excel" (see Figure 3.13, Step 1). As a first rule, you should only import the information needed. In our case, this refers to the OrderCost sheet and OrderRevenue sheet. Advantages of importing only the required information into the PBI map include less memory consumption, faster processing and simplicity. When importing data, loading errors can occur. In our case, the message displayed in Figure 3.14 appears. Rather than closing the message box, we will view the errors.

FIGURE 3.13 Power BI Desktop with frequently used elements highlighted.

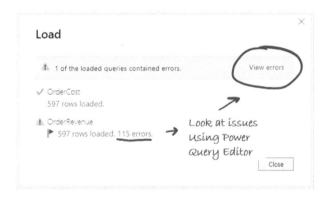

FIGURE 3.14 Import error message identifying issues.

Power Query Editor

This opens up the Power Query Editor (PQE), which can assist with many data manipulation tasks. In our case, we will focus on understanding the errors and finding a solution. Figure 3.15 shows the query errors. Investigating the errors, we find they are triggered by orders which have not been paid. In the data source, the related Excel cells are empty. This is an interesting insight, as we will see when displaying the KPIs. Rather than removing the entire record, we will replace the errors with NULL values. Figure 3.15 shows how to do this on the query errors group. However, we are actually interested in fixing the Order Revenue table rather than the "Errors in OrderRevenue". That means delete the Query Errors group [right click on Query Error » Delete Group] and replace the errors (with value null) in the Order Revenue table instead. Further, the import with errors led to the Revenue and Gross Profit column having the wrong data type in the OrderRevenue table, which needs to be changed to a decimal number [shift click on Revenue and Gross Profit » Transform » Data Type » Decimal Number]. Figure 3.16 illustrates these steps. Once these steps are done, we can close the PQE and apply the changes.

This brings us back to PBI, where the Data tab includes the OrderCost and Order-Revenue tables. By the way, at this point, data changes can be easily refreshed in PBI [Home » Queries » Refresh].

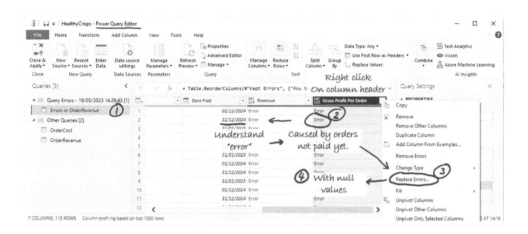

FIGURE 3.15 Power Query Editor – analysing import errors.

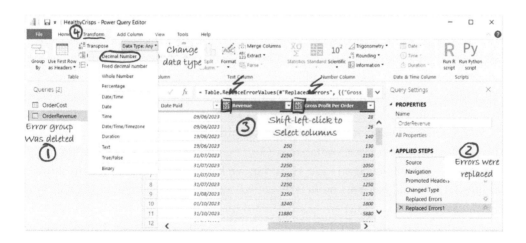

FIGURE 3.16 PQE steps to "fix" Revenue and Gross Profit column.

Model View

Next, let us verify that there is a relationship between the two tables by entering the model view (see Figure 3.13 Step 3a). Figure 3.17 visualises a 1:1 relationship between the tables. That means each record in OrderCost has exactly one corresponding record in OrderRevenue. It is always a good idea to check that the cross filter direction works both ways [double-click on relationship or Relationships » Manage relationships]. This is important for the interactivity of the visuals in the report view.

FIGURE 3.17 One-to-one relationship between two tables.

Report View – Financial KPIs

Let us now enter the Report view (Figure 3.13 Step 3c) and add a text box (Step 4). Start typing "Financial Performance" and the text will appear. This will be our header (font size 32 and bold). As mentioned before, this PBI page is all about the gross profit. Hence, we will add a card that displays the total gross profit. Step 5 (Figure 3.13, Card) creates an empty card. In the Data tab, expand OrderRevenue and tick Gross Profit. In the Visualizations » Data tab, you will find Fields; the top one displays the "Sum of Gross Proft Per Order". We want to rename this and call it "Gross Profit" [right-click field » Rename for this visual]. Let us create two more cards for Net Sales and Cost (COGS). The Net Sales are reflected in the Revenue column with the OrderRevenue table, and the COGS can be found in the OrderCost table as CostOfGoodsSold. Let us rename the page to Gross Profit [double-click on Page 1]. So far, we have created the dashboard shown in Figure 3.18. Recall that gross profit is the difference between net sales and COGS. However, a simple check 7.23M - 4.47M = 2.53M makes us wonder why the gross profit is not 3.93M. We encountered the answer when importing the data. (Net sales and gross profit for unpaid orders are missing.). That means adding a time horizon (filter = slicer)

Financial Performance

3.93M	7.23M	4.47M
Gross Profit	Net Sales	Cost (COGS)

FIGURE 3.18 Financial Performance intermediate dashboard.

resolves this issue. We will add a Slicer (see Figure 3.13 Step 5) for the years, which will be a year-drop-down slicer. This is achieved with the following three steps:

1. Add a slicer [Visualizations » Slicer];

2. Select the year data [Data » Order Revenue » Date Paid » Date Hierarchy » Year];

3. Format as dropdown list [Visualizations » Format » Slicer settings » Options » Drop-down].

We test that the gross profit is OK for the year 2023 by applying the created slicer. The gross profit is 432.86K when calculating the difference between net sales (824.64K) and COGS (391.78K). Similarly, slicers for quarters and months are created (or via copy and paste and ticking quarter/month in the Data tab).

Report View – Timeseries

It would be interesting to see the development of the gross profit over the quarters. This is best visualised as a bar chart with the X-axis made up of the year and quarter and the Y-axis having the sum of gross profit per order. The required steps for this are [Visualizations » Stacked column chart + Data » OrderRevenue » Date Paid » Date Hierarchy: Year, Quarter + Data » OrderRevenue » Gross Profit Per Order]. Let us label the y-axis as Gross Profit [Visualizations » Y-Axis » Rename for this visual] and remove the x-axis label [Visualizations » Format » X-axis » Title » Off]. Data labels allow us to have concrete values available [Visualizations » Format » Data labels » On].

Generally, in businesses, financial measures are reported in quarters. This allows setting targets and assessing the performance of the business. Quarterly reports are issued to the stakeholders to increase transparency and provide clarity about the company's financial situation. This allows analysts and investors to assess the financial health of the business.

Internally, the company is also interested in refined reports such as monthly performance and its trend. Hence, we add this visual to our report. This is achieved with the following steps:

1. Reuse previous visual [copy and paste quarterly report];
2. Change chart type [Visualizations » Area chart];
3. Turn off data labels: Visualizations » Format » Data labels » Off;
4. Add zoom slider [Visualizations » Format » Zoom slider » On » Y-axis » Off];
5. Add months [Data » OrderRevenue » Date Paid » Date Hierarchy: Year, Quarter, Month];
6. Add trend line [Visualizations » Analytics (analyses) » Trend line » On].

The visual shows us that the profit has a strong incline. At this point, the dashboard should look like the one shown in Figure 3.19. We have a functional dashboard which can be used for the business.

Dashboard – Visual Improvements

Visual effects: Further formatting increases the aesthetics. For instance, we can reformat the slicers by placing them in an empty text box with a light blue background and rounded corners [Format (textbox) » Effects » Background » Color: Theme color 1, Transparency: 50%; Visual border: On, Rounded corners: 30px; Format (menu bar) » Arrange

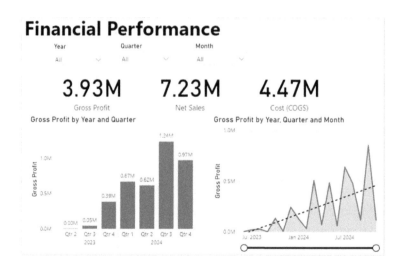

FIGURE 3.19 Financial performance dashboard including quarterly profits and a timeseries with time slicers and trend line.

» Send to back]. Similarly, we format the other visuals by changing their background colour and border effects [Visualizations » Format » General » Effects].

Conditional formatting: The bar chart would benefit from gradient colour scheme based on the gross profit [Visualizations » Format » Columns » Default » fx] (see Figure 3.20).

Default color - Columns - Colors ×

Format style

Gradient ⌄

What field should we base this on?   Summarization   How should we format empty values?

Sum of Gross Profit Per Order ⌄   Sum ⌄   As zero ⌄

Minimum   Maximum

Lowest value ⌄   Highest value ⌄

FIGURE 3.20 PBI gradient colour format.

Buttons can be integrated for navigation. We will use icons (images) for our buttons; they can be found at IconScout. I have created a few images using PowerPoint shown in Figure 3.21.

Let us create buttons for gross profit, net sales and COGS with the icons shown in Figure 3.21. For instance, the gross profit button is created via [Insert » Buttons » Blank + Format » Button » Style » Icon » Icon Type: Custom » Browse . . . : images » profits.PNG, Horizontal Alignment: centre, Padding: 0px]. The other two buttons are created in a similar fashion. Generally, images can be displayed using buttons. To use the buttons for navigation, we will need more pages. Let us create a Net Sales and COGS page [⊞ New Page]. Now we can add an action to the Net Sales button [select Net Sales button » Format » Action » On » Type: Page navigation, Destination: Net Sales] and – similarly – for the COGS button. Now we can navigate to these two empty pages via Ctrl + mouse clicking.

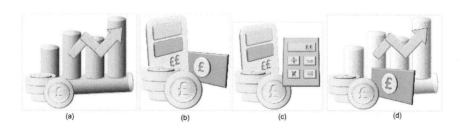

(a)   (b)   (c)   (d)

FIGURE 3.21 Images for (a) profits, (b) net sales, (c) COGS and (d) forecast.

Tooltips are added to provide clarity about the meaning of certain measures. Let us create a tooltip for the gross profit card. First, we need to create the tooltip page [⊞ New Page: Tooltip Gross Profit]. Now, we can format the page to be a tooltip [Visualizations » Format Page » Format » Page information » Allow use as tooltip: On; Canvas background » Color: Theme color 7, Transparency: 0%]. Let us add a textbox as shown in Figure 3.22. Finally, we link the gross profit card with the tooltip page [Select Gross profit card » Visualizations » Format » General » Tooltips: On » Type: Report page, Page: Tooltip Gross Profit]. Now, when we hover over the card, the tooltip page appears.

> **Gross Profit** = Net Sales – Cost of goods sold (COGS).
>
> **COGS** may include labour and product cost, cost of raw materials and inventory cost.
>
> **Net sales** = Sales after discounts, returns and allowances.

FIGURE 3.22 Tooltip page.

KPI visual: A *key performance indicator* (KPI) visual is a compact representation of a measure's value, graph and target. We will create a monthly KPI visual for the gross profit. First, we will create a column that maps the date to the month. The PQE offers a convenient way to achieve this. Let us open the PQE [Home » Transform data] and add a month column to the Order Revenue table [Select OrderRevenue query and the Date Paid column followed by Add Column » Date » Month » Start of Month]. We rename the column Date Paid Month [double-click on column], close the PQE and apply the changes. Now we can add the KPI visual to the gross profit page [Visualizations » Build visual » KPI, Value: Gross Profit Per Order, Trend axis: Date Paid Month]. You can set the callout value font size to 20 and turn the trend axis date on.

Currency: In order to show the pound symbol, we need to convert the type of the required columns to currency. We can do this in the Table View and in the Report View's Data tab by selecting a column which we want to format. The Column tools tab allows us to make the appropriate change [select OrderRevenue » click on Gross Profit Per Order column » Column tools » Format: Currency, $: "£ English (United Kingdom)"]. The Revenue and CostsOfGoodsSold columns can be similarly changed.

Figure 3.12 shows the final dashboard. Similarly to the previously created gross profit dashboard, we can create a dashboard for net sales. Figure 3.23 provides such a dashboard. Here, the hexagon buttons on the left allow us to navigate to the other pages. For consistency, the same layout is used for the COGS page as well, as shown in Figure 3.24.

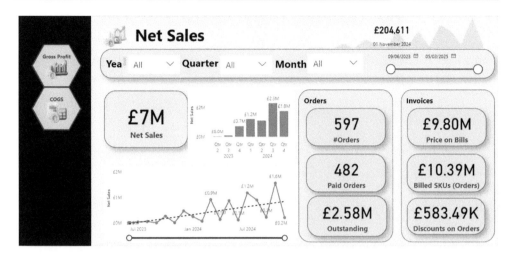

FIGURE 3.23 PBI net sales dashboard.

FIGURE 3.24 PBI COGS dashboard.

Publishing

Mobile layout: A PBI desktop dashboard can easily be transformed into one suitable for mobile devices. This is achieved by using the menu bar's View ribbon and activating the mobile layout tool [Mobile » Mobile layout] (Figure 3.25). Now, you can drag and drop the existing visuals into the mobile view. Figure 3.12 (b) and (c) show the layout as seen on a Samsung mobile phone. On android devices, the Microsoft Power BI App can be installed using the Google Play Store. In order to view the dashboards created on a desktop computer on a mobile phone, the PBI map has to be published.

FIGURE 3.25 PBI mobile view.

Publishing and sharing: Sharing and making dashboards available to a wider audience are important steps in Business or Data Analytics projects. They allow stakeholders and users to utilise the information for decision making. In PBI, this is achieved via the Home ribbon's share group [Home » Share » Publish]. First, you need to select a destination such as "My workspace". After this, PBI uploads all the files and returns a success message, which includes an openable link. In Figure 3.26, the link is called Open "HC.pbix".

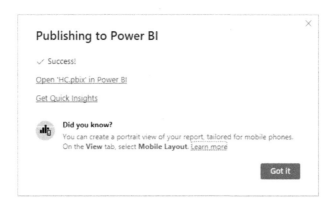

FIGURE 3.26 PBI desktop success message for publishing a report with link.

Following the link provided, opens the corresponding PBI service in a web browser. Here, you can share the report with colleagues within your business and, depending on the PBI licence type (free, pro or premium), with external collaborators. Without sharing the report, it can already be accessed from the PBI mobile app via Workspaces and selecting the report. The mobile layout of the gross profit dashboard is shown in Figure 3.12 (b) and (c).

Power BI service: The PBI service is similar to the desktop version, especially when the edit function is activated. Figure 3.27 shows the PBI service with the edit window activated. Exploring the workspaces provides an interesting view of the projects because it reveals the data sources and gateways needed to update the data for published reports. This requires the setup of gateways. A *gateway* is a software that usually runs on the data server (or a computer with access to the databases) and manages the connection with the PBI service. This allows periodic synchronisation (refreshing) of the data and makes the PBI reports more of a life system (pro license: 8 refreshes/day, premium: 48 refreshes/day). The installation of the standard gateway is straightforward (De Boer, 2023).

FIGURE 3.27 PBI services edit window.

As mentioned previously, another main advantage of the PBI service is the possibility of sharing and collaborating on PBI projects.

Financial measures: We have only used a few financial measures in this report. However, there are several more interesting terms and formulas.

$$Gross\ Profit\ Margin = Gross\ Profit\ /\ Net\ Sales \qquad (3.2)$$

Fluctuations (volatility) in the gross profit margin indicate issues with management or products.

$$Operating\ Profit = Gross\ Profit - Indirect\ Operational\ Expenses \qquad (3.3)$$

Usually, indirect operational expenses include administration, overhead, sales cost and marketing cost.

Operating Profit = Operating Earnings

$$= \text{Earning Before Interest and Taxes (EBIT)} \tag{3.4}$$

$$\text{Operating Profit Margin} = \text{Operating Earnings / Revenue} \tag{3.5}$$

$$\text{Net Profit} = \text{Operating Profit} - (\text{Taxes} + \text{Interest}) \tag{3.6}$$

Here, the handling of taxes and annual interest is the focus. For instance, business growth (investments) is rewarded by paying less interest. A quick word about the operational expenses (Opex) to sales ratio. A high ratio indicates little profit. Typically, organisation have to provide income statements. An income statement includes gross profit and net profit. Another interesting term is gross sales, which are the sales before discounts, returns and allowances.

Forecast the anticipated profit: Forecasting the profit helps the business determine its investment strategy, so it is of interest to shareholders and investors. Figure 3.28 (a) shows the gross profit for the next three months. We cans see that oscillations (up-down-up) are expected. The grey shaded region shows the 95% "confidence" interval (it is likely that they meant the prediction interval). Figure 3.28 (b) can be used to verify the quality of the forecast. Here, we see that the forecast roughly captures the existing months. However, the first month forecast is too high, the second one is too low and the third month is too high again. More details about forecasting are discussed in the Analytics section.

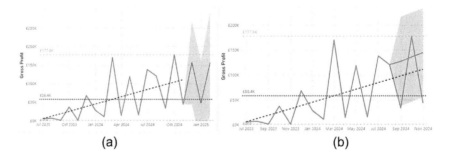

(a)   (b)

FIGURE 3.28 (a) Forecasting next three months and (b) comparing last three months.

Next, we will analyse and compare products by profit and demand. The graphs in Figure 3.29 were created using the Order (Units) and OrderRevenue (Gross Profit) data for each product (id) over the entire time horizon.

We can see that the top products are AO (Apple Orange) and AL (Apple Lime). Next, we can investigate the reasons ABB has the lowest demand and profit. By considering the product development, we can see that ABB was introduced later than the other products. That means the product development is much better than the other four products. This implies that ABB seems to be the company's top choice to focus on. The other

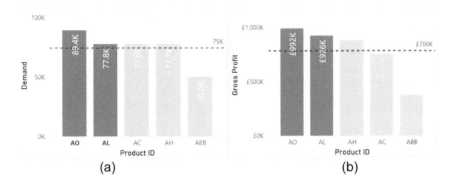

FIGURE 3.29 PBI product (a) demand, (b) profit for entire period.

four products seem to be fairly balanced. Next, we should consider the product development in the most recent months. This will reveal that the product AL needs attention.

Customer analysis is important to identify potential opportunities or churns. It also helps us know who are (were) the top customers. Hence, we compare the customers demand and profit. Figure 3.30 (a) provides an overview table identifying Texo as the top customer. Figure 3.30 (b) shows a steady increase in customer demand over the visualised period for most customers. However, it appears Leedl's demand dropped in Q4 of 2024. The creation of the table in PBI is straightforward. However, we need to import the customer table and link it with the order data. Please ensure that the relationship's cross filter supports both directions (Figure 3.31). The creation of the demand chart is done in the usual way mostly, but the individual customers can be displayed by adding the customer name into the visuals legend field. The last quarter is removed using a date slicer within the PBI page.

Next, we will display the location of the customers. Figure 3.32 identifies all delivery locations. We can see that the majority of goods are sold in London. There are several other cities which Healthy Crisps provides with goods. The map indicates that there is plenty of growth opportunity.

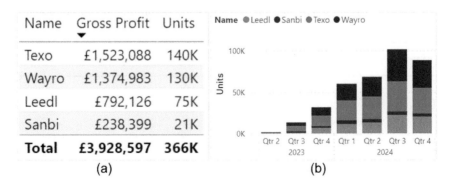

FIGURE 3.30 PBI customer (a) profit and demand, (b) demand chart.

FIGURE 3.31 PBI relationship between order and customer that enables cross filtering in both directions.

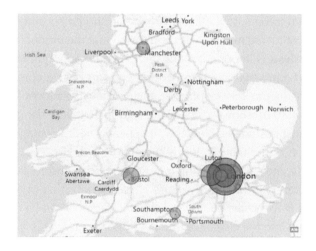

FIGURE 3.32 PBI map showing total demand in current delivery postcodes.

For operations, weekly demand predictions are important. Previously, we forecasted the gross profit for the next three months. Since we do not have a weekly date column, we will have to create one [Select Order table » right-click » New Column]. Insert the following text to create a date that records Monday as the first day of the week.

```
Delivery Week = [Delivery Date] - Weekday([Delivery Date],2) -1
```

This allows us to create a weekly forecast. Figure 3.33 shows the weekly demand forecast for eight weeks.

The forecast can be created using PBI's built-in feature. First, a line chart is created based on the order data [Visualizations » Line Chart, X-axis: Delivery Week, Y-Axis: Units]. Then we add a 50% and 90% quantile line. Next, we add an average demand line and a trend line. These are used to verify the forecast. Finally, we add the forecast

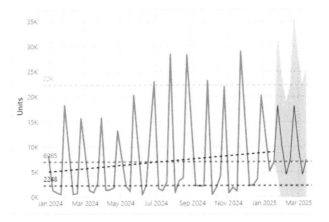

FIGURE 3.33 PBI weekly demand forecast of all products.

[Visualizations » Analytics » Forecast: On, Units: Points, Forecast length: 8]. A time slicer is also added to select the relevant period for the forecast. This is achieved by taking general knowledge into account, such as the irrelevance of the product introduction period and the final week in January being incomplete.

This concludes our crash course in PBI.

3.3.3 PBI General Considerations

Simplicity

Data models in PBI should focus on the business challenge under consideration. That means only the data needed should be imported. The data model is the same as the entity relationship model in databases. In databases, "normalisation" (see database section) is of great importance (more generally in OLTP), whereas "simplicity" is more desired for analytical considerations (or more generally in OLAP). That means that, in a database, we may have twenty tables describing a car sales system, but in PBI, we might just have three (Figure 3.34). As a consequence, the data model in PBI can have redundant data, integrated lookup tables and other non-normal data structures. Moreover, since "simplicity" is a main focus, it is recommended to drop any columns that are not needed. Hence, it is recommended to import customised views rather than tables from a database. PBI allows the execution of queries when importing from traditional SQL databases. The fewer tables the better. Also keep in mind that the import may be done repeatedly or that data needs to be refreshed. PBI provides the Power Query Editor, which allows data manipulations. However, the original data source systems (e.g. Excel) may have "easier" (or more familiar) preprocessing opportunities. Hence, data preprocessing in the data source system can be an advantage.

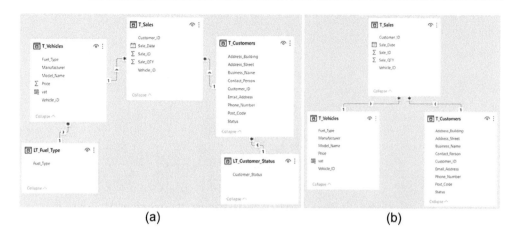

(a)   (b)

FIGURE 3.34 PBI relationships and simplicity.

We conclude that when importing "good" model data, simplicity is key to a successful operation. The following steps can be done to achieve this simplicity.

- Only use important tables;
- Remove all unneeded columns (or concise SQL/view on table);
- Use simple table and column names;
- Manipulate data before importing (if possible).

It is not necessary to de-normalise data before importing it. In fact, it is better to have the normalised data scheme. This has similarities to a star scheme. A star scheme consists of a fact table and corresponding dimension tables. For instance, a sales table constitutes a fact table; it has columns such as sold product identifier, sales date, order quantity, sales price and sales staff. Corresponding dimension tables are products and staff.

Relationships

Once the tables are imported, it is important to know the relationship between them.

Let us continue with the car sales example. The sale table depends on the vehicles and customers (Figure 3.35). Let us have a closer look at the relationship between sales and vehicles. To understand the relationship (business rule), we need to define the meaning of a vehicle record (e.g. [10, Volkswagen, Golf, petrol, £ 16,500]). We will say this record represents an available vehicle category with a fixed price rather than an individual car. For instance, 328 Volkswagen Golf petrol cars were sold (i.e. revenues of 328 × £ 16,500 = £ 5,412k). That means that one record in the vehicle table can have

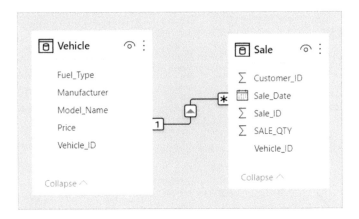

FIGURE 3.35 Car sales example with vehicle and sales table relationship.

many records in the sale table. This is visualised by 1-▸-∗ , where the arrow indicates the direction of reading.

This is known as cardinality one-to-many (1:*). If the direction changes, then its cardinality is many-to-one (*:1). One seeks to avoid the cardinality many-to-many (.) since it ambiguous. The many-to-many cardinality can be avoided by introducing an intermediate table. The cardinality (1:1) indicates that each record in one table has one record in the associated table.

Power Query

In the Data view, click on open the Power Query Editor. Now create a blank query by right-clicking in the Queries pane as shown in Figure 3.36. Now, you can use the *m-language* (m for mashup) to create the dates. The m-language is for formulas and is part of the Power Query tool: for details, see Klopfenstein (2023).

```
= List.Dates(#date(2016,11,21), 1095, #duration(1,0,0,0))
```

Data Design Questions

Do the reports have to be updated frequently? Will the structure of the data sources remain the same (i.e. only the content changes)? Who is responsible for updating the data?

For instance, the data can reside in SQL databases, Excel maps and other software systems. The advantage of having a "static" report is that it does not affect ongoing changes and is a snapshot at a certain point in time. It does influence the performance of the live services. A dynamic report has the advantage of providing a current view of the business, which can be updated at regular intervals.

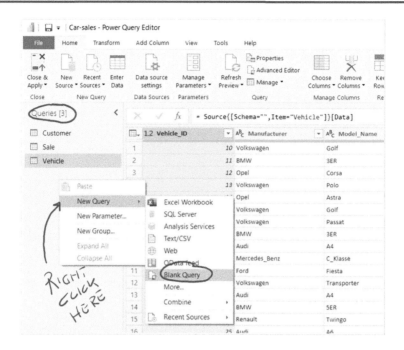

FIGURE 3.36 Power Query Editor – creating a new query.

A static report can be stored locally without any disadvantages. Dynamic reports require the organisation and delegation of responsibilities to update the data sources and at what time. In this case, databases, shared drives (e.g. OneDrive, GoogleDrive, Nextcloud) or shared sites (SharePoint) are needed to efficiently delegate the updating of various data sources.

3.4 Analytics

PBI provides access to analytics via specific visuals such as charts and key influencers. The PBI tool provides basic analytics for most charts in the form of the minimum, maximum and average. Medians and percentiles are statistics that are also provided in some chart visuals. PBI *line chart* analytics include slightly more advanced methods, such as trend lines and forecasts. Some background to trend lines and forecasts is provided next. The key influencers are particularly interesting for predictions. We will hear about the technical details in a later chapter. However, the usage and meaning of this PBI visual is explained here. More advanced analytical visuals can be created using the R script and Python visuals. Several chapters of this book are dedicated to creating and understanding those methods. In this chapter, we will restrict ourselves to demonstrating the principle integration of an R script into PBI. Finally, DAX functions are often heard in context with analytics. Hence, we will provide a guide to this domain as well.

3.4.1 Trends and Forecasts

For a business, it is essential to understand the development of its profit, sales and demand – to name a few. Trends, timeseries analysis and forecasts help in this endeavour. *Trend* is the general direction in which something is developing. *Timeseries* analysis tries to create a mathematical model to describe given data over time. This model is then used to *forecast* (predict) future time periods.

Trend: The most commonly used trend line is the linear regression. We will consider linear regression in detail in Chapter 6. Chapter 5 provides numerous examples in domains such as operations, finance and marketing. Here, we will briefly mention the linear regression and other popular trend lines. In the previous section, we added trend lines to visualise the overall development of gross profit, net sales and demand. The underlying line equations are of the form:

$$\text{Predicted Gross Profit}_i = \beta_0 + \beta_1 \text{time}_i, \tag{3.7}$$

where i is the time index. That means we have a series of $n = 17$ points describing gross profits y = (789, 18429, 25904, 1031, 136872, 4723, 245115, 130787, 32357, 506073, 72264, 484060, 60630, 639606, 478148, 119340, 856138, 116330). The specific month information is disregarded, and discrete sequential equidistant time steps are assumed. The data is used to learn the parameters (β_0, β_1) such that the "error" between the predicted gross profit $\hat{y}$ and the given gross profit y is minimised. The details for this and the resulting formulas are given in Section 6.4.1. Applying these formulas to the gross profit example gives us as intercept $\beta_0 = 28002.75$ and slope $\beta_1 = 28783.36$. The trend line is shown in Figure 3.37. There are other ways to model trends, such as using polynomial, exponential or logarithmic functions. Figure 3.38 visualises them using the Data Science language R (see Chapter 4). Trend lines or other trend functions can be used for forecasting.

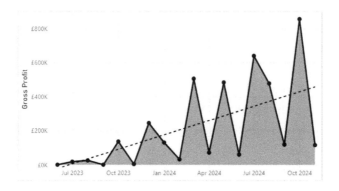

FIGURE 3.37 PBI trend line.

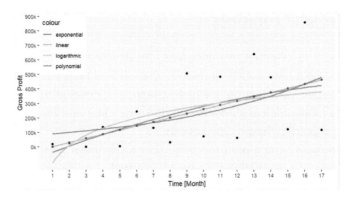

FIGURE 3.38 Alternative trend models.

Forecasts: Forecasts are important for business, finance, economics, production, governments and many more areas. They are used to making qualified decisions about growth targets, quantities and employment figures, to name just a few. Yet it boils down to a forecast being a guess about the future. However, with quantitative methods, we can evaluate the forecast's quality.

On top of a trend, a forecast can identify seasonality. Seasonality refers to patterns that are repeated on a yearly basis. Cycles describe any patterns or dynamicity that is not covered by trend or seasonality. Three popular models that cover cyclicity are moving average (MA), autoregression (AR) and their combination ARMA. The interested reader is referred to Diebold (2007) for details. Probably one of the most universal forecasting methods is called autoregressive integrated moving average (ARIMA), which is a generalisation of the ARMA model.

Power BI uses the ETS(AAA) and ETS(AAN) algorithms (according to a Microsoft employee's blog in 2016; unfortunately, not too much background about forecasts is revealed in the official documentation). ETS is the abbreviation for error trend seasonality and represents an exponential smoothing algorithm with increased weights for later data points. The three characters in the brackets (AAA, AAN) specify the handling of error, trend and seasonality. The error can be additive (A) or multiplicative (M). Trend can be additive (A), multiplicative (M), additive-damped (Ad) or not considered (N). Finally, seasonality can be additive (A) or multiplicative (M), or there is none (N). Hence, in both models, we have additive error and additive trend. However, they differ in using additive or no seasonality. ETS(AAN) is also known as Holt's linear method with additive errors or ARIMA(0,2,2). ETS(AAA) is also known as Holt Winter's triple smoothing model. In our example (Figure 3.28), the first forecast matched the ETS(AAA) model as best fit and the second forecast matched the ETS(AAN).

3.4.2 PBI Key Influencers Visual

The PBI key influencers visual identifies and ranks the features that affect a target variable. For instance, a company may want to know the factors (salary, gender, other existing insurances etc.) that influence a customer to purchase insurance. The key influencers (KIF) visual is based on logistic regression for categorical variables. Logistic regression is introduced in Chapter 6 in detail. The key influencers visual also runs several steps in the background, such as one-hot encoding, missing value imputation and standardisation and the logistic regression based on the limited memory Broyden-Fletcher-Goldfarb-Shanno method.

Figure 3.39 (a) shows a key influencers visual. The example was created using the Caravan data, which can be found in the Various database (Chapter 2) or within R in the ISLR2 package. As target field, we identified the purchase field. In PBI, this represents the analyse field. This will be explained by various features (variables, factors). For this example, we chose the ones which have the highest correlation coefficients to the purchase-yes value. These correlations can be obtained in R using the lares package and corr_var function, which can be easily integrated into PBI using the R code in Figure 3.40. Figure 3.39 (b) displays the top correlated variables using the R script. We can replace the variable names with descriptions in the key influencers visual (e.g. MKOOPKLA represents the purchasing power class). The purchasing power class has a 0.0959 correlation to the purchase-yes variable. In the key influencer visual, this variable is identified to increase the likelihood of insurance

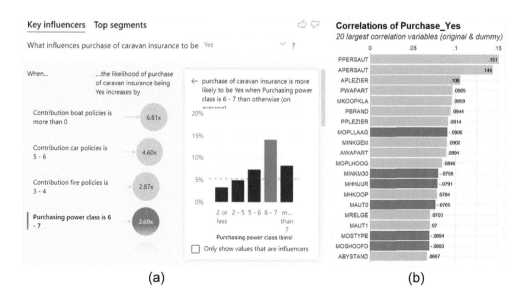

(a) (b)

FIGURE 3.39 (a) PBI key Influencers visual, (b) correlations.

```
R script editor                                    ˅ ↗ ⚙ ⊙
1 library(pacman); p_load(lares)
2 D<-dataset # ensure dataset got an index otherwise data is lost
3 D$Index <- NULL # but index is not needed for correlations
4 D$Purchase <- factor(D$Purchase);
5 levels(D$Purchase)= c('No','Yes')
6 D |> corr_var(Purchase_Yes)
```

FIGURE 3.40 R script code for correlations.

being purchased. The factor implies that potential customers with a purchase power being in class 6–7 are 2.69 times more likely to purchase insurance than customers with other purchase power. This kind of information allows us to target specific individuals for sales activities. However, there is also a segmentation within the key influencers visual, which accelerates the identification of customer groups interested in purchasing insurance. Figure 3.41 displays four segments. The first segment contains 359 records (data points). It is formed by factors such as car policies, fire policies and purchasing power but defined by specific factor categories (e.g. category 5 or 6 in car policies).

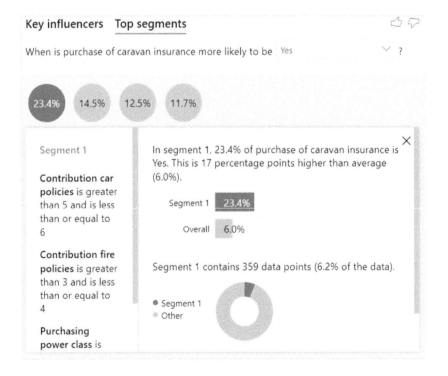

FIGURE 3.41 Segmentation of customers.

In case the target field (column to analyse) is a continuous (numerical) variable rather than a discrete (categorical) variable, then a linear regression is used (see the earlier trend line example and more details in Chapter 6). The actual algorithm's implementation is in the ML.NET library as SDCA-regression (Stochastic Dual Coordinated Ascent). Shalev-Shwartz and Zhang (2013) discuss methods for regularised loss minimization in the context of SDCA. More details about the KIF and its context to ML.NET can be found in Microsoft's Power BI documentation (ML.NET, 2023).

3.4.3 DAX Functions

Data Analysis Expressions (DAX) is a library of functions and operators that can be combined to build formulas and expressions in Power BI. DAX is a universal functional language which can be used to create new columns or derive tables. Typical DAX functions are average, max, min, count and concatenate for aggregation. It also includes functions for filtering, finance, information logic, statistics, tables and text manipulation. Microsoft's DAX reference document (Minewiskan, 2023a) provides more details. Here, we provide a few introductory examples. DAX functions can be created in Power BI's data view and report view (e.g. New Column).

DAX for dates: Let us create a table called DatesExp which generates dates for a year [Data view » Table tools » New table]. In the formula bar, enter:

```
DatesExp = CALENDAR(date(2023,06,17), date(2024,06,16))
```

Let us derive several date details columns [Data view » Table tools » New column]. That means repeatedly pressing "New Column" in Column tools and entering each of the following lines:

```
Year        = YEAR(DatesExp[Date])
MonthNb     = MONTH(DatesExp [Date])
WeekNb      = WEEKNUM(DatesExp [Date])
Weekday     = FORMAT(DatesExp [Date],"DDDD")
Weekend     = or(WEEKDAY(DatesExp[Date],2)==6,
              WEEKDAY(DatesExp [Date], 2)==7)
```

Figure 3.42 shows a snapshot of the created table. We started by entering the Data view (A). Then we created the DatesExp table (Blue numbers 1 and 2). Automatically,

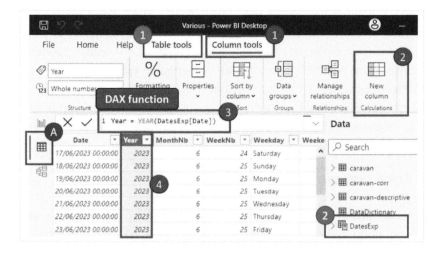

FIGURE 3.42 Workflow to create DAX functions in PBI.

we switched to the Column tools ribbon (1). Here, we clicked New column (2) and (3) wrote in the formula bar Year = YEAR(DatesExp[Date]), which returned the Year column.

We can use this table to derive an entirely new table. For instance, let us derive the table MonthExp, which includes the distinct months from the DatesExp table. First, go to Table tools » New table, then write the following DAX function:

```
MonthsExp = DISTINCT(DatesExp[MonthNb])
```

Another important application is to compute the difference with dates utilising the DATEDIFF function.

DAX for Aggregation

We continue with the MonthsExp table and add an average, min, max and count column.

```
avg = AVERAGE(MonthsExp[MonthNb])
min = MIN(MonthsExp[MonthNb])
max = MAX(MonthsExp[MonthNb])
count = count(MonthsExp[MonthNb])
```

DAX for Text Manipulations

For instance, let us concatenate the year and week from the previously created DatesExp table:

```
YearWeek = CONCATENATE(DatesExp[Year],DatesExp[WeekNb])
```

Slightly simpler is the following:

```
Year-Week = DatesExp[Year] & - & DatesExp[WeekNb]
```

Here, the and-operator is used for concatenating strings.

There are many more functions such as find, lower, search, left and right (see the text functions overview). An overview of these text functions can be found in Minewiskan (2023b).

DAX for Logical Decisions

Often, conditional creation of columns is necessary. For instance, let us reuse the MonthsExp table and create a column that decides if it is the first or second half of the year.

```
year-half = IF(MonthsExp[MonthNb]<7, "1st half" , "2nd half" )
```

DAX for Linked Tables

For the next example, we need the car sales data. The data can be found at smartana. org/db in the Access database car-sales-solution.accdb. Next, we create a PBI map and import the Sale and Vehicle table. (Renaming the tables is suggested.) Now, we can make a revenue column from two related tables: [Report View » click on Sale table » New column] (Note: revenue = sale's quantity times vehicle price).

```
Revenue = CALCULATE(min(Sale[SALE_QTY]) * min(Vehicle[Price]))
```

To highlight columns in bar charts, we can add a rank column to a table. For instance, let us create a column that ranks the profit (Table: Sale, Column: Profit).

```
Rank = rankx('Sale',[Profit])
```

3.5 Miscellaneous

3.5.1 Best Practices/Shared Experiences

- Only import parts from database;
  - o Do not attempt to import entire database;
- Create relationships between entities from scratch;
  - o Do not trust relationships in PBI;
- Best to remove them all and recreate (check ERM);
  - o Less information is more;
- Avoid information overload;
  - o Only have three to four pages per PBI.

3.5.2 Bit-Sized Challenges

Example 3.5.1 (Unpivot cross-table). Data is given as cross-table (pivot Table 3.2). How can you unpivot the data?

TABLE 3.2 Table data (cross-table) to be pivoted.

Month	Audi	BMW	Mazda	Mercedes	Volkswagen
Jan	78	159	1	112	246
Feb	100	112		88	202
Mar	122	110		61	218
Apr	78	132		97	196
May	113	128	2	128	227
Jun	100	137		90	279
Jul	75	123	6	54	189

Solution: Power Query Editor (PQE) » Transform » Unpivot Columns » Unpviot Other Columns (see Table 3.3).

Example 3.5.2 (Inconsistent date link). Two tables are given. The first table contains dates like 15/7/2022 and the second table only contains the name of the month. We want to link these two tables. For instance, all July dates from the first table need to be linked to the first of the month from the second table.

TABLE 3.3 Unpivoted (normalised) table.

Month	Attribute	Value
Jan	Audi	78
Jan	BMW	159
Jan	Mazda	1
Jan	Mercedes	112
Jan	Volkswagen	246
Feb	Audi	100
Feb	BMW	112
Feb	Mercedes	88
Feb	Volkswagen	202
Mar	Audi	122
Mar	BMW	110

TABLE 3.4 Data from Excel map, which contains two sheets called (a) Revenue and (b) Cost.

Date	Income
15/07/2022	£ 1,742
27/07/2022	£ 1,561
03/08/2022	£ 1,974
08/08/2022	£ 2,792
15/08/2022	£ 1,898
30/08/2022	£ 2,330
02/07/2022	£ 1,629
17/07/2022	£ 3,869
19/07/2022	£ 1,963

Month	Expenses
July	£ 6,000
August	£ 6,500
September	£ 7,000

(a)   (b)

Solution: Create a new column in the first table, where the date is mapped to the first day [PBI » Fields » select Revenue » right click » New column] (Figure 3.43). The following text was entered in the formula bar.

```
Month = Date(YEAR([Date]),MONTH([Date]),1)
```

Now you can link the two month columns (Figure 3.44). This allows you to select and display related data (Figure 3.45).

Example 3.5.3 (Transforming pivoted data and year-quarter format). The tool SimVenture exports data in the following format. The first column contains the feature

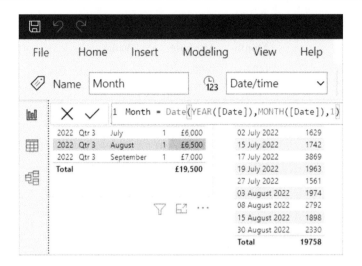

FIGURE 3.43 PBI new month column.

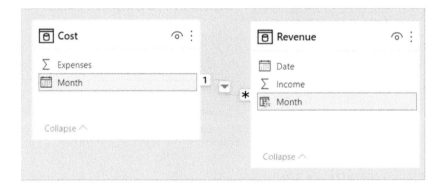

FIGURE 3.44 PBI link cost and revenue via month.

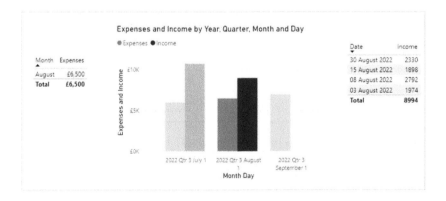

FIGURE 3.45 Monthly comparison of expenses and income.

(variable) to be the column headers. The subsequent columns have date headers (e.g. Y2, Q1) and numerical values.

Solution: in Power BI, add a year and quarter column:

```
Year = convert(RIGHT(LEFT([Year and Quarter],2),1),INTEGER)+2000

Quarter = Convert(Right([Year and Quarter],1),INTEGER)
```

Next, create a new date column which designates the first day of the quarter:

```
Date = Date([Year],[Quarter]*3-2,1)
```

Example 3.5.4 (Missing identifier). When creating an R script visual, the duplicated rows are removed. Hence, it is important to provide an identifier. Often, the data does not contain an identifier; thus, it has to be created [Power Query Editor » Add Column » Index Column]. Once the data frame is submitted, the Index column can be removed within the R script editor: `Dataset$Index=NULL`.

Example 3.5.5 (Aggregation by date using the Power Query Editor (PQE)). Assume you have daily revenue data (in a PBI table with columns revenue_date and revenue), and you'd like to have them for each quarter. Note: only use this if you do not need the daily data any-more; in PBI, quarterly information can be displayed directly. First, start PQE via [PBI » Home » Transform Data » Transform]. Then use the date field (i.e. revenue_date) and transform it to quarterly dates using [Date » Quarter » Start of Quarter]. Lastly, use ["Group By" (Start of Quarter) » New column name: revenue_quarter; Operation: Sum; Column: revenue].

Example 3.5.6 (Highlight top three items (and add average)). A sales-table is created; conditional formatting is added to highlight the profit of the top three products (see Figure 3.46).

The detailed steps for this example are as follows:

1. Create a sales table and add a few values [PBI » Home » Enter Data] (Figure 3.46);
2. Create a column that automatically ranks the profit using table Sales and column Profit [Data » New Column: `Rank = rankx('Sales',[Profit])`];
3. Create a stacked bar chart with product and profit [Visualizations » Stacked bar chart; Data » Sales » select Product and Profit];
4. Add conditional formats [Visualizations » Format » Bars » Colors » Conditional Formatting: Format style: Rules; Field: Rank; Summarization: Minimum; Rules: if 0<value<=3 then "red"].

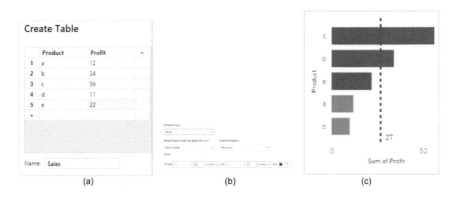

FIGURE 3.46 (a) Create sales table, (b) conditional formatting rule, (c) highlighted profit.

An average line is added by using the Analytics tab . The steps are: Constant line »
Add » Value: function » Field value based on average profit.

Example 3.5.7 (How to substitute the built-in gauge with a custom visual). We use
the sales data from the previous example. Let us create a Target table for each product
(Figure 3.47) and link it with the Sales table (Model View » check relationship exists or
create one).

Let us first create a built-in gauge: (1) insert gauge [Visualizations » Gauge]; (2) add
measure [Sales » Profit]; (3) specify target and maximum value (Figure 3.47 (b)). This
results in Figure 3.47 (c). It is possible to use conditional formatting [Visualizations »
Format » Visual » Colors » fx)], but this is tedious. Instead, I recommend getting a third-
party visual such as the tachometer from Annik Inc. [Visualizations » Add Data » . . . »
Get more visuals » Tachometer (Annik) » Add]. You should see the ⬩ icon in the Visualizations tab. Use this to create visual (b) in Figure 3.47. This is achieved via the settings
shown in Figure 3.48 (a) and formatting the range colours.

FIGURE 3.47 PBI usage of built-in gauge (a) underlying data, (b) configuration of visual and (c)
gauge visual.

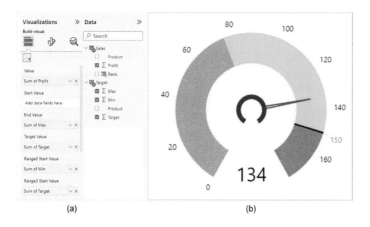

(a)   (b)

FIGURE 3.48 Custom gauge integration (a) configuration and (b) custom gauge visual.

Example 3.5.8 (How to add a new column based on a column in another table). A column from another table can be used with the RELATED function when there is a one-to-one relationship between the two tables. Assume you have an Order table which contains the units and a OrderRevenue table which contains the information on whether or not the order has been paid. Your goal is to have a new column in the Order table which shows the sold units. This is achieved by adding a "New column" to the Order table.

```
Units Sold = RELATED(OrderRevenue[Paid true])*[Units]
```

3.5.3 Create Custom R Visual for PBI

Preparation

You need to install the JavaScript runtime environment called node.js (which can be downloaded from https://nodejs.org/en/). This is needed to install the pbiviz package, which we need to build customised PBI visuals. To install the pbiviz package, open cmd and

```
run npm i -g powerbi-visuals-tools@latest
```

Verify that the installation was successful by running pbiviz. This should return an output like the one shown in Figure 3.49 (a).

Next, go to the folder where you would like to have your custom visual: e.g. create the folder myPBIvisuals and use the change directory command (cd c:\myPathTo\myPBIvisuals). Note: sometimes the path is really long in front of the command prompt. You can remove it by typing: prompt $g. Now, create the folder rTest for our visual using the rvisual template via: pbiviz new rTest -t rvisual and enter it with the

(a)   (b)

FIGURE 3.49 PBI Custom Visual (a) pbiviz tool for creation, (b) top: creating a new template; bottom: the resulting files.

command "dir"; we can see the generated files (Figure 3.49 (b)). The file script.r will contain our R-code. There are a few json-files, which we will modify.

R Code

We begin by creating a new PBI desktop file and saving it in C:\myPathTo\myPBIvisuals as customRvisual.pbix. We will assume that RStudio are R are installed. Let's get some test data (e.g. house prices from the database called various; see Section 2.2). Follow the following four steps: Step 1 is to create an R visual (click R). Step 2: In the Fields panel, select the features Price, SqFt and Home. Step 3: In the R script editor, write plot (dataset$SqFt, dataset$Price). Then click the Run script icon ⊙ (Step 4). These four steps are shown in Figure 3.50. The R-Code is specific for the house price dataset at the moment by using the Price and SqFt feature. So we will need to make it neutral to be used as a universal custom visual ("add-in"). Usually, this is best done in an external editor such as RStudio. Click the external R editor icon ↗ in PBI's R script editor.

```
D <- dataset  # rename to D
x <- D[,1]  # first column is x
y <- D[,2]  # second column is y
# use feature names for x and y label; and big red dots
plot(x,y,xlab=names(D)[1],ylab=names(D)[2],col= red ,
    pch=20,lwd=4)
```

As we can see, no specific feature names are used anymore, which makes the code functional for any two numeric fields.

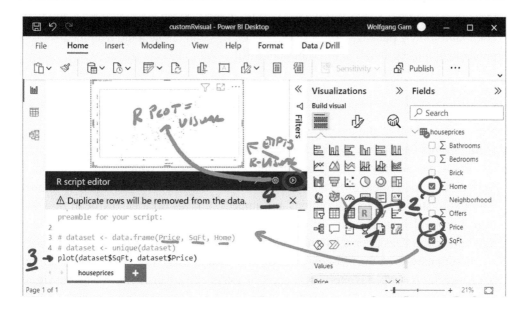

FIGURE 3.50 Creating an R visual.

Custom Visual Creation

Now the actual creation of the custom visual begins. The R code is copied into the script.r file replacing `plot(values);`. The file [capabilities.json] needs to be modified to have [dataRoles:name:dataset] instead of [dataRoles:name:Values], and similarly, the [data-ViewMapping »in:Values] needs to be changed. The software Notepad++ can be used. I'd suggest installing the JSON Viewer plugin via [Plugins » Plugins Admin . . . » JSON Tools]. This allows you to format the files properly via [Plugins » JSON Viewer » Format JSON]. Most likely you will use R libraries; these can be added in the [dependencies.json] file.

Add information about the new visual into the [pbiviz.json] file. I'd suggest providing the author's name and email address. You must provide a description. You can also provide a speaking name and display name. Optionally, you can add your own icon in the [asset] folder. I like the [ToYcon.exe] tool for converting images to icons and icons to png. However, we only need to provide a 20×20 png-image, which provides some flexibility: i.e. you can also use the Windows Snipping Tool.

Optionally, you may want to also allow the resizing of the image element in the [src/visual.ts] file by adding the following two lines in the [onResizing] method:

```
this.imageElement.style.height = finalViewport.height + px ;
this.imageElement.style.width = finalViewport.width + px ;
```

Once you are done modifying these files, it is time to "package" them by running the command [pbiviz package] in the [rTest] folder. This will create a file with the extension pbiviz (e.g. [rTest.pbiviz]) in the subfolder [dist].

Usage

Now you can import the created visual into Power BI: [Visualizations » . . . » Import a visual] from a file. The removal is similar [Visualizations » . . . » Remove a visual].

There are already many prefabricated custom visuals which can be found on Microsoft's AppSource. For instance, Chiclet Slicer allows you to aesthetically improve the built-in slicers by adding buttons and images. Images on their own can be added using the simpleImage add-in, although this visual could be quickly created using RStudio. Infographic Designer is another nice-to-have visualisation add-in.

In summary, even the first-time creation process and usage of a custom visual are simple. Once this is done, it is effortless to copy the folder and create multiple different visuals.

3.6 Summary

Power BI facilitates the transformation of data into actionable insights for an organisation's strategic and tactical business decision making. Several BI tools were identified, and Power BI was chosen in this chapter. We introduced several visualisations and made the reader aware of the appropriate use of bar charts, pie charts, line charts and others. Further, we gave guidance in creating business tables. Storytelling with visuals showed us how to prepare data for decision making.

A Power BI crash course introduced many essential steps from data import to sharing the final reports. This included the creation of dashboards. We focused on financial dashboards and introduced several popular measures. We continued with general considerations when using PBI and offered some best practices.

The analytics section described related PBI visuals such as trend lines, forecasts and key influencers. Furthermore, we introduced Data Analysis Expressions (DAX) to assist with basic date manipulation, aggregation and calculations.

We provided several bit-sized challenges, which are typically encountered in practice and can be solved in PBI. We introduced the creation of custom R visuals for PBI integration and demonstrated how to use them.

Annotated Bibliography

A practical book about storytelling with data:

1. Knaflic, C. N. (2015). *Storytelling with Data: A Data Visualization Guide for Business Professionals*. Hoboken, NJ: John Wiley & Sons.

A concise and easy-to-follow introduction:

2. Diebold, F. X. (2007). *Elements of Forecasting*. (4th ed.) Mason, OH: Thomson South-Western.

Contains a good BI definition:

3. Adam, F. and Pomerol, J.-C. (2008). Developing practical decision support tools using dashboards of information. In: *Handbook on Decision Support Systems 2: Variations*. Ed. by Burstein, F. and Holsapple, C. W. Berlin, Germany: Springer, pp. 175–193.

A top-level managerial view of PBI:

4. Deckler, G. and Powell, B. (2022). *Mastering Microsoft Power BI: Expert Techniques for Effective Data Analytics and Business Intelligence* (2nd ed.). Birmingham, UK: Packt Publishing.

A technical introduction to PBI with examples:

5. Deckler, G. and Powell, B. (2021). *Microsoft Power BI Cookbook: Creating Business Intelligence Solutions of Analytical Data Models, Reports, and Dashboards*. (2nd ed.). Birmingham, UK: Packt Publishing.

A good introduction to Power BI:

6. Knight, D. et al. (2018). *Microsoft Power BI Quick Start Guide: Build Dashboards and Visualizations to Make Your Data Come to Life* (3rd ed.). Birmingham, UK: Packt Publishing.

External PBI Links

*   Power BI tutorial: What is Power BI? Why use? DAX examples: www.guru99.com/power-bi-tutorial.html.

*   Find the right Power BI training for you: learn.microsoft.com/training/powerplatform/power-bi.

*   Become a Power BI data analyst: learn.microsoft.com/djwu3eywpk4nm.

*   Tutorial: Create an R-powered Power BI visual: learn.microsoft.com/power-bi/developer/visuals/create-r-based-power-bi-desktop.

*   A BPI tutorial: www.guru99.com/power-bi-tutorial.html.

*   PBI examples: projectpro.io/article/power-bi-microsoft-projects-examples-and-ideas-for-practice/533, Microsoft PBI examples: learn.microsoft.com/power-bi/create-reports/sample-datasets and HEVO examples: hevodata.com/learn/top-10-best-power-bi-dashboard-examples.

*   Microsoft's AppSource – search for Power BI on: appsource.microsoft.com.

*   An excellent blog about Power BI's forecasting: https://pawarbi.github.io/blog/categories.

TWO

Coding and Frameworks

Data Science languages such as R provide a platform to access the state-of-the-art methods for analysing business data. Data Analytics frameworks such as the Machine Learning roadmap give the essential steps in approaching typical Data Analytics projects.

Datatypes: double, integer, ...

Vector, matrix, list

Data frame, class

Controls, functions

Projects, Packages

4. Data Science Languages

4.1 Introduction

Many business challenges require advanced, adapted or new data-mining techniques. For this endeavour, Data Science languages are needed. Often Business or Data Analytics tasks have to be automatised, and programming using Data Science languages such as R or Python comes in handy.

This chapter aims to provide:

- An introduction to prototype programming;
- Insights to fundamental vector and matrix operations.

Section 4.2 introduces essential data types, which are the starting point of each programming language. Basic operations such as addition and multiplications are taken to the next level by introducing them in the context of matrices. This allows the efficient handling and formulation of challenges. Controls such as if-statements and loops are at the heart of programming and are introduced with several examples in Section 4.3. These "controls" function to solve re-occurring data challenges. Hence, they are stored as functions or objects. To develop a set of useful functions, projects are used and can be "packaged" and shared with others in form of libraries (Section 4.1.2).

DOI: 10.4324/9781003336099-6

4.1.1 Language R

Probably the most used Data Science language for statistics and Data Analytics is R.

Online and desktop version: For R, the most popular online *integrated development environment* (IDE) is Rstudio.cloud. After registering, you can create a new project. This returns the screen shown in Figure 4.1. This is similar to the desktop version. To install

FIGURE 4.1 R online version: rstudio.cloud default screen for a new project.

the desktop version, first download the language R from r-project.org. Then obtain the RStudio IDE from rstudio.com. The free desktop version is sufficient for our purposes. Once RStudio is running, you can create a new script (Ctrl+Shift+N), save it as test.R and write a few lines as shown in Figure 4.2. Execute the script via "Source" (Ctrl+Shift+S). In the console, you will see the text output. When activating the Plots tab, you will see a figure based on the variables displayed in Environment window.

4.1.2 Projects and Libraries

A **project** helps keep related files together. In most cases, this will be your first choice for most of your Data Science tasks. In RStudio, a new project can be based on an entirely new folder (or an existing one). For instance, let us create the project DSL [RStudio » File » New Project . . . » New Directory " New Project » Directory name: DSL]. This project will be used in Sections 4.2 and 4.3. I suggest doing these two sections now and then returning to this section to learn about packages.

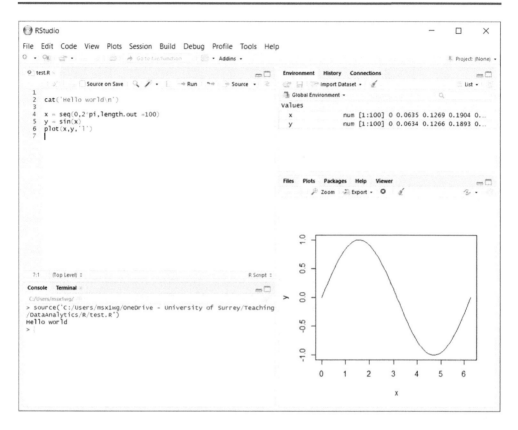

FIGURE 4.2 RStudio with a simple example.

When you have functions, markdown documents or datasets that you intend to reuse or share with other people, then you will end up converting a project to a **package**. A package is the natural next step to release, share and publish a project.

In RStudio, a package is created via [File » New Project . . . » NewDirectory » R Package] (Figure 4.3). After building a package, you will get a single file in source tarball (tar.gz) format. Given that you are still in RStudio's package project, the build can be achieved with: Build » Build Source Package. For instance, if the package project is called ptest1 then a file ptest1_0.1.0.tar.gz is built, where _0.1.0 is the version of the package.

This file can now be distributed to others or reused in your projects. You will need to install the package. Any package in source tarball (tar.gz) format can be installed using: `install.packages(path_to_file, repos = NULL, type= source )`. Please note that the file name usually contains the version number (e.g. _0.1.0). Hence, when you load the package/library, omit the version number. The installed libraries must be in one of the paths returned by the `.libPaths()` function. Hence, going to that folder allows you to see a package's entire content. Another way is to use the list command, e.g. `ls("package:titanic")`. A package can be uninstalled using: `remove.packages("ptest1")`. Deleting the corresponding folder is equivalent to

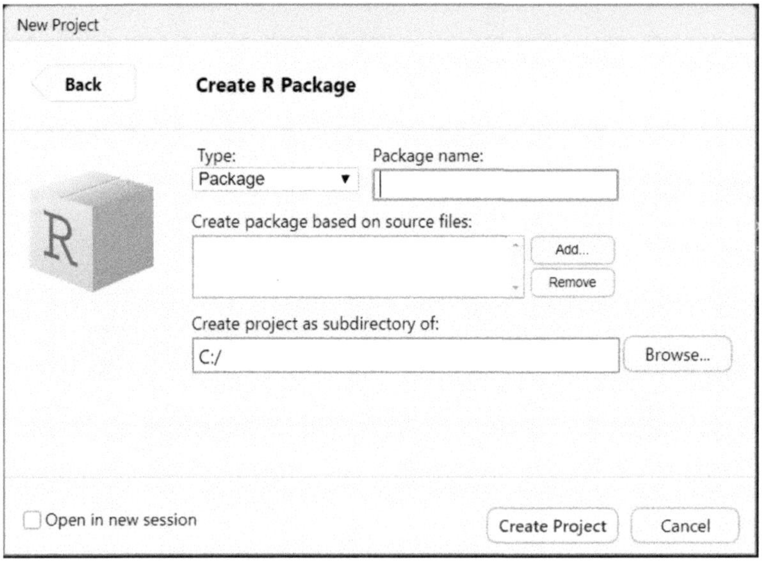

FIGURE 4.3 Input mask to create a R package.

uninstalling the package. A package can be unloaded using `detach( package:my_package , unload=TRUE)`.

https://github.com/ is a popular platform to share and store any kind of projects (papers, presentations, courses etc.) on the web, but it is primarily related to coding. In order to use it, you need to register a Github account. That means we should use Github to store our R packages or projects.

Now that we know the framework, we can begin learning the Data Science language R's details.

4.2 Data Types and Operations

This section will be an adventure that will take you from a data jungle to the radiant sky of knowledge. Don't worry, you won't be bitten by pythons (none will be here), but lots of R will get you to your destination.

We will begin our journey with a "Hello World" scream and wrestle with math. Our first data jungle encounter will show us the atomic types of R. Eventually, we will meet our new best friend data.frame.

4.2.1 Arithmetic and Basic Data Types

Hello World and Arithmetic

It is custom to begin programming with a "Hello World" example. In the console window, write:

```
cat('Hello World\n')
```

This prints the text Hello World. Here, we used the function cat, which concatenates and prints. The string `'Hello World\n'` could have been split into three parts.

```
cat('Hello','World','\n')
```

By the way, \n means new line and ensures the command prompt will not be next to the string. Strings are identified by single or double quotes.

```
'Hello'
"World"
```

The output in the console can be cleared using the keyboard shortcut `Ctrl+L` or executing `cat('\014')`. The console executes commands immediately.

Try fundamental arithmetic's $1+2$, $2-1$, 3×4, $\frac{9}{3}$

```
1+2; 2-1; 3*4; 9/3
```

You can concatenate and display this with cat.

```
cat(1+2, 2-1, 3*4, 9/3)
## 3 1 12 3
```

Let's try powers such as 2^4, 3^{-1}. Add the math for square root of 16 and 16 to the power of 1/2, so, that it agrees with the code below.

```
cat(2^4, 3^-1, sqrt(16),16^(1/2))
## 16 0.3333333 4 4
```

Practice makes perfect: Display the sum of the numbers one to five divided by five.

```
cat((1+2+3+4+5)/5)
## 3
```

The average (aka sample mean) is computed this way:

$$\bar{x} = \frac{1}{n}\sum_{i=1}^{n} x_i = \frac{x_1 + x_2 + \cdots x_n}{n}$$

Display the text: "The golden ratio is:" and concatenate it with the calculation $\frac{1+\sqrt{5}}{2}$. By the way, the background of the golden ratio (Wikipedia, 2023a) is intriguing.

```
cat("The golden ratio is: ", (1+sqrt(5))/2)
## The golden ratio is: 1.618034
```

Scalars, Vectors and Matrices

Scalars: In the previous exercises, scalars were used. Now we will use them via variable names.

```
a = 1; b = 2; # this is a comment: declaration
c = a + b      # addition
c              # show result
## [1] 3
```

Let us analyse this code. The first line assigns values to the variables *a* and *b*. The first *command* is to assign the value 1 to a via a=1. In R, it is very common to use <- as assignment operator. Try it – replace all = with <- in the code. You can even assign variables from right to left – e.g. a+b → c – which "feels" really strange if you have used other programming languages. The second command is b=2. Commands in the same line are separated by a semicolon (;). We have added a *comment* at the end of line 1. Comments are identified with a hashtag (**#**), and they are not computed.

Vectors: A vector is formed by concatenating scalars using the c() function. Next, we show two ways to create the vector x.

```
x = c(1,2,3) # easiest way
a = 1; b = 2; c = a + b # or using the previous variables
x = c(a,b,c)
```

The vector $x = \begin{bmatrix} 1 & 2 & 3 \end{bmatrix}$ has three elements. This can be confirmed using the function length. Each element of the vector can be accessed via its index using square brackets.

```
x = c(1,2,3)
cat('length =', length(x), '\n')
## length = 3
cat('x1 =', x[1], ', x2 = ', x[2], 'etc.')
## x1 = 1, x2 = 2 etc.
```

Note that the first element has index one, unlike in other programming languages, which start with index zero.

Vectors are commonly known as *arrays*. Mathematicians prefer the term *vector*. Computer scientists like the term *array*. In machine learning, we will often call them *features*. In statistical learning, the term *variable* will come up frequently.

Several elements in vectors can be accessed using index vectors. For example, let us access the elements at positions 2, 3, 2 and 5 within the vector $x = \begin{bmatrix} 11 & 22 & 33 & 44 & 55 \end{bmatrix}$ simultaneously.

```
x <- c(11,22,33,44,55)
I <- c(2,3,2,5)  # index vector
x[I]
## [1] 22 33 22 55
```

Addition and Transpose: Let $x = \begin{bmatrix} 1 \\ 2 \\ 3 \end{bmatrix}$ and $y = \begin{bmatrix} 4 \\ 5 \\ 6 \end{bmatrix}$ be vectors and $x + y$ their sum.

```
x = c(1,2,3)
y = c(4,5,6)
x + y
## [1] 5 7 9
```

Although this result looks like a row vector, it is not. The transpose of it (x^T) makes it clear. Generally, the transpose means that a row becomes a column vector or vice versa.

```
x = c(1,2,3)
t(x)
##      [,1] [,2] [,3]
## [1,]   1    2    3
t(t(x))
##      [,1]
## [1,]   1
## [2,]   2
## [3,]   3
```

That means that by default, x and y are already column vectors. Further, the transpose function returns the array as a one-dimensional matrix.

Multiplication: There are several ways to multiply the vectors x and y. We will look at *element-by-element* multiplication and the *scalar product*.

The former is also known as *Hadamard product* $x \odot y$. For a vector with three elements, we obtain: $x \odot y = \begin{bmatrix} x_1 y_1 & x_2 y_2 & x_3 y_3 \end{bmatrix}$. For instance,

```
x = c(1,2,3)
y = c(4,5,6)
x * y
## [1]  4 10 18
```

The *scalar product* $x \cdot y$, also known as the *dot product* (or matrix multiplication – we will get to this in a jiffy), is computed via $x \cdot y = x_1 y_1 + x_2 y_2 + \cdots + x_n y_n$. In R, this is achieved with %*%.

```
x = c(1,2,3)
y = c(4,5,6)
x %*% y
##      [,1]
## [1,]   32
```

These results pushed us to the frontier of the world of matrices because a vector is just a one-dimensional matrix.

Practice makes perfect: Create a vector y with elements one to ten using the colon operator (:), then retrieve the second and ninth elements. You can try to break up your solution approach into little chunks. First, you could write 1:10; then, assign it to y; and at last, calculate $y_2 + y_9$.

```
y = 1:10; y[2]+y[9]
## [1] 11
```

Assume you have two vectors $u = \begin{bmatrix} 5 & 2 \end{bmatrix}^T$ and $v = \begin{bmatrix} 2 & 4 \end{bmatrix}^T$. They are visualised in Figure 4.4. What is $u + v$?

```
u = c(5,2); v=c(2,4)
u+v
## [1] 7 6
```

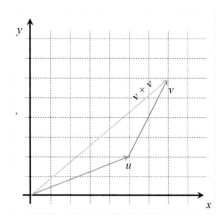

FIGURE 4.4 Vector addition.

You can verify the result in the previously mentioned figure. How can you double the size of vector $\begin{bmatrix} 7 & 6 \end{bmatrix}$? You could use scalar multiplication or add the same vector twice.

```
z = c(7,6); 2*z # or z+z
## [1] 14 12
```

Assume $u = \begin{bmatrix} 1 & 2 & 3 \end{bmatrix}$ and $v = \begin{bmatrix} 2 & 1 & \frac{1}{3} \end{bmatrix}$. Hadamard product $u \odot v$?

```
u = c(1,2,3); v=c(2,1,1/3)
u*v
## [1] 2 2 1
```

Given are $u = \begin{bmatrix} 1 & 2 & 3 \end{bmatrix}$ and $e = \begin{bmatrix} 1 & 1 & 1 \end{bmatrix}$. What is the dot product $u \cdot v$?

```
u = c(1,2,3); e=c(1,1,1)
u%*%e
##      [,1]
## [1,]   6
```

Beautiful side effect – the dot product of a vector u with a one-vector e is just the sum of the vector elements, i.e. $u \cdot e = \sum_{i=1}^{n} u_i$.

Matrices: A matrix $A = \begin{bmatrix} 1 & 4 \\ 2 & 5 \\ 3 & 6 \end{bmatrix}$ can be created from vectors using the row or column bind functions:

```
x = c(1,2,3); y = c(4,5,6)
A = cbind(x,y)  # column bind
B = rbind(x,y)  # row bind
A;B
##        x y ##      [,1] [,2] [,3]
## [1,]  1 4 ## x      1    2    3
## [2,]  2 5 ## y      4    5    6
## [3,]  3 6
```

Another way to create A is by using the matrix function with the input ncol = 2.

```
    A = matrix(c(1,2,3, 4,5,6), ncol = 2)
```

Now, it is interesting to access individual elements of the matrix. To access an element in a matrix, two indices are needed. For instance, assume you want to return the element located in row 3 and column 2.

```
A[3,2]
## [1] 6
```

We expand the matrix to make the extraction of elements more interesting.

```
B = cbind(A,A); B
##             [,1] [,2] [,3] [,4]
## [1,]          1    4    1    4
## [2,]          2    5    2    5
## [3,]          3    6    3    6
```

The display of matrix B identifies the rows [i,] and columns [,i]. For instance, let us return the second row and third column.

```
B[2,];               B[,3]
## [1] 2 5 2 5     ## [1] 1 2 3
```

Let's return the second and fourth column of B in one go using an index vector.

```
B[,c(2,4)]
##          [,1] [,2]
## [1,]       4    4
## [2,]       5    5
## [3,]       6    6
```

Basic Data Types

In this section, we will look at classic R data types. We have looked at vectors, which are the most fundamental type in R. Previously, we had the example x=c(1,2,3). There are six basic data types: logical (binary number), integer (natural number), double (real number), complex, character (string) and raw (bytes), which are all in the form of vectors. The function typeof() will return these data types.

By default, a numeric vector has a double data type.

```
x = c(1,2,3)
typeof(x)
## [1] "double"
```

In order to get an integer vector, we need to add an L (long integer) to the numeric value.

```
x = c(1L,2L,3L)
typeof(x)
## [1] "integer"
```

Next, we will look at the data types logical and character.

```
b = c(TRUE,FALSE,TRUE)
s = c('one', 'two', 'three')
cat('type of b: ', typeof(b), ', length of b:', length(b))
## type of b: logical, length of b: 3
cat('type of s: ', typeof(s), ', length of s: ', length(s))
## type of s: character, length of s: 3
```

The last output is interesting because it returns the length of the vectors. The vector s contains three string elements. Usually (e.g. Java), a string consists of characters. So, actually, the data type character should be called string.

The question arises on how we can get characters out of a string. The function we need is substr(). Let's extract the first two characters and characters 6 to 8.

```
s = 'Data Analytics'
cat(substr(s,1,2), substr(s,6,8))
## Da Ana
```

By the way, *nchar()* returns the number of characters in a string. There are two more basic data types: complex and raw. The first one allows us to use complex numbers.

```
u = 1+1i
v = 1+0i
cat(u + v, u - v, u*v, u/v)
## 2+1i 0+1i 1+1i 1+1i
```

The second one deals with byte operations. Let's begin with a few numbers translated into bytes.

```
as.raw(c(0,2,8,9,10,15,32,64,128,255))
## [1] 00 02 08 09 0a 0f 20 40 80 ff
```

Note the hexadecimal representation of the bytes. The bit representation can be achieved with:

```
rawToBits(as.raw(7))
## [1] 01 01 01 00 00 00 00 00
```

Practice makes perfect: Considering integer, long int, float, double and raw – which ones are basic data types? Answer: integer, double and raw.
Determine the *type of* 123.45:

```
typeof(123.45)
## [1] "double"
```

Extract the first character of str.

```
str = 'Data Analytics'
substr(str,1,1)
## [1] "D"
```

Extract the last two characters of str using nchar().

```
str = 'Data Analytics'
substr(str,nchar(str)-1,nchar(str))
## [1] "cs"
```

What data type do you expect for `c(1.1, 2.3, 3.3)`? Answer: double.

4.2.2 Compound Data Types

Data Frames and Lists

Data Frames: Probably the most important data structure is the data.frame. In the previous section, we created several vectors with different basic data types. Now we can put them together in a data.frame.

```
x = c(1,2,3)
b = c(TRUE,FALSE,TRUE)
s = c('one', 'two', 'three')
c = c(1+0I,1+1I,-1+0I)
D = data.frame(x,b,s,c)
D
##   x     b     s      c
## 1 1  TRUE   one  1+0i
## 2 2 FALSE   two  1+1i
## 3 3  TRUE three -1+0i
```

This is similar to a matrix. However, a matrix only contains elements of one type. We observe that each column vector must have the same length.

```
cat(length(x),length(b),length(s),length(c))
## 3 3 3 3
```

We obtain the number of rows and columns via the following three functions:

```
dim(D);              ncol(D);    nrow(D)
## [1] 3    4        ## [1] 4    ## [1] 3
```

Elements can be accessed in the same way as in matrices. For instance, let us extract the element in the second row and third column.

```
D[2,3]
## [1] "two"
```

Similarly to matrices, rows and columns can be extracted: e.g. second row and third column.

```
D[2,];                              D[,3]
##      x      b      s      c      ## [1]"one"  "two"   "three"
##      2 2    FALSE  two    1+1i
```

Tip: Should I use a matrix or a data frame? If you can, always use the "simpler" struc-ture. When all elements have the same data type, a matrix is simpler than a data frame. By the way, also use a vector instead of a one-dimensional matrix.

Let us have a look at another example. Assume you have several customers and information about them. You can create the following data frame.

```
customer <- c('Wolfgang', 'Eleanor', 'Vikas', 'Patrick')
salary   <- c(100,90,120,60)
years    <- c(10,3,8,1)
df       <- data.frame(customer,salary,years)
df
##          customer      salary      years
## 1        Wolfgang      100         10
## 2        Eleanor       90          3
## 3        Vikas         120         8
## 4        Patrick       60          1
```

This data frame has four rows, also known as *observations*, and three columns, aka *variables* or *features*.

A feature can be extracted from a data frame using the *access operator* $. Let us extract all customers from the data frame.

```
df$customer
## [1] "Wolfgang" "Eleanor" "Vikas" "Patrick"
```

An observation can be obtained using square brackets:

```
df[2,]
##   customer  salary  years
## 2 Eleanor       90      3
```

Lists: A list is a sequence of elements. For instance,

```
L = list(a_number=1, words=c('one', 'two'), binvec = c(T,F,T))
```

By the way, for the binary vector, we used R's feature to autocomplete T and F to TRUE and FALSE.

Elements in a list are accessed differently to data frames using [[]]. For instance, let us get the second element in the list, which is vector s.

```
L[[2]]
## [1] "one" "two"
```

In a way, a data.frame is a special list in which all elements are vectors with the same length.

It is possible to access column vectors in lists and data frames by their name, using the list subset operator $. The function names() returns the list elements' names as expected.

```
names(L)
## [1] "a_number" "words" "binvec"
```

The $ access operator can also be used for data frames, e.g. D$x ## [1] 1 2 3.

Practice makes perfect: Determine the number of rows and columns (use nrow() or ncol()).

```
cars = mtcars
nrow(cars)
## [1] 32
```

List all column names of mtcars.

```
names(mtcars)
## [1] "mpg" "cyl" "disp" "hp" "drat" "wt"
## [7] "qsec" "vs" "am" "gear" "carb"
```

Generally, all datasets can be listed using library(help = datasets), which includes mtcars.

```
library(help = "datasets")
help(mtcars) # get more information (opens in new window)
```

Determine the average number of miles per gallon.

```
mean(mtcars$mpg)
## [1] 20.09062
```

Now, let's get to the **extreme** level. List all cars that are above the average mpg value. Your "cooking ingredients" are rownames for the cars, mean for the average, the logical comparison > and logical indices [TRUE, FALSE, . . .].

```
# put it all together using logical indices
rownames(mtcars)[mtcars$mpg > mean(mtcars$mpg)]

# [1] "Mazda RX4" "Mazda RX4 Wag" "Datsun 710" "Hornet 4 Drive"
# [5] "Merc 240D" "Merc 230" "Fiat 128" "Honda Civic"
# [9] "Toyota Corolla" "Toyota Corona" "Fiat X1-9" "Porsche 914-2"
# [13] "Lotus Europa" "Volvo 142E"
```

Classes and Objects

This is advanced material. You can skip this section, but if you decided to do so, you should go through the Controls and Function tutorial next.

Previously, we heard about lists. A list can be converted into an object (more specifically, into an S3 object). The *class* represents the common structure; an *instance* or *object* of a class contains specific values.

Let us create the list c1 and state that it is an object with class name customer.

```
c1 <- list(name = 'Wolfgang', salary = 100, years = 10)
class(c1) <- 'customer'; c1
## $name            $salary        $years         attr(,"class")
## [1] "Wolfgang" [1] 100        [1] 10         [1], "customer"
```

A *constructor* is a function that creates objects. Usually, the constructor's name and class name are identical. That means we integrate the customer object into a function.

```
customer <- function(n,s,y){
   cr <- list(name = n, salary = s, years = y)
   class(cr) <- 'customer'
   return(cr)
}
wolfi <- customer('Wolfgang', 100, 10); print(wolfi)
##     $name           $salary        $years         attr(,"class")
## [1] "Wolfgang" [1] 100 [1] 10             [1] "customer"
```

Let us write a customised print function for the customer class.

```
print.customer <- function(obj){
   cat("Name: ", obj$name, "\nSalary: ", obj$salary)
}
print(wolfi)
## Name: Wolfgang
## Salary: 100
```

This is cool! The function print.customer was automatically associated with the class. This is the first benefit of classes we have noticed. That means there is a generic function print that is usable across many classes (see methods(print)).

It is possible to create new generic methods. For instance, let us create the generic function salary and implement a default function.

```
salary <- function(obj) {UseMethod("salary")} # generic method
salary.default <- function(obj) {# try this for any class
  cat("The salary is", obj$salary, ".\n")
}
salary.customer <- function(obj) {#use this for the
customer class
  cat("The salary of",obj$name, "is", obj$salary, ".\n")
}
salary(list(salary=77))
## The salary is 77.
salary(wolfi)
## The salary of Wolfgang is 100.
```

Practice makes perfect: Create a generic, default and specific purchase function for the customer class which allows a customer to buy a car.

```
# generic method
purchased <- function(obj) {UseMethod("purchase")}

# try this for any class
purchased <- function(obj, purchased_object) {
  obj$purchased_object <- purchased_object
  cat("The object:", obj$purchased_object, "was purchased.\n")
  return(obj)}

# use this for the customer class
purchased <- function(obj, car) {
  obj$car <- car
  cat(obj$name, "purchased a", obj$car, ".\n")
  return(obj)}
wolfi <- purchased(wolfi, "MG ZS EV")
## Wolfgang purchased a MG ZS EV.
```

A class consists of *attributes* (attributes(c1)) and *methods*. The S3 class system introduced earlier is probably the most popular one. Generally, object-oriented programming (OOP) attempts to provide coding with a more natural language. For instance, "Wolfgang purchased a BMW" translates into wolfi <- purchased(wolfi, BMW).

However, there is another object-oriented programming approach in R, known as **R6**. This one is more closely related to traditional programming languages such as C# and Java. I will give an example which should suffice to explain how this class concept works. For more details, please see Hadley's R6 and Chang's documentation. The earlier example's translation becomes a bit more natural: wolfi$purchased(BMW).

```
library(R6)
Customer <- R6Class(
  classname = "Customer",
  public = list(
    name = '', salary = 0, car = '',
    initialize = function(name = '', salary = 0) {
      self$name = name; self$salary = salary},
    purchased = function(car) {
      self$car = car
      cat(self$name, "purchased a",self$car, "\n")}))
wolfi <- Customer$new("Wolfgang",100)
wolfi$purchased("BMW")
## Wolfgang purchased a BMW
```

4.2.3 String Operations and Regular Expressions

The most efficient way to deal with characters is by using regular expressions. A *regular expression* is a sequence of characters that expresses a pattern, which is searched for within a string.

We will look at a few challenges found in practice. Often, it will be necessary to extract text between a begin and end marker. Any pattern can be detected using `str_detect(string, pattern)`.

```
str = 'some text BEGIN interesting bit END more
  BEGIN good END,one more BEGIN excellent END stop.'
  str_detect(str, 'BEGIN')
## TRUE
```

There are two ways to extract a begin-end block from str. Both extractions will use the BEGIN and END tag in our example. The greedy extraction tries to get as many characters as possible before hitting the end of the line.

```
str_extract(str, ' (BEGIN)(.+)(END) ')
## "BEGIN interesting bit END more BEGIN good END, one
## more BEGIN excellent END"
```

As we can see, the greedy extraction went up to the very last END keyword. That is why this is called greedy matching.

Let us explain the pattern `(BEGIN)(.+)(END)`. The parentheses are used for structuring. The characters `BEGIN` and `END` specify the beginning and end of the pattern. Generally, such markers are known as *tags*. The dot character in `(.+)` represents "any" character (even numbers but not line breaks). The plus symbol means that there must be at least one character, but there could be many. By the way, an asterisk (*) matches any number of characters – including zero characters. Without further symbols, the plus and asterisk cause greedy matching.

Typically, we would like to stop the extraction when the first `END` keyword is found. This is known as *lazy matching*. Personally, I would call it kind extraction. The question mark behind a greedy match (e.g. plus symbol) transforms it into a lazy match. The following code uses a lazy regular expression to extract the first block.

```
str_extract(str, '(BEGIN)(.+?)(END)')
## "BEGIN interesting bit END"
```

The lazy matching allows us to extract three blocks from str.

```
str_extract_all(str, ' (BEGIN)(.+?)(END) ')[[1]]
## "BEGIN interesting bit END" "BEGIN good END"
## "BEGIN excellent END"
```

Note `[[1]]` removes the list environment. Lists are explained in the next section.

Almost always, you will need to remove the begin and end tags. This can be done via additional `str_remove` commands or integrated into the regular expression. Here, the begin tag needs to be preceded by ?<= and the end tag by ?=. The following code extracts the blocks without tags (markers).

```
str_extract_all(str, ' (?<=BEGIN)(.+?)(?=END) ')[[1]]
## "interesting bit" "good" "excellent"
```

Matched patterns are replaced using str_replace_all().

```
str_replace_all(str, 'BEGIN', 'START')
## "some text START interesting bit END more START good END,
## one more START excellent END stop."
```

Words can be removed using str_remove_all().

```
str_remove_all(str, 'BEGIN|END')
## "some text interesting bit more good, one more . . ."
```

Here, we used the pipe symbol (|)as an or-clause. That means if the word BEGIN or END is found, it is removed. The or-clause, in conjunction with str_count(), can be used to get an idea of the sentiment of a text.

```
str_count(str, 'good|excellent|interesting|terrific')
## 3
```

Regular expressions use *special characters* such as \^$.?*|+{}()[]. However, these characters could occur in the text. In this case, we need to "escape" their regular expression meaning. The backslash (\) is the character for escaping. However, in R, we need two of them for escaping. It gets even "wilder" when we want to escape the backslash. In that case, we will need four backslashes. Here is an example dealing with special characters.

```
sstr <- 'text before \\begin{T} great \\end{T} stuff'
str_extract(sstr, '(\\\\begin\\{T\\})(.+?)(\\\\end\\
{T\\})')
## "\\begin{T} great \\end{T}"
```

Let us conclude our introduction of regular expression by extracting some numeric values.

```
nstr <- 'a=123, b=12.3, c:32.1, the end' str_extract_all(nstr,
'(\\d|\\.)+')
## "123" "12.3" "32.1"
```

Here, we used \d to identify digits and \. for the dot. Generally, there are several character classes defined. We could have also used [:digit:] or [0-9] for the numbers zero to nine. Similarly, we can define a character class [a-z]. Please see visit the Regular Expression in R website (www.smartana.org/blogs/regexp.html) for more details.

4.3 Controls and Functions

Please be sure you have done the data types section. We are continuing the R adventure by learning essential survival skills. First, you need to know how to decide. Your life may depend on it, so you need to be able to execute "if in danger do the right thing then

I will be fine else there is trouble". Once this is mastered, you need to learn how to *keep on going*. The for and while loops will help with that.

4.3.1 If Conditions

Change the Boolean variable to `FALSE` and you should be in trouble.

```
doing_the_right_thing = TRUE
if (doing_the_right_thing == TRUE){
  cat('I will be fine.\n')
} else {
  cat('I am in trouble.\n')
}
## I will be fine.
```

Warning: `}` `else` must be on the same line.

Next, we create a Boolean variable rain and set it to false. Write an if clause that displays: "There is a risk of flooding" or "everything is fine" (don't forget \n).

```
rain = FALSE
if (rain == TRUE){
  cat('There is a risk of flooding.\n')
  cat("Please move to higher grounds. ")
} else {
  cat('everything is fine\n')
}
## everything is fine
```

4.3.2 Loops – Control Flow

For loops: We print the numbers 1 to 50 on the console to demonstrate the benefits of loops.

```
for (nb in (1:50))
  {cat(nb, ", ", sep = " ")
}
## 1, 2, 3, 4, 5, 6, 7, 8, 9, 10, 11, 12, 13, 14, ...
## 38, 39, 40, 41, 42, 43, 44, 45, 46, 47, 48, 49, 50,
```

Assume you have several machine learning algorithms rpart, knn, neural-net, randomForest, lm and xgbTree. Iterate through these algorithms.

```
algos = c('rpart', 'knn', 'neuralnet', 'RF', 'lm', 'xgbTree')
for (alg in algos){
  cat(alg, ", ", sep = " ")
}
## rpart, knn, neuralnet, RF, lm, xgbTree,
```

Now display the iteration number as well.

```
algos = c('rpart', 'knn', 'neuralnet', 'RF', 'lm', 'xgbTree')
nb = 1
for (alg in algos){
  cat(nb, ". ", alg, "\n", sep = " ")
  nb <- nb+1
}
## 1. rpart        ## 4. RF
## 2. knn          ## 5. lm
## 3. neuralnet    ## 6. xgbTree
```

This will come in handy when comparing algorithms.

Loops are often used for aggregation purposes. For instance, you can compute the sum or product of multiple numbers.

Write a for loop that computes the cumulative product using a for loop. That means multiply the number $e \in \{2,4,\ldots,10\}$ and output as variable s.

```
s = 1
for (e in 2*(1:5)){
  s = s*e
}
s
## [1] 3840
```

In order to decipher a code, you will need seven Fibonacci numbers, the first one being greater than two.

$$F_1 = 1, F_2 = 1, F_n = F_{n-1} + F_{n-2}$$

```
F[1]=1; F[2]=1;
for (n in 3:10){
  F[n]  =  F[n-1] + F[n-2]
}
F[F>2]
## [1]  3  5  8 13 21 34 55
```

While loop: The following example demonstrates the usage of the while loop.

```
energy = 10
while (energy > 5){
   cat('Energy level ', energy, '\n ')
   energy = energy - 2
}
## Energy level 10
## Energy level 8
## Energy level 6
```

We begin with a high energy level: i.e. we set the energy variable to the value of ten. Then the while loop starts by checking whether the condition to run a loop is fulfilled. Here, the condition is that the energy must be above five. Since the energy level is above this, the loop is entered. In the while loop's body, the energy level is printed, and the energy level is reduced by two levels to level eight. Now, the while loop condition is checked again and the loop's body is executed again and again until the condition is false.

4.3.3 Functions

There are many built-in functions already. What are typical base functions? For instance, `sum()`, `mean()`, `min()`,`max()`. (Run `library(help = "base")` for a comprehensive list)

How do we develop a function? The following steps are a possible approach. Let us re-implement sum as a script using a for loop. Assume that we want to write a function that determines $2 + 1 + 4 + 7$. We will derive the function slowly for educational purposes.

We begin by simply writing down the sum, saving the numbers in a vector x and then adding up the elements in that array.

```
2+1+4+7 # simple
## [1] 14
x <- c(2,1,4,7) # save numbers as vector x
s <- x[1]+x[2]+x[3]+x[4] # still fourteen
```

116

In the last line, we added the elements one by one to the sum. This is the same as:

```
s <- 0
s <- s + x[1]
s <- s + x[2]
s <- s + x[3]
s <- s + x[4]
```

Now we can compress these lines by using a for loop.

```
s = 0 # our summation variable
for (k in 1:4) {# btw. length(x) = 4
  s = s + x[k] # add element to sum
}
s # display result
## [1] 14
```

Next, let us insert this "body" into a function definition: mySum()

```
# define a function
mySum <- function(x){
  s = 0
  for (k in 1:length(x)){
    s = s + x[k]
  }
  return(s)
}
```

Here, mySum is the function name. The symbols <- assign a function block function(x){}, where x is an *input variable*. The function return() returns the results from within the function's body to the environment (workspace) in which it was called.

Since we have the mySum function, it can be applied to various vectors.

```
# use the function
x = c(1,2,3,4) # given vector
mySum(x) # call the function
## [1] 10
mySum(c(2,1,4,7))
## [1] 14
y <- c(10,2,1,4,7,5); mySum(y)
## [1] 29
```

Practice makes perfect: Write the function myMin, which determines the minimum. Then write x=c(65,70,24,26,36,65,83,34,42,34) and return the minimum using your function.

```
myMin <- function(x){
  m = INF # special means m is at infinity
  for (k in 1:length(x)){if (x[k]<m) m = x[k]}
  return(m)
}
# use function
x=c(65,70,24,26,36,65,83,34,42,34); myMin(x)
## [1] 24
```

What if we have **several input variables?** Let us have a function that multiplies three numbers.

```
multi3 <- function(a,b,c){return(a*b*c)}
multi3 (2,3,4)
## [1] 24
```

What if we have several output variables? Let us return the variables a, b and c.

```
ret3 <- function(){
  L = list(); # initialise empty list
  L$a = 1; L$b = 2; L$c = 3;
  return(L)
}
ret3()
## $a $b $c
## [1] 1 [1] 2 [1] 3
```

Practicalities: What do you do if you have written many functions you will use several times in your project? The easiest way is to collect them in one r-file and then use the source command to load them.

What do you do if you have written many functions you will use several times in many projects? In this case, it pays to create a package. The creation of a package is explained in Section 4.1.2.

4.3.4 Coding with GPT

For RStudio, there is an add-in called GPTstudio created by Nivard (2024). This lets you use the generative pre-trained transformer (GPT) for all kinds of things:

- Writing code from a simple spec (I am very impressed with this);
- Adding comments to your code;
- Spell checking;
- Translating languages (e.g. German to English, R to Python).

Here is a quick start: register for an openai account and get an API key. In RStudio, do the following (assuming you have installed pacman: install.packages("pacman")):

```
openai_api_key = "enter your key here "
Sys.setenv(OPENAI_API_KEY = openai_api_key)
library(pacman); p_load(devtools, openai)
install_github("MichelNivard/gptstudio ")
p_load(gptstudio)
```

You will probably have to restart RStudio. Now you should see the add-ins (see Figure 4.5).
Now you can do some simple experiments. Open a new R script window and write: "Cans yoou hep me wit mi speling?" ChatGPT outputs "Can you help me with my spelling?"

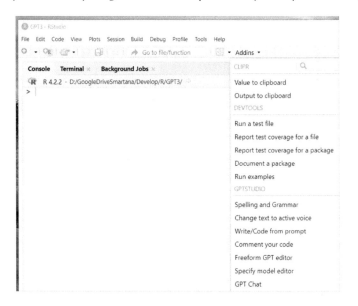

FIGURE 4.5 RStudio ChatGPT add-ins.

Now, let us apply it to write a code snippet. In our R script window, we write: *"visualise iris data using ggplot"*. The provided ChatGPT output is:

```
library(ggplot2)
ggplot(iris, aes(x = Sepal.Length, y = Sepal.Width,
  color =Species)) + geom_point()
```

We can verify that the code is functional; moreover, it is the most common way to write it.

We can also use it to help us write passages of text. We ask ChatGPT: *"Write 500 words about UAV supporting delivery services. The implications of UAVs to the last-mile delivery and its benefits to sustainability"*. An excerpt of the ChatGPT output is as follows: *"Unmanned Aerial Vehicles (UAVs) have been gaining traction in the last-mile delivery industry due to their potential to reduce costs, improve efficiency, and increase sustainability. UAVs are a type of drone that can be remotely operated and are capable of carrying goods from one location to another. UAVs have the potential to revolutionize the last-mile delivery industry by providing a cost-effective and efficient solution for delivering goods to customers"*. Overall, ChatGPT delivers a well-written text. However, at the time of writing, it struggles with providing evidence and references. That means provided references are invented.

Generally, for simple coding tasks, ChatGPT can be efficiently used.

This allows you to create code in almost-natural language and have it translated into code. It can help you translate existing code from one programming language to another one. Further, it can improve existing code. However, you will have to check the generated code since it has its own "creative" elements. That means some lines are simply wrong.

In coding, it is common to do a web search to find useful code snippets that answer the challenge you are facing. Often, Stack Overflow/Exchange will provide a concise example. The GPT allows you to shortcut this step within the programming environment.

4.3.5 Data Transfer Function

How do I create a SQL connection in RStudio? Let us assume we would like to connect to an existing MySQL database called HealthyCrisps hosted on a local computer with a given username and password.

The following steps open a dialogue box [RStudio » Connections » New Connection » MySQL ODBC 8.0 Unicode Driver]:

```
library(pacman) p_load(DBI,odbc)
con <- DBI::dbConnect(odbc::odbc(),
  driver = 'MySQL ODBC 8.0 Unicode Driver',
  dbname = 'HealthyCrisps', host= 'localhost', port=3306,
  user   = 'healthy', password = 'healthy.')
```

After the connection is created, click on your new connection (e.g. HealthyCrisps@ localhost) and select Connect » R Console. This will show the available databases and their tables.

What is the most convenient way to import data from an Excel map? A convenient package is rio, which uses the file extension to select the appropriate import method.

```
library(pacman); p_load(rio)
dbf <- import_list("BusinessData.xlsx")
```

This reads all sheets from an Excel map into a list of data frames. If you are only interested in a single sheet, use

```
import("../BusinessData.xlsx", sheet="Product").
```

How do I transfer a data frame from R into a table in a MySQL database? Establish a DB connection as explained earlier and execute

```
dbWriteTable(con, "myTableName", myDataFrame).
```

You may want to suppress the `row_names` column via `row.names = FALSE`.

4.4 Summary

The Data Science language R was introduced. Several fundamental data types were introduced, and we realised that they are used for storing data of different types. We advised using simpler types over more complex ones when given the choice. Several basic operations were introduced, especially for vectors. For instance, vector addition and multiplication were discussed. It was stated that data frames are the most often used data types in machine learning. The if control was introduced to decide about cases. The for and while loops are used when repetitive steps occur. Functions help structure the code and are useful if code has to be reused. Overall, the basics of programming were introduced. These skills can be transferred to other languages, such as Python or Matlab.

Annotated Bibliography

A very short introduction to R:

1. Brauer, C. (2020). *A-Very-Short-Introduction-to-R.* [Online]. https://github.com/ ClaudiaBrauer/A-very-short-introduction-to-R/ (Accessed 13 December 2023).

Data Analytics Tutorial for Beginners – From Beginner to Pro in 10 Mins – DataFlair:

2. Data Analytics Tutorial for Beginners – From Beginner to Pro in 10 Mins *DataFlair* (2019). https://data-flair.training/blogs/data-analytics-tutorial (Accessed 20 October 2020).

Discovering Statistics Using R and RStudio:

3. Field, A. P. (2021). *Discovering Statistics Using R and RStudio* (2nd ed.). London: SAGE.

A Hands-on Introduction to Data Science:

4. Shah, C. (2020). *A Hands-on Introduction to Data Science*. Cambridge, England: Cambridge University Press.

An explanation of the golden ratio:

5. Wikipedia (2023). *Golden Ratio – Wikipedia, the Free Encyclopedia*. https://en.wikipedia.org/wiki/Golden_ratio (Accessed 26 January 2023).

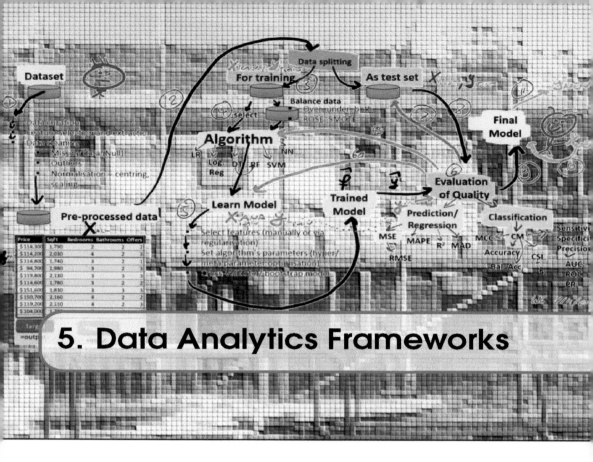

5. Data Analytics Frameworks

5.1 Introduction

It is always good to follow a strategic roadmap. We motivate Data Analytics roadmaps by first developing a business scenario and introducing associated modelling. Here, formal definitions for real and prediction models are provided. These are of foremost importance. We will use them to derive one of the most commonly used measures – the mean squared error (MSE) – to evaluate the quality of a data mining model. Several business applications are mentioned to give an idea of which kind of projects can be built around a simple linear model. The models and quality measures provide us with a solid foundation for the frameworks. This chapter introduces the methodology of knowledge discovery in databases (KDD), which identifies essential steps in the Data Analytics life-cycle process. We discuss KDD with the help of some examples. The different stages of KDD are introduced, such as data preprocessing and data modelling. We explore the cross-industry standard process for data mining (CRISP-DM).

This chapter works towards the following learning outcomes:

- Data Analytics and a methodical approach to analysing data;
- Communicating and providing results to the management and stakeholders for decision making and implementation.

DOI: 10.4324/9781003336099-7

5.2 Modelling and Applications

In order to better relate to the modelling frameworks introduced in subsequent sections, we begin with the modelling of property prices.

5.2.1 Business Scenario Example

You are the manager of a properties agency, and you have three employees named Smart Genius, Common Sense and Silly Often. Smart Genius has compiled a list of properties. You are contemplating using the list, but you want to get a "feeling" about the team's thoughts. Silly often tells you it is a waste of time to look at a list because he knows the prices inside-out, and there is nothing you can do with that data anyway. Common Sense thinks it could be helpful, would like to learn more about it and has heard about data-driven decision making. Smart Genius states that the list can support the agency in predicting the sales price of a house, devising a strategy to maximise profitability subject to insights in the data and revising house prices. Smart continued with several more suggestions. So you decided to have a look at the list (Figure 5.1). *Business understanding:* selling all properties with a 10% commission is possible.

Model 1: (Sum of all house prices) × 10% = $16.7Mx10% = $1.67M

HomeID	Price	SqFt	Bedrooms	Bathrooms	Offers	Brick	Neighborhood
1	$114,300	1,790	2	2	2	No	East
2	$114,200	2,030	4	2	3	No	East
3	$114,800	1,740	3	2	1	No	East
4	$ 94,700	1,980	3	2	3	No	East
5	$119,800	2,130	3	3	3	No	East
6	$114,600	1,780	3	2	2	No	North
7	$151,600	1,830	3	3	3	Yes	West
8	$150,700	2,160	4	2	2	No	West
9	$119,200	2,110	4	2	3	No	East
10	$104,000	1,730	3	3	3	No	East

FIGURE 5.1 House prices and other features.

Evaluation: The reliability and testing of the model is trivial. The model can be easily explained. Does the model make sense? Actual fees are more like 1.42% or in the range [0.75%, 3.0%]. Selling all properties this year may not be possible. At this point, you may decide against the deployment of the model and start with the second cycle of the CRISP-DM. In the next cycle, you may consider adapting the commission fee, estimating the effort of recording the historical data to estimate the sale's speed or accommodating this as an estimated factor. Your next model tells you that you will have a turnover of

$330k per year. But your target is $1,000k; since the business is scalable, you increase the staff by a factor of three and succeed in reaching your target.

As a second challenge, you want the data analyst to build you a model that predicts house prices given some property information. Figure 5.2 shows the house prices, with some numerical information about the properties circled in green. As before, the house price is our target variable. Some of the potential numerical input is circled in green. In statistical and machine learning, it is common to call these input features. By the way, a row is also known as an *instance*, a *data point*, a point, an example and an *observation*. Confusingly, sometimes the target on its own is called an observation. A dataset contains the target and features.

HomeID	Price	SqFt	Bedrooms	Bathrooms	Offers	Brick	Neighborhood
1	$114,300	1,790	2	2	2	No	East
2	$114,200	2,030	4	2	3	No	East
3	$114,800	1,740	3	2	1	No	East
4	$ 94,700	1,980	3	2	3	No	East
5	$119,800	2,130	3	3	3	No	East
6	$114,600	1,780	3	2	2	No	North
7	$151,600	1,830	3	3	3	Yes	West
8	$150,700	2,160	4	2	2	No	West
9	$119,200	2,110	4	2	3	No	East
10	$104,000	1,730	3	3	3	No	East

Target
=output

Features
=input

FIGURE 5.2 House prices illustrating target and features.

Business question: What is the house price given the square footage? That means we are only using one of the features (at least for now). The model we are building can be visualised as shown in Figure 5.3. This schematic can be translated into pseudo-math (business style) notation:

$$\text{House price} = \text{Model}(\text{Square Feet}) \tag{5.1}$$

A specific implementation of the model is:

$$\text{House price} = -\$10,000 + \$70 \times (\text{Square - Foot}) \tag{5.2}$$

Target ← Model ← Input

FIGURE 5.3 Input, model and target schematic.

This linear equation has a negative offset of $10k. Further, we see that the house price increases by $70 for each square foot (i.e. $7k for a 100 SqFt).

Figure 5.4 represents the evaluation of the model presented to you, the manager or the analyst. You sense check the first record by computing the modelled price:

$$-\$10,000 + 70 \times (1,790) = \$135,300$$

Price	Model	Error	SqFt
$114,300	$135,300	$-21,000	1,790
$114,200	$152,100	$-37,900	2,030
$114,800	$131,800	$-17,000	1,740
$ 94,700	$148,600	$-53,900	1,980
$119,800	$159,100	$-39,300	2,130
$114,600	$134,600	$-20,000	1,780
$151,600	$138,100	$ 13,500	1,830
$150,700	$161,200	$-10,500	2,160
$119,200	$157,700	$-38,500	2,110
$104,000	$131,100	$-27,100	1,730

FIGURE 5.4 House prices model evaluation data.

Considering the *error:* $114,300 – $135,300 = -$21,000 seems to be too much. The other errors are also quite large. From the sample, it appears that the model is over-estimating the house prices. This error is also known as a *quality or accuracy measure.* We tell the data scientist that an overall quality measure of the model would be great; a quality visualisation would be nice and, actually, a better model is required. As a business/data analyst, you can address these recommended improvements, and as a manager, you should understand them.

5.2.2 Real World and Prediction Model

We will now introduce supervised statistical learning more formally, inspired by the previous example.

We begin with the real-world model formula shown in Figure 5.5. A model is a simplified version of reality to serve a purpose.

The example of house prices introduced the concept. We may be tempted to identify the model House price = -$10,000+$70×(Square-Foot) as a real-world model and the later determined error as a random error. However, we will find that the model can be improved, and the error is currently systematically overestimating. Hence, it is better to state that -$10,000+$70×(Square-Foot) is the prediction model, and its output is the prediction (see Figure 5.6). Our task (or the statistical learning task) is to learn the

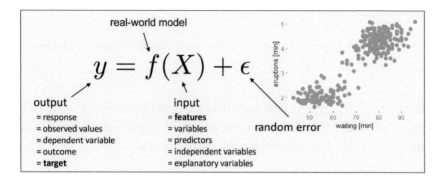

FIGURE 5.5 Real-world model formula.

prediction model from the dataset. The dataset includes the target and features (input). Once we have learned the prediction model sufficiently well, new data can be "fed" into the prediction model, which results in modelled values. Often, lots of real-world data is neglected, but that is good because it allows us to focus on the important features.

Let us approach this a bit more formally. A *real-world model f* (systematic information) is explained by:

$$y = f(X) + \varepsilon \tag{5.3}$$

where y is the output (response, observed values), $X = \left(x_1, \cdots, x_p\right)$ is the input (known also as predictors, variables, features) and ε is the random error. All inputs and outputs are real with $X \in \mathbb{R}^{n \times p}$ and $y \in \mathbb{R}^n$. Here, n is the number of observations, and p is the number of features.

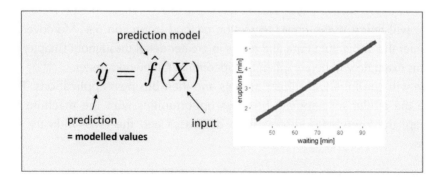

FIGURE 5.6 Prediction model.

A *prediction model* $\hat{f}$ (estimate for f) generates predictions $\hat{y} \in \mathbb{R}^{n \times 1}$ using existing (real) input $X = [X_i] = [x_j]$ (rows X_i, columns x_j):

127

$$\hat{y} = \hat{f}(X).$$

Using the multivariate linear regression model, the prediction model becomes:

$$\hat{y} = \hat{f}(X) = Xb,$$

where $b \in \mathbb{R}^{1 \times p}$ is a row-vector. Note that one of the features of X is a one-vector (i.e. all elements are ones). The lm (linear model) method, implemented in the Data Science language R, computes b by minimising the *mean squared error:*

$$MSE = \frac{1}{n}\sum_{i=1}^{n}(y_i - \hat{y}_i)^2.$$

Please note that the MSE is introduced with great care in Section 6.1, amongst other quality measures. Let us return to the house price example. Now the prediction model can be written in mathematical notation $\hat{y} = \beta_0 + \beta_1 x$. Figure 5.7 (a) shows the context for the previous formulations given. Instead of using the lm method, linear regression (LR) can be used. Figure 5.7 (b) illustrates that LR finds the "orange line" by minimising the MSE between observed and modelled values.

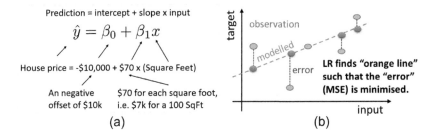

FIGURE 5.7 (a) Linear model formulations, (b) linear regression to find linear model.

We will return to the linear regression method in Section 6.4. Moreover, we will reconsider the underlying data and errors in greater detail throughout Chapter 6. However, this example will help explain the upcoming frameworks better.

We will continue with linear models and their business applications. This shall enable the reader to associate business opportunities with the machine learning roadmap, the knowledge discovery in databases and the cross-industry standard process.

5.2.3 Business Applications

Exercise 5.1 (Specify linear models). Identify three business scenarios, which fit the following format:
Target $= \beta_0 + \beta_1$ Feature

Replace the parameters target and feature with business-related terms. You can leave the intercept and slope variables unspecified. This exercise should lead to scenarios like the ones mentioned later in this section.

We have structured the following business applications, which can be approximated by linear models according to business domains. (Occasionally, we also provided classification examples.) The business domains used are operations, marketing, sales and human resources.

Operations

- Predict best/reliable/quality supplier based on lead time/correct quantity/inspection failure rate, on-time order completion rate, beyond acceptable quality limits;
- Predict machine breakdown (logistic) based on previous breakdowns, service level, maintenance, temperature, oil level etc. (see also Machine Learning Techniques for Predictive Maintenance);
- Demand $= \beta_0 + \beta_1$ (historic demand), e.g. predict customer demand for each SKU to support production later;
- Crop yield $= \beta_0 + \beta_1$ (amount of fertilizer) $+ \beta_2$ (amount of water);
- Number of complaints $= \beta_0 + \beta_1$ (wait times of callers);
- Shelf life of cookies $= \beta_0 + \beta_1$ (baking temperature).

Finance

- Predict profit margin based on previous margins;
- Trend and forecast for cost, revenue and profit based on time;
- Revenue $= \beta_0 + \beta_1$ (historic revenue);
- Credit card default based on customer profile (logistic);
- Fraud detection based on history and location (logistic).

Marketing

- Campaign effectiveness dependent on promotions and pricing for specific brands using radio and TV;
- Revenue $= \beta_0 + \beta_1$ (ad spending);
- Market research based on a customer survey.

Sales

- Revenue from ice cream (or lemonade or hot dogs or . . .);

- Sales $= \beta_0 + \beta_1$ (temperature);
- Revenue $= \beta_0 + \beta_1$ (opening hours);
- House price $= \beta_0 + \beta_1$ (#rooms);
- Meat sales $= \beta_0 + \beta_1$ (season);
- #Alarm systems sold $= \beta_0 + \beta_1$ (burglaries in area).

Human Resources

- Employee attrition $= \beta_0 + \beta_1$ (stock options) $+ \beta_2$ (job role) $+ \beta_3$ (work-life balance);
- Wage $= \beta_0 + \beta_1$ (Age) $+ \beta_2$ (Education).

Others

- Car insurance premium table based on claims, declared value, driver information, demographics etc.;
- Caravan insurance based on potentially 85 features (logistic);
- #Car accidents $= \beta_0 + \beta_1$ (gender);
- Car price $= \beta_0 + \beta_1$ (brand) $+\beta_2$ (mileage).

5.3 Machine Learning Roadmap

We will now provide the general roadmap for approaching most Data Analytics challenges. The roadmap can be illustrated by the schematic in Figure 5.6. We begin with a dataset and preprocess it. We split the data into training and test data. The training dataset is used to learn a model. The learning of the model is guided by quality metrics. We evaluate the learned model with test data. We might now return to the learning phase to further improve the model. Once we are happy with the evaluation, we apply the final model to new data.

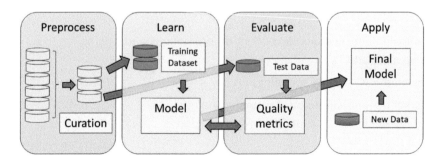

FIGURE 5.8 Roadmap for statistical/machine learning.

We will refine this roadmap by deriving the process illustrated in Figure 5.9, which is commonly used to solve supervised statistical and machine learning challenges.

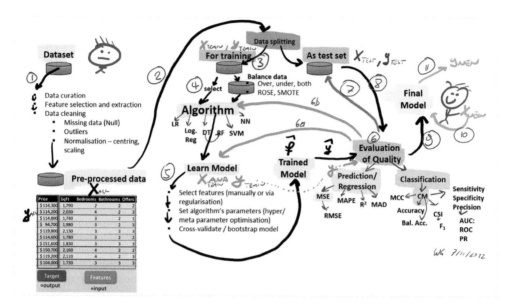

FIGURE 5.9 Supervised statistical/machine learning process.

The term *supervised* refers to the fact that the target guides (supervises) the learning of the underlying model. The previous schematic can be extended to accommodate the "unsupervised" learning process: i.e. the target is unknown. Unsupervised learning will be discussed in Chapter 8. We will give an idea about the steps mentioned in this road-map and use them throughout this book.

5.3.1 Preprocessing, Splitting and Balancing

Stage 1: Preprocessing. Our starting point is a dataset. *Data curation* is the process of obtaining, organising, describing, cleaning, enhancing and preserving data (Mixson, 2021; SuperAnnotate, 2021). The data can be obtained from a single dataset or a set of data. For instance, the dataset can be based on (organised in) several database tables (see Chapter 2) or heterogeneous sources (see Section 3.2). Data descriptions can be in the form of data dictionaries, which are simple natural language explanations of each feature. A preliminary feature selection and extraction (creation) can happen at this point. Data descriptions can also go into explanatory data analysis, which includes summary statistics. Often, these statistics identify null values. Depending on the scenario, records with null values may be omitted or imputed. Removing rows is simple, but valuable information may be lost. *Imputing* null values attempts to predict the missing (null) value. This can be as simple as replacing the null values with the feature's sample mean or using "chained" (sequential) predictions (e.g. linear regression). Outliers can represent wrongly recorded values or real values differing from their peers. In the first case, it would be good to "repair" the wrongly recorded values. In the case of correct outliers, we either consider them separately or ensure that we consider them appropriately. Depending on the machine learning method used, later normalised data may be necessary. Normalisation often refers to reducing (scaling) the feature's domain to the interval [0, 1]. An interesting question is whether normalisation can always be done; this will be explored later.

Eventually, we obtain a single preprocessed data frame, which contains the target y and features X of all records.

Stage 2: Data splitting. In this stage, we divide the data into *training* and *test data*. Often, this is done with an 80:20 or 70:30 split. An 80:20 split means that a random sample (without replacement) of 80% of the data is taken for training (learning) a model, and the remainder is used to test (evaluate) the learned model. The training data contains the target y_{train} and feature X_{train} subset. The test data consists of y_{test} and X_{test}. The test data is also known as a *hold-out set*. Documentation is sparse about data split details.

Since we are taking a random sample, each split will lead to different learned models. This randomness is well acknowledged in Stage 5 but, interestingly, not used in Stage 2. Limited computing resources might be a contributing reason for this. Conceptually, we would like to split the data such that the model's evaluation is reliable and representative of unseen data. On the other hand, we want the training data to be sufficient to learn an accurate model.

Stage 3: Data balancing. Generally, data balancing is associated with classifications, but it may prove useful for learning continuous predictions, especially when they contain real desirable outliers. In the first instance, you may want to omit data balancing to derive a base model. That means to derive a model for comparison purposes. Some machine learning techniques will not require data balancing at all (e.g. logistic regression). Other methods, such as neural networks, benefit from more balanced data. *Imbalanced data* with a binary target consists of two classes. For instance, you may only have a few customers who buy insurance. These constitute the *minority class*, and the others are the *majority class*. In such a case, it is beneficial to balance the data. It is interesting that perfectly balanced data is usually not the best for learning a model. Here, perfectly balanced refers to having equally sized (50:50) classes. So it may be necessary to experiment with different balance ratios (minority: majority, 20:80, 30:70, 40:60). The simplest balancing technique is *undersampling*, which is achieved by reducing the majority class by selecting a sample to obtain the desired balancing ratio. *Oversampling*, is achieved by duplicating records from the minority class until the desired ratio is achieved. *Both* simply combines over- and undersampling.

Random over-sampling examples (ROSE) is a library containing the previously mentioned balancing techniques and synthetically generated data points (records). The generation is based on kernel density estimators (roughly speaking, the continuous form of histograms). As the name *synthetic minority oversampling technique* (SMOTE) indicates, new data points are created from the minority class by oversampling. A new synthetic data point for the minority class is created by considering the line segment between neighbouring points. For details, consider Chawla et al. (2002).

5.3.2 *Learning*

Stage 4: Select algorithm. This is probably the phase most spoken about: which algorithm should be used. An algorithm is a list of instructions to solve a problem. The best-studied and most-often used algorithm is the linear regression (LR). Section 6.4 explains it in detail. In Section 5.2.3, we saw several business applications. We observed that the target variable is in the continuous domain. So it is suitable for predictions. If the target variable has a categorical output such as the customer buys or does not buy insurance, then we need an algorithm capable of classification. *Logistic regression* (Log. Reg.) is the prime example of those (Section 6.5). Tree-based algorithms can be used for predictions and classifications. Decision trees (DTs) have a high degree of interpretability because of the ease of reading and comprehending the learned model. It is called DT because features are used to make decisions (see Section 7.2). A "random" combination (ensemble) of DTs forms a random forest (RF). The RF leads to better predictions but sacrifices interpretability. So we begin to see a typical trade-off between the accuracy (or other quality metrics) and interpretability of algorithms. Support vector machine (SVM) and neural network (NN) algorithms are also prominent choices. Deep learning neural network algorithms in particular have recently gained great popularity. We will discuss them in Section 9.2. There are hundreds of other algorithms which could be chosen. Generally, one begins by selecting one algorithm to gain first insights. Then a set of algorithms is used and compared. Sometimes an ensemble of algorithms is used to improve the accuracy (or other quality metrics) further. Eventually, you might want to invent your own algorithm.

Stage 5: Learning the model. The previously chosen algorithm is used to learn a model. The model can then be used to predict the target given new unseen data. In Stage 1, features were selected and extracted. The algorithms often can help with the feature selection using a so-called *regularisation term* in their learning objective (Section 6.5). Another way is to use stepwise forward/backward feature selection (James et al., 2013, Section 6.1), which requires us to run the algorithm multiple times. The *stepwise-forward* procedure adds one feature at a time such that the quality of the model improves most. The *stepwise-backward* procedure starts with all features and reduces the model by removing one feature at a time such that the quality of the model is reduced the least. These stepwise algorithms are heuristics because they only look at removing one feature rather than the combination of features. Often, features are manually selected using intuition or subject matter expertise. In Stage 1 a "rough" feature selection/extraction is done, and in Stage 5, we refine the selection/extraction. This step prepared the input to learn the model. Most algorithms have *hyper (meta) parameters* that control the learner's behaviour. For instance, the DT allows us to set the minimum number of observations required for a split. We can also control the tree's depth and many more characteristics. Beginners rely on the default configuration, which should be suitable for commonly encountered scenarios. Experts fine-tune the meta parameters. However, a systematic approach using *experimental designs* (e.g. as discussed in Jain, 1991, Part Four) should lead to better results. Learning the models on one fixed dataset can lead to overfitting. That means the model will have great evaluation quality on the training set but poor quality on the test set. To overcome this, random sampling methods are used within the training dataset. Prominent sampling approaches are cross-validation and bootstrapping (James et al., 2013, Section 5.1 and 5.2). At this point, some authors start to distinguish between three datasets: *training-, test- and validation dataset*. The validation set is used for learning the model (Stage 5), whilst the test data is used at the end of the process (Transition 8). Note that sometimes validation data is not used. Overall, after this stage, a trained model $\hat{f}$ is obtained.

5.3.3 Evaluation and Application

Stage 6 with transition 7 and 8: evaluation of quality. The evaluation of the trained model is based on its output $\hat{y}$. There are two evaluations. One is used for learning the model. It is based on the training data and feeds back into Stage 5. In Figure 5.9, this is shown as the green Transition 6a. The training data evaluation may even prompt the reconsideration of the choice of algorithm (shown as Transition 6b). Most prediction algorithms have the mean squared error (MSE, Section 6.3) as evaluation metrics internally (implicitly) implemented. That means the training data evaluation does not need to be done by the user of the algorithm. Classification algorithms vary their evaluation metrics and sometimes offer to provide or select a measure. Knowing or setting the algorithm's evaluation function is important to justify the test data evaluation. The test data evaluation is our primary concern because the analyst will have to read and explain its output. This is probably the most essential deciding factor in choosing the final model. The evaluation of the quality of the trained model is based on its computed values $\hat{y}_{\text{test}} = \hat{f}(X_{\text{test}})$ and the observed values y_{test}.

We will explain the prediction and classification quality metrics in Section 6.3 and Section 6.1 respectively. The prediction/regression quality abbreviations shown in

Figure 5.9 are mean squared error (MSE), root MSE (RMSE), mean absolute percentage error (MAPE), coefficient of determination (R^2) and mean absolute deviation (MAD). The classification quality metrics abbreviations are confusion matrix (CM), Matthew's correlation coefficient (MCC), balanced accuracy (Bal. Acc.), critical success index (CSI), F-score (F_1), area under curve (AUC), receiver operating characteristic (ROC) and precision recall (PR).

Stage 9 with transitions 10 and 11: final model. The final model is chosen by comparing multiple models based on one or several quality measures indicated in Stage 6. The final model is exposed to entirely new and unseen input data (not yet available to us, Transition 10) and predicts the target variable (Transition 11). At this point, the analyst stops. However, it is debatable whether, at this stage, the test data should be reintegrated (at least to a certain extent) into training the model further. Furthermore, as soon as new data becomes available, we could continue improving the final model.

The preceding was a rough description of the overall roadmap for the machine learning process. To further enhance the ML process, a closer view of the business applications and the project management aspects is required. This motivated the creation of knowledge discovery in databases.

5.4 Knowledge Discovery in Databases (KDD)

The *KDD process* is introduced to extract useful knowledge from volumes of data (Fayyad et al., 1996). The process involves several steps: data selection, data preprocessing, data transformation, data mining and interpretation/evaluation of data. Figure 5.10 shows these steps. One of the steps in KDD is data mining, which may have motivated the second meaning of the abbreviation KDD: *knowledge discovery and data mining.* Generally, the process transforms raw data into knowledge, which can be used for decision making. The usefulness of the gained knowledge gives value to data. This is based on patterns discovered through data mining or, more specifically, statistical analysis or machine learning methods. The knowledge can be in the form of reports, identifying events, deriving trends, supporting decisions or policy. These should assist in achieving business or operations objectives. In the context of research, the scientific goals are addressed (ibid.). KDD encourages investing a "large portion" of effort in stating the challenge instead of optimising algorithmic details. Despite this business objective–oriented view, the process steps are mainly concerned with presenting data manipulation steps. However, at the knowledge step, one can formulate actionable data insights beneficial to a business's objectives. Debuse et al. (1999) provide a series of roadmaps detailing the KDD process steps and enhance it with a resourcing and exploitation step. The visuals contain actual USA roadmap symbols. I have provided a European version in Figure 5.11.

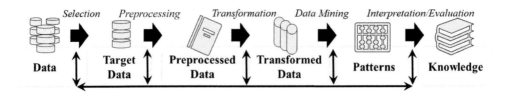

FIGURE 5.10 Original KDD process steps.

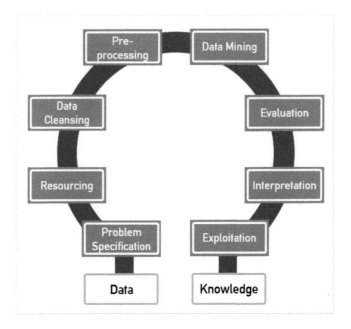

FIGURE 5.11 KDD roadmap.

5.4.1 KDD – Problem and Resourcing

In the beginning, goals for the future application need to be established, which requires domain-specific knowledge. A rough problem formulation will follow, which needs to be refined into a concise problem specification. This requires a preliminary data examination to check the data's availability and feasibility for the business challenge. This will lead to some familiarity with the data. Figure 5.12 shows the roadmap for the problem specification. We begin by having a rough business opportunity (problem) description (or idea) about the Data Analytics project. The first "stop" is to record a travel log entry. That means recording the task, person and time needed. Ideally, this is done for each task in each phase. This helps plan and control the project. Next, we check the basic technicalities of the database: for example, is it a single database or a heterogeneous set of data sources (variety)? This should lead to an idea about the data's volume, access rights and access

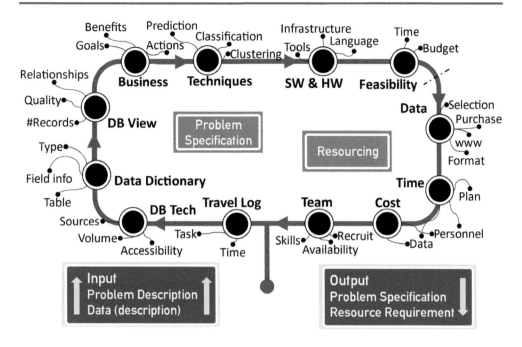

FIGURE 5.12 KDD roadmap problem specification and resourcing phase.

speeds (velocity). In *Big Data* terminology, these are known as the three Vs – variety, volume and velocity. Given the project's objective, a data dictionary lists relevant tables. This will eventually lead to specifying fields. The fields should be explained with textual and visual descriptions. Detailed descriptions may be done at a later stage in the project, which can include a density plot and summary statistics. The type of field (categorical or numerical data) is already useful at the beginning of the project. The next task is to become more familiar with the database. This can be as simple as knowing the number of records in the relevant tables. How many NULL values (missing data) are present in tables. This is a quality measure of the data, indicating whether enough data is available for a successful analysis or if additional data needs to be collected. The relationship between tables reveals the business rules and parts of the business process. It allows us to link various data sources or tables with each other. This will prove useful later when the data needs to be transformed. Once the data has been screened, it should be easier to return to the business opportunity idea and refine it to a proper goal/objective. The benefits to the business need to be clearly specified. Furthermore, clear actions (steps) have to be specified for how the "potential" business opportunities can be manifested. Typical Data Analytics projects deliver predictions, classifications or cluster solutions. At this stage, strategic decisions about the Data Science language (R, Python, Matlab), tools (Power BI, Tableau, SPSS Modeler) and infrastructure (computing power, shared drives) should be made. What is realistically feasible to achieve the project, considering the needed time and budget cost? The last task paves the way for detailing the resource requirements.

The roadmap was inspired by Debuse et al. (1999). I have modified some specifics, which – in my opinion – are more appropriate and capture the gist. Overall, one will notice the immediate closeness of the project specification to data. This is fine for projects, which are less focused on business objectives. We will refrain from this since it is covered in the CRISP-DM framework. However, based on the original ideas of KDD, this phase could be substituted to accommodate the business problem formulation.

The next phase of Debuse's KDD roadmap concerns resourcing. Resources come in various forms. The primary resource for a Data Analytics project is the data. In most businesses, extensive data collection is taking place already. Often, these are stored in relational databases (structured data) or in unnormalised form (e.g. spreadsheets). Sometimes, data collection processes and database designs have to be initiated. Other times, data has to be purchased. The World Wide Web (WWW) offers plenty of data sources with structured and unstructured data. These may be utilised for Data Analytics projects. One of the aspects that can be considered during these data resourcing plans is the data format control (e.g. age coded as integers or in ranges, customers identified differently for marketing and sales etc.). In the project-specification phase, the data aspects have been discussed, and this should have led to a clear picture of the availability and need for data.

Traditional resources are cost and time. The cost of purchasing data and the time required to obtain and organise it need to be considered. Typically, cost and time are associated with personnel – their availability and skills play important roles. Here, the decision has to be made about the team members' responsibilities. A project plan should be derived as an output.

These days, the cost of software can be negligible when Data Science languages such as R and Python are used exclusively. However, the larger the businesses, the more likely it is that substantial software costs can occur when solutions have to be integrated into Enterprise Resource Planning (ERP) tools or special management software needs to be customised. Business intelligence tools are relatively cost-effective (see Section 3.2). Hardware or, more commonly, cloud computing resources need to be considered as well.

5.4.2 KDD – Data Cleansing and Preprocessing

Despite the efforts of the database administrators, data engineers, software engineers and other staff, the gathered data's quality may not be as intended. Often, there will be missing values, partial records or wrongly entered data. The saying "Rubbish (data) in, rubbish (results) out" can be avoided by preparing the data. Some sources claim that this could take up about 80% of a Data Science project. The data cleansing and preprocessing to ensure data quality are of high importance to encourage trust into the subsequent analyses and business decisions. That means quality data is essential to create valid business reports. The data preparation begins by connecting to the data sources, cleaning the data and transforming it to meet the business challenge's requirements. This can include anonymisation of the data to conform with legislative rules. Obviously, the data cleansing and preprocessing phases have similarities to the machine learning process discussed in Section 5.3 (Stages 1 to 3).

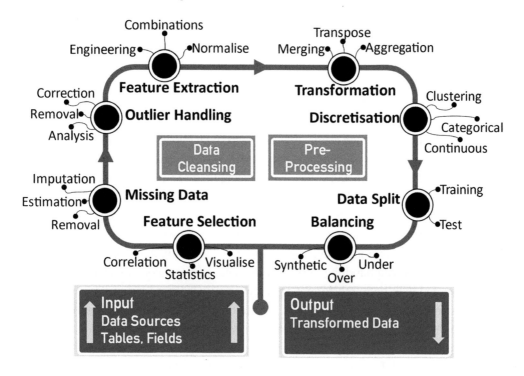

FIGURE 5.13 KDD cleansing and preprocessing in KDD.

In the previous two phases (problem specification and resourcing), a very good understanding of the data sources, tables, relationships, fields and descriptions has been gained. This served as a pre-selection of features. In this phase, we commit to selecting a subset of features. Visualisations such as histograms (density plots) or boxplots may help in determining the usefulness of features. Correlation between non-target variables may identify them as redundant information. Often, this means that a single representative variable is more objective. Features having high correlations to the target are of interest as this indicates that they may have great predictive power. Obviously, one needs to filter out variables, which are generated from the target. Variables with no correlations to the target may be omitted as well. Visualising correlations may reveal non-linear patterns that can be used at this stage to identify potentially useful learning algorithms. Summary statistics about the variable give an idea about the count, min, max, average, deviation and null values.

The null values identify missing data. If the percentage of missing data is minimal and has no systematic structure, records may be omitted. Otherwise, one can attempt to "repair" the missing data. An easy way to achieve this is to use the average value for a missing value. Another way to approach the repairing of data is to set the feature with the missing value as a target temporarily. This allows it to predict the missing values. If there are several features with missing values, then a chained approach of predictions can be used. Generally, these approaches are known as *data imputation*.

The visualisations of features and summary statistics may reveal outliers. A typical *outlier detection* is based on the assumption that the data is normally distributed. Here, an observation beyond a certain deviation (e.g. three standard deviations) from the average is classified as an outlier. Clustering can be used to identify outliers. Garn and Aitken (2015) provide a review of outlier detection techniques. After detecting outliers, one needs to decide whether they have to be kept as an important minority class or if they are erroneous and need to be removed or corrected. Corrections methods are similar to the missing data techniques mentioned earlier. Data cleansing is primarily associated with missing data and outlier handling.

Once the existing relevant features have been repaired, one can consider *engineering* new features. For instance, the value of an existing field can be squared or the logarithm taken. Features can be combined by multiplying powers of the individual values (e.g. x^2y) to create a new feature. In the data mining phase, algorithms may require *normalised data*. Hence, normalisation can take place at this stage. However, several of today's algorithms detect whether normalisation is required and scale the data appropriately.

The previous data handling steps (missing data, outlier detection, feature extraction) are associated with data transformation. However, we have added this as an extra step to emphasise that if the data came from various data sources, it needs to be merged. This is due to the nature of data mining algorithms requiring a single "table" (data frame) as input. The features have to represent the columns. If this is not the case, then the columns must be transposed. This step is usually done before the data cleansing tasks. Depending on the desired results, the data has to be aggregated. For instance, if monthly results are expected and the data is given on a day-by-day basis, then aggregations have to happen.

The business objective may indicate whether a prediction, classification or clustering approach is required. If the data is continuous but a classification is demanded, then the target has to be discretised (i.e. transformed to a categorical type). Sometimes, the later evaluation phase may show unsatisfactory quality; in this case, you may decide to switch from a prediction problem to a classification challenge.

At this point, the data should be clean and is almost ready for data mining algorithms. However, to verify that the algorithm works properly we hold out some test data (see Section 5.3, Stage 2 for details). If we identified some minority classes during data preprocessing, it may be necessary to balance the data (see Section 5.3, Stage 3 for details). Please note that the test data is not balanced because synthetic data may affect the evaluation. Additionally, balanced test data would provide a false expectation of the business users.

5.4.3 KDD – Data Mining and Evaluation

In the previous section, we explained the steps to prepare the data. Once the data is prepared, the data mining process can begin. In this stage, machine learning methods and other AI techniques are used to offer the methods which will lead to the answers to the initial business challenge.

We discussed these phases in the machine learning roadmap in Section 5.4 – please see Stages 5 and 6 for details.

5.4.4 KDD – Interpretation and Exploitation

Visualisation plays a major part in interpreting the gained data insights. For instance, a sales demand forecast can reveal an increase. As a consequence, the underlying supply chain may have to be adjusted.

Sharing BI reports and dashboards allows the collaborative exploitation of the actionable business insights (knowledge) discovered in this process.

5.5 Cross-Industry Standard Process for Data Mining

In 2000, the cross-industry standard process for data mining (CRISP-DM) 1.0 data mining guide was published by Chapman et al. (2000). It was inspired by the KDD but itself motivated the KDD roadmap, which was published shortly afterwards. After more than 20 years, an updated version would have been expected, but none was published. Nevertheless, it is still the most widely used process for Data Analytics/data mining projects. On Google Trends, the topics CRISP-DM and knowledge discovery have similar search scores. On sites such as KDNuggets, CRISP-DM outperformed the KDD process by roughly a factor of five from 2002 to 2014.

CRISP-DM can be seen as guide to doing Data Analytics projects. It consists of six phases: business understanding, data understanding, data preparation, modelling, evaluation and deployment. Figure 5.14 is a typical representation of these phases. A few benefits of the CRISP are ensuring quality of results for knowledge discovery projects, being of general purpose and being tool independent. In an analogy to project management, each phase is broken down into generic tasks. The phases and generic tasks are defined as the CRISP process model. The corresponding specialised tasks and process instances are known as the CRIPS process.

5.5.1 Understanding

Business Understanding

There are four essential tasks in this phase. The first one is to determine the business objectives. This involves providing some background and defining what qualifies as success criteria. The second task is assessing the situation. How many resources are available? What are the requirements, assumptions and constraints? What risks are involved in the project? What are the contingency measures? It also includes providing the terminology, costs and benefits. The third task is more specific to data mining challenges and requires specifying the data mining goals and success criteria. The final task is the creation of a project plan, which should include envisaged tools and techniques.

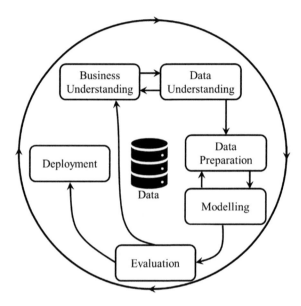

FIGURE 5.14 Typical representation of the CRISP phases.

Compared to the KDD process and roadmap, this phase is on a higher level and disentangles the project planning from data details.

Data Understanding

The phase of understanding the data is concerned with creating reports about collection, description, exploration and quality of data.

Fayyad, Piatetsky-Shapiro, and Smyth (1996) emphasise the business challenge aspects in the text of their KDD paper. Yet their process flow diagram does not reveal this aspect. Debuse et al. (2001) show in their KDD roadmap – in an interlaced way – the data understanding and project specification part. So it could be seen as a step forward to have a more clear separation between those two different topic areas. The business understanding is on an managerial level whilst the data understanding enters the realm of the data analyst. The arrows between business and data understanding highlight the importance of communication between manager and analyst to capture the right level of insight about opportunities and challenges.

5.5.2 *Preparation and Modelling*

Data Preparation

This phase aims to deliver a dataset with a description. The selected data needs to be justified with a rationale. The data cleaning should be documented. This phase also includes the task of constructing data. This involves deriving attributes (features) or the generation of records (observations). Another important task is to integrate data, which can be done through merging operations. It may also be necessary to reformat the data. Now it becomes obvious that CRISP-DM is derived from KDD. That means we can fall back on the details mentioned in the previous sections.

Modelling

The four essential tasks are (1) selecting the modelling techniques, (2) generating the test design, (3) building the model, and (4) assessing the model. The first task should provide justification for selecting the technique and be clear about the assumptions made. The generation of the test design could include a description of the experiments (e.g. systematic trial and errors) or even experimental designs. Building the model usually includes the investigation of several methods, each of which might be run with various differing parameter configurations. This is usually done in conjunction with assessing the model's quality.

5.5.3 *Evaluation and Deployment*

Evaluation

In this context, evaluation refers to the results of the data mining output in context with the business success criteria specified previously. This will require the approval of the models from the stakeholders. This phase should also include reviewing the process and listing the next steps (decisions and actions).

In the KDD and machine learning processes, we used evaluation in conjunction with the data mining algorithms. Here, the business context is emphasised.

Deployment

Once the project has completed the evaluation phase successfully, it needs to be made ready for deployment. This requires the creation of a deployment plan. Further, a monitoring and maintenance plan will ensure that the project's success will last. It should also produce a final report (presentation) and a review of the project.

5.6 Summary

We began by modelling a business scenario. In this context, formal functions providing real world and prediction models were defined. These functions were used to introduce one of the most important quality metrics in machine learning: the mean squared error (MSE). After having gained insights from a specific business scenario and equipped with fundamental evaluation metrics (the MSE), the general machine learning process was discussed. This process was supported with typically used tasks, tools, measures and algorithms. The knowledge discovery process in databases (KDD) integrated the machine learning process into its roadmap. Here, we added the project specification and resourcing part in an interlaced way. Additionally, steps for data cleansing and data preprocessing were discussed in detail. The deployment of the model was mentioned in the KDD context. The CRISP-DM and its essential phases and tasks were stated. We observed that the CRISP-DM offers better separation between business- and data-related tasks. Overall, three closely related frameworks were provided.

Annotated Bibliography

The following two references give a brief overview of CRISP:

This is the ultimate (original) reference for CRISP. It explains all aspects of CRISP in 78 pages in an easily accessible manner:

1. Chapman, P. et al. (2000). *CRISP-DM 1.0: Step-by-Step Data Mining Guide*. SPSS Inc., pp. 1–73.

Section 10.1 introduces the CRISP-DM methodology. He provides a short history and the process model and explains the phases of the reference model:

2. Du, H. (2010) *Data Mining Techniques and Applications: An Introduction*. Andover, England, UK: Cengage Learning.

The development of the CRISP-DM framework is discussed 20 years after its publication and compared to other evolving frameworks:

3. Martínez-Plumed, F. et al. (2019). CRISP-DM twenty years later: From data mining processes to data science trajectories. *IEEE Transactions on Knowledge and Data Engineering* 33 (8), 3048–3061.

An overview of the CRISP-DM process is given in Chapter 2:

4. Provost, F. and Fawcett, T. (2013). *Data Science for Business: What You Need to Know About Data Mining and Data-Analytic Thinking*. CA: O'Reilly Media.

THREE

Learning

Predictions, classifications and clusters are obtained using Machine Learning techniques. Business operations and strategies rely on their outputs. Statistical learning provides well-established linear and logistic regression for common predictions and classifications. Supervised machine learning techniques support business in their decision making when one can learn from a given target and input. Unsupervised machine learning can discover clusters without a specified target.

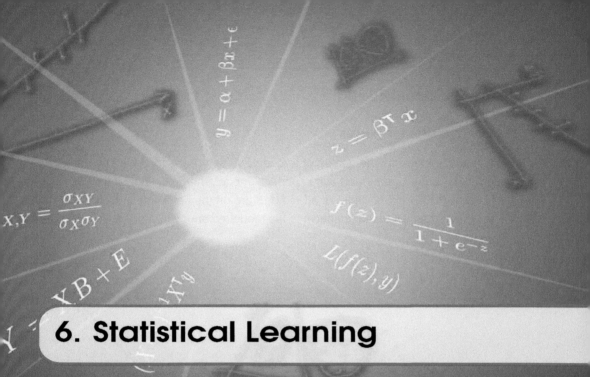

6. Statistical Learning

6.1 Introduction

Classic statistical learning methods are linear and logistic regression. Both methods are supervised learners. That means the target and input features are known. Linear regression is used for predictions, whilst logistic regression is a classifier. These methods are well-established and have many benefits. For instance, a lot of the theory of the methods is understood and the resulting models are easy to interpret. To evaluate the quality of the prediction and classification models, we need to understand the errors. This chapter uses an example to introduce the concept of errors.

Section 6.2.1 introduces common error measures such as the mean squared error and the mean average percentage error to measure the quality of predictions. The quality of classification is based on the so-called confusion matrix, which is discussed in Section 6.2.2. In order to get a better idea about the target and the input features, we will use descriptive statistics (Section 6.3). For linear and logistic regression, it is important to understand the correlation of the input features and the correlation to the target variable. We will introduce this in the same section. Section 6.4 gives the technical details of linear regression. Logistic regression is discussed in Section 6.5. The concepts introduced in this chapter will be used repeatedly in the remaining chapters.

DOI: 10.4324/9781003336099-9

6.2 Models and Quality Measures

6.2.1 Quality Measures

How can we determine the quality of a model? Which of the following two models is better? What is the best model? For a "perfect" model, the modelled values are exactly the same as the observed values. If all red dots are on the black line in Figure 6.1, then all observed target values are identical to the modelled ones. This implies that the closer

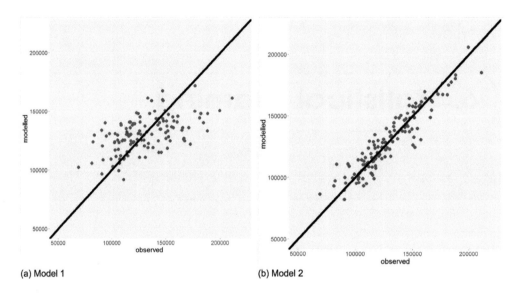

(a) Model 1 (b) Model 2

FIGURE 6.1 Observed versus modelled values for two models.

the red dots are to the black line, the better the quality of the model. That means that Model 2 is better than Model 1. These two models are based on the business scenario which was discussed in Section 5.2 using the MSE.

The quality of the model is determined by the frequency of errors. We will use the annotated Figure 6.2 to introduce quality and error measures.

This contains ten observed house price values $y_1 = 114,300$, $y_2 = 114,200$, $\cdots$, $y_{10} = 104,000$. Similarly, it shows modelled values $\hat{y}_1 = 135,300$, $\hat{y}_2 = 152,100$, $\cdots$, $\hat{y}_{10} = 131,100$. All the observed and modelled values are stored in vectors y and $\hat{y}$ respectively. The difference between an observed and modelled value is known as an *error*. For instance, the error between the ninth observed and modelled value is $\varepsilon_9 = y_9 - \hat{y}_9 = -38,500$. We could look at the mean error, but since there are positive and negative values, the mean error is not too meaningful. However, we can compute absolute values $|y_i - \hat{y}_i|$. The *mean absolute error* (MAE) is a useful quality metric:

$$\text{MAE} = \frac{1}{n}\sum_{i=1}^{n}|y_i - \hat{y}_i|. \tag{6.1}$$

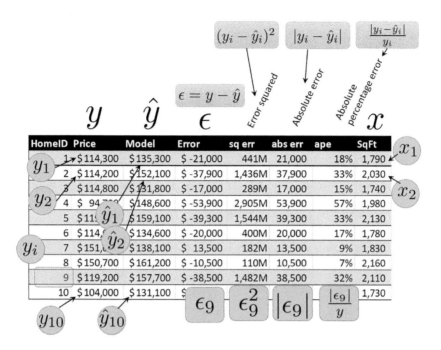

FIGURE 6.2 Errors and notation.

Here, n represents the number of data points. The MAE can be contrasted with the average house price value, which then tells us the expected absolute deviation from this average. In order to get an idea about the relative deviation between each observed and modelled value, we compute the absolute percentage error $\frac{|y_i - \hat{y}_i|}{|y_i|}$. If all observed values are positive, we can omit the absolute operator in the denominator. The mean absolute percentage *error* is defined by:

$$\text{MAPE} = \frac{1}{n} \sum_{i=1}^{n} \frac{|y_i - \hat{y}_i|}{|y_i|}. \tag{6.2}$$

The fundamental flaw with the MAPE is that a zero observed value renders the MAPE into an undefined expression. Additionally, values close to zero can generate large absolute percentage errors.

The *mean squared error* (MSE) is the most popular metric in statistical and machine learning for predictions. It is defined by:

$$\text{MSE} = \frac{1}{n} \sum_{i=1}^{n} (y_i - \hat{y}_i)^2. \tag{6.3}$$

In order to get an idea of the magnitude of deviation, the square root of the MSE is taken. This defines the *root mean squared error*:

$$RMSE = \sqrt{\frac{1}{n}\sum_{i=1}^{n}(y_i - \hat{y}_i)^2}$$

(6.4)

Example 6.2.1 (RMSE and MAPE). Previously, we introduced models about house prices. Model 1 is defined via the formula: House price = -$10,000 + 70 × (Square Feet). Computing the RMSE gives us $29,714. If the errors are normally distributed, then 68.3% of all house prices are within the interval average house price minus RMSE and average house price plus RMSE. The MAPE for Model 1 is 22%. That means Model 1 is simple and easy to explain but has a 22% error.

Let us introduce a second model, which considers three additional features:

$$y = -17k + 62x_1 + 9kx_2 + 13kx_3 - 14kx_4$$

with the following details:

	x1	x2	x3	x4
-17347.4	61.8	9319.8	12646.3	-13601.0
Intercept	SqFt	Bedrooms	Bathrooms	Offers

The RMSE is 14,703, which is half of Model 1's RMSE. This is also reflected in the 9% MAPE. Model 2 is a bit more complex but has a lower error.

What is a good enough model? This depends on the application. For instance, most people would agree that predicting the employee of the month is less important than detecting a medical condition correctly. Figure 6.3 shows a typical curve representing this trade-off and provides an indication of the term *good enough*.

The term *accuracy* is used loosely (i.e. it just stands for a generic quality measure rather than the definition given later). When the accuracy is 50%, then the prediction

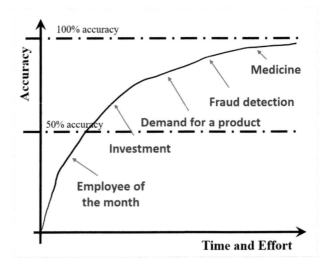

FIGURE 6.3 What is a good enough model?

model is as good as tossing a coin. A prediction model below 50% tells us that the model gets it wrong most of the time. Models above 50% accuracy are of interest to us. Usually, more time and effort invested in creating a model rewards us with better accuracy.

Assuming time and effort are not issues, how good should we make the model so that it works well for unseen data? This forces us to look into the trade-off between bias and variance. Figure 6.4 illustrates on the right that high bias implies that the model underfits the real data.

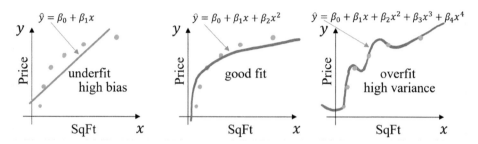

FIGURE 6.4 Bias versus variance.

The figure in the middle demonstrates a good fit. By the way, we extracted a new feature by squaring the SqFt feature. On the right, we see an overfitted model. Although it has the highest accuracy for the training data, it will perform badly for new data. Generally, the error between the real world model and the prediction model is:

$$\text{Error} = \text{Bias}^2 + \text{Variance} + \text{IrreducibleError}, \tag{6.5}$$

or, in a mathematical style:

$$\text{Error}(x) = \left(E\left[\hat{f}(x)\right] - f(x)\right)^2 + E\left[\left(\hat{f}(x) - E\left[\hat{f}(x)\right]\right)^2\right] + \sigma_e^2. \tag{6.6}$$

This explains the importance of bias and the influence of variance. Figure 6.5 (a) shows four possible scenarios.

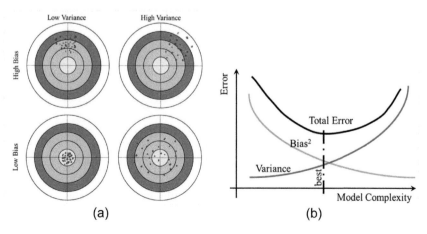

FIGURE 6.5 (a) Bias and variance scenarios, (b) model complexity and errors.

When the bias and variance are low, then we predict the target best (given these four scenarios). If the bias is low and the variance is high, we will still have some hits in the target. In case of high bias and low variance, the target is systematically missed. High variance and high bias mean the target is missed in all aspects. These bias and variance dynamics in context of model complexity are shown in Figure 6.5 (b). It demonstrates that a trade-off between bias and variance needs to happen, guided by the model's complexity. Previously, when we discussed the machine learning process, several methods were mentioned that help us find the right model complexity. These methods included regularisation and stepwise model selection techniques.

6.2.2 Confusion Matrix

In the previous section, we discussed quality metrics for predictions of target variables with a continuous range. However, if the target variable has only a binary output or a discrete set of outputs, then we need to reconsider whether there are better options than the MSE. The confusion matrix is the basis for various "accuracy" (quality) statements.

Let us have a look at three examples with binary target outputs. The examples compare actual target outcomes to predicted ones. The three examples are insurance policies, fraud detection and advertisement effectiveness. We want to explore the meaning of the confusion matrix elements.

The confusion matrix consists of four elements illustrating the combination of observed (actual) and predicted (modelled) values: true positives (TP), true negatives (TN), false positives (FP) and false negatives (FN). These elements would be easier to understand if they were correctly called predicted positives, correctly predicted negatives, falsely predicted positives and falsely predicted negatives.

Typically, in a binary target, the numeric value one is used to identify positive cases, and the numeric value zero is used for the negative cases. We can identify the confusion matrix elements via the following logical combinations, where y and $\hat{y}$ are vectors for the actual and predicted values:

$$TP = (y = \hat{y}) \wedge (y = 1) \tag{6.7}$$

$$TN = (y = \hat{y}) \wedge (y = 0) \tag{6.8}$$

$$FP = (y \neq \hat{y}) \wedge (\hat{y} = 1) \tag{6.9}$$

$$FN = (y \neq \hat{y}) \wedge (\hat{y} = 0). \tag{6.10}$$

These can also be derived using the following mathematical formulas, where the square brackets are used as *Iverson brackets*: i.e. if the expression within the brackets is true, then it is evaluated as one; otherwise, it is zero.

$$TP = \sum_{i=1}^{n} |y_i = \hat{y}_i| [y_i = 1] \quad (6.11)$$

$$TN = \sum_{i=1}^{n} |y_i = \hat{y}_i| [y_i = 0] \quad (6.12)$$

$$FP = \sum_{i=1}^{n} |y_i \neq \hat{y}_i| [\hat{y}_i = 1] \quad (6.13)$$

$$FN = \sum_{i=1}^{n} |y_i \neq \hat{y}_i| [\hat{y}_i = 0] \quad (6.14)$$

Example 6.2.2 (Confusion matrix). An arbitrary confusion matrix is created, and the previously introduced logical formulas are used to derive its elements.

```
#       TP            TN            FP            FN
y   = c(rep(1,9), rep(0,80), rep(0,3), rep(1,8))
yh  = c(rep(1,9), rep(0,80), rep(1,3), rep(0,8))
sum (y == yh & y   == 1)  # TP
## [1] 9
sum (y == yh & y   == 0)  # TN
## [1] 80
sum (y != yh & yh == 1)  # FP
## [1] 3
sum (y != yh & yh == 0)  # FN
## [1] 8
```

The created matrix is shown in Table 6.1. Table 6.1 shows a simple numeric example of a confusion matrix.

TABLE 6.1 Confusion matrix example.

		Predicted		Actual
		Positive	Negative	Total
Actual	Positive	TP = 9	FN = 8	P = 17
	Negative	FP = 3	TN = 80	N = 83
Predicted	*Total*	PP = 12	PN = 88	100

In the context of the insurance policy's test data, there are $P = 17$ observations that actually purchased insurance and $N = 83$ that did not. P and N abbreviate the total number of positive and negative cases respectively. The model predicted that $PP = 12$ would purchase insurance and that $PN = 88$ would not. PP and PN stand for the total number of *predicted positive* and *predicted negative* cases. TP=9 tells us that the model correctly predicted 9 cases (out of 17) that would purchase insurance. That means the prediction model *hit* the target. It also correctly predicted TN=80 cases out of 83 would not buy insurance. We say that the model *correctly rejected* those who would not buy insurance. Now, on the flip side, the model falsely predicted that FP=3 customers would purchase insurance. That means that the model *overestimated* (OE) the number of who would buy insurance. We say that the model gave a *false alarm*. This also known as a *Type I* (TI) error. Additionally, the model falsely predicted FN=8 negative cases. These cases are actually positive. That means it underestimates the desired outcome. This is why we also call FN *underestimates* (UE) or *misses*. Another more abstract name for FN is *Type II* (TII) error.

For the fraud application, we interpret TP as 9 fraudulent transactions correctly identified by the model. TN means 80 flagged cases were correctly rejected. However, the model missed 8 fraudulent transactions, which, of course, leads to financial losses. Lastly, falsely predicted positives (FP) means that the model will raise a false alarm for 3 transactions. Again, this can cause inconvenience to the customer by blocking the transaction. This can result in the customer not purchasing a product and both merchant and customer losing out. Additionally, it causes unnecessary fees for the bank investigating these FPs.

In general, the confusion matrix gives an objective view of quality and allows a focus on TP. Table 6.2 shows the confusion matrix with the terms introduced. Additionally, it provides the confusion matrix in two relative version.

The first one is based on rates dividing by P and N. The second one is obtained by dividing by PP and PN. The first relative confusion matrix elements are true positive rate (TPR), false negative rate (FNR), false positive rate (FPR) and true negative rate (TNR).

TABLE 6.2 Confusion matrix, rates and ratios.

| | | Predicted | | | Rates |
		PP	**PN**		
Actual	P	hit TP	miss FN	recall TPR	FNR
	N	false alarm FP	cor. rej. TN	FPR	specificity TNR
Ratios		precision PPV	FOR		
		FDR	NPV		

The first relative (rate) confusion matrix is obtained by dividing the CM elements by P and N. The elements are $TPR = \dfrac{TP}{P}$, $FNR = \dfrac{FN}{P}$, $FPR = \dfrac{FP}{N}$ and $TNR = \dfrac{TN}{N}$. The most essential value of this matrix is probably TPR. It has several synonyms such as hit rate, sensitivity, probability of detection and recall. It would be wise to use these terms in the context of application.

For instance, "recall" for products (cars, washing machines etc.) that need to be recalled or when dealing with fraud, the "probability of detection" is appropriate. The TNR is also known as *specificity* and *selectivity*.

The second relative (ratio) confusion matrix is obtained by dividing the CM elements by PP and PN. The elements are $PPV = \dfrac{TP}{PP}$, $NPV = \dfrac{TN}{PN}$, $FDR = \dfrac{FP}{PP}$ and $FOR = \dfrac{FN}{PN}$. The corresponding names are positive predicted value (PPV), negative predicted value (NPV), false discovery rate (FDR) and false omission rate (FOR). Again, the measure based on TP deserves an additional name: i.e. PPV is also known as *precision*.

There are several quality metrics with a single value that are based on the confusion matrix or its relative versions. The most prominent metric is accuracy:

$$\mathcal{A} = \frac{TP+TN}{P+N} \tag{6.15}$$

Accuracy can be used when the data is balanced. Imbalanced data renders its meaning useless. For instance, imagine 99% of the observed data is negative. A model that predicts only negative values will have a 99% accuracy rate. But the true target class is 100% wrong.

Hence, to accommodate imbalanced classes, *balanced accuracy* is introduced:

$$\mathcal{B} = \frac{1}{2}\left(TPR+TNR\right) \tag{6.16}$$

If the objective is to predict positives and negatives equally well, this is a good measure. If it is more important to focus on the true positives, the Jaccard index (aka *Critical Success Index* (CSI) and threat score (CS)) is more appropriate. It is defined as:

$$J = \frac{TP}{TP+FP+FN} \tag{6.17}$$

The importance of TPs can be emphasised even more using the F_1 score:

$$F_1 = \frac{2TP}{2TP+FP+FN} \tag{6.18}$$

The last two measures neglect true negatives.

A famous balanced relative quality measure takes the root product of all correctly predicted relative measures and subtracts the root product of all falsely predicted measures:

$$MCC = r_\rho = \rho = \sqrt{TPR \times TNR \times PPV \times NPV} - \sqrt{FPR \times FNR \times FDR \times FOR} \tag{6.19}$$

There are two more useful measures. They determine the area under the curve (AUC) for relative confusion matrix measures.

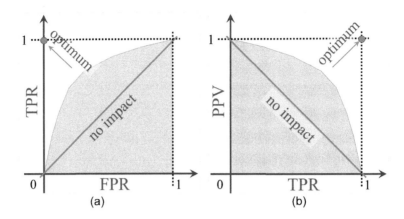

FIGURE 6.6 Area under curve (AUC) for (a) receiver operating characteristic (ROC) and (b) precision and recall.

The following two visualisations (Figure 6.6) show their concept. The first curve is called the *receiver operating characteristic* (ROC). It is based on the observation of the TPR (recall) and FPR. If the AUC has value one, then the model is optimal. This happens when FPR is zero and recall is one. If the measure is less than 0.5, then it is better not to use the model at all. This measure is good when false positives have to be avoided. However, they are scaled by the actual negative observations. That means that when the data is imbalanced, a high ROC-AUC value is easily achieved, which makes this measure less attractive.

The second visual shows the *precision recall* (PR) curve. Again, the value one represents an optimal model and 0.5 an unusable one. Remember, recall is TPR and precision is PPV. This AUC completely avoids the true negatives. Hence, if TNs are irrelevant, then this is a good measure. So, for imbalanced data, this measure seems to be more suitable.

6.3 Descriptive Statistics

Descriptive statistics are introduced using several examples, which are supported with R code. In Section 5.2, a business scenario about house prices was introduced. We will continue with this scenario.

6.3.1 Exploring Data

We will explore the structure and the first few records (i.e. rows) of the data. Some basic descriptive statistics for each feature (i.e. column) will be looked at. This will give us a basic understanding of the data.

Structure, preview and statistics

Table 6.3 shows some of the data about the homes. The first column gives an identifier for the home. The price is given in USD. The area of the home is in square feet; 1,000 square feet equals about 92.9 square meters. The data shows the number of bedrooms and bathrooms and the number of offers the home has received so far. It also states whether the walls are made out of brick or not. It provides the geographic location by means of the neighbourhood column. This data can be obtained from ywchiu's GitHub repository, or it can be accessed from the database various (see Chapter 2). You can use R to obtain the data.

```
root    <- 'https://raw.githubusercontent.com/'
folder <- 'ywchiu/riii/master/data/'
fn      <- 'house-prices.csv'
H       <-   read.csv(paste0(root,folder,fn))
```

TABLE 6.3 A preview of data about homes.

Home	Price	SqFt	Bedrooms	Bathrooms	Offers	Brick	Neighborhood
1	114300	1790	2	2	2	No	East
2	114200	2030	4	2	3	No	East
3	114800	1740	3	2	1	No	East
4	94700	1980	3	2	3	No	East
5	119800	2130	3	3	3	No	East
6	114600	1780	3	2	2	No	North
7	151600	1830	3	3	3	Yes	West

This table extract can be shown with the head function. Here, we will only display the first three entries.

```
head(H, n=3)
## Home Price SqFt Bedrooms Bathrooms Offers Brick Neighb. . .
## 1    1 114300 1790       2         2      2    No         East
## 2    2 114200 2030       4         2      3    No         East
## 3    3 114800 1740       3         2      1    No         East
```

Its structure can be seen with str. (Again, we only show the first few features.)

```
str(H)
## 'data.frame':        128 obs. of 8 variables:
## $ Home          : int 1 2 3 4 5 6 7 8 9 10
## $ Price         : int 114300 114200 114800 94700 119800
## $ SqFt          : int 1790 2030 1740 1980 2130 1780 1830. . .
## $ Bedrooms      : int 2 4 3 3 3 3 3 4 4 3 . . .
## $ Bathrooms     : int 2 2 2 2 3 2 3 2 2 3 . . .
## $ Offers        : int 2 3 1 3 3 2 3 2 3 3 . . .
## $ Brick         : chr "No" "No" "No" "No"
## $ Neighborhood: chr "East" "East" "East" "East" . . .
```

The *structure of the data* details the number of observations and variables. It is common to abbreviate the *number of observations* with n. That means there are n = 128 homes.

We'd like to explore the business data.

- How can you get an overall idea about the homes?
- How many homes are there?
- What is the average price of a home?
- Which are the smallest and largest homes?

The answers to these questions can be obtained by considering descriptive (summary) statistics. Summary statistics reveal key characteristics for each variable.

```
summary(H)
#       Home                  Price          SqFt            Bedrooms
# Min.   :   1.00  Min.   :  69100  Min.   :1450  Min.      :2.000
# 1st Qu. :  32.75  1st Qu.: 111325  1st Qu.: 1880  1st Qu.   :3.000
# Median :  64.50  Median : 125950  Median : 2000  Median    :3.000
# Mean   :  64.50  Mean   : 130427  Mean   : 2001  Mean      :3.023
# 3rd Qu. :  96.25  3rd Qu.: 148250  3rd Qu.: 2140  3rd Qu.   :3.000
# Max.   : 128.00  Max .  : 211200  Max.   : 2590  Max.      :5.000
#
# Bathrooms              Offers           Brick       Neighborhood
# Min.   :2.000  Min.      :1.000  Length: 128       Length :128
# 1st Qu. :2.000  1st Qu.  :2.000  Class :character  Class  :char
# Median :2.000  Median   :3.000  Mode :character    Mode  :char
# Mean   :2.445  Mean     :2.578
# 3rd Qu. :3.000  3rd Qu.  :3.000
# Max.   :4.000  Max.     :6.000
```

Looking at the home variable, we observe that it is a unique identifier for each home.

Let us define that each house price is an observed value and abbreviate it with y_i, where i represents the ith home. The average house price is \$130k (abbreviated as y). Generally, we use the variable y for the target variable and x for a feature. The smallest home is 1450 square feet (i.e. 135m^2), and the largest home is 2590 ft^2 (i.e. 241 m^2). The average home is 2001 ft^2. Here, we will use the variable x to represent the square footage feature.

The most prominent statistic is the expectation. The expectation deals with the entire "population". However, usually only a sample from the entire population is known. The sample expectation is known as average. The *sample mean* is defined via:

$$\bar{x} = \frac{1}{n}\sum_{i=1}^{n} x_i \qquad (6.20)$$

We can apply the formula on our square foot feature.

```
x = H$SqFt; n = length(x);
sum(x)/n; mean(x)
## [1] 2000.938
## [1] 2000.938
```

If we are interested in the entire population, then expectation (mean) is used $\mathbb{E}[X]$, which is also abbreviated with μ_X. This is known as the first moment.

To get an understanding of the sample deviations of the observations from the sample mean, we introduce the sample variance. The *sample variance* is defined as:

$$s^2 = \frac{1}{n-1}\sum_{i=1}^{n}(x_i - \bar{x})^2. \qquad (6.21)$$

Again, when considering the population, the notation $VarX$ is used for variance.

The *data range* is identified by the minimum (smallest value) and maximum (largest value). The range combined with the quartiles give us an idea of the data distribution. The first quartile q_1 indicates that 25% of the data are below the q_1 threshold. The second quartile q_2 is also known as median and tells us that 50% of the data are below q_2. The third quartile q_3 reveals that 75% of the data are below q_3. The range between the first and third quartiles is known as *interquartile range*.

Visual Inspection

Histograms and boxplots – To get an even better understanding of the house prices, we will look at their distribution. Basically, we would like to find out whether the distribution is symmetric. If yes, then the average house price is the most frequent one. This information can help the business develop a sales and purchase strategy: for instance, ensuring enough homes are available in the targeted price categories. The following code creates a *histogram* and displays the sample mean (Figure 6.7).

```
library(ggplot2)
c <- ggplot(H, aes(Price)) + geom_histogram(bins = 20) # Histo
c + geom_vline(xintercept = mean(H$Price)) # average line
```

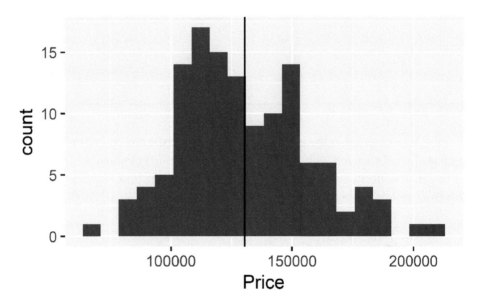

FIGURE 6.7 Histogram showing distribution of house prices and their average.

A *boxplot* provides essential statistics in a concise form. Let us consider the price distribution one more time.

```
boxplot(H$Price, horizontal=TRUE)
```

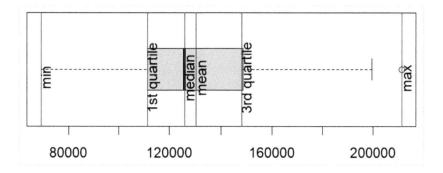

FIGURE 6.8 Boxplot and meaning (read lines).

That means the boxplot is a visualisation of the summary statistics.

This can assist us in specify the marketing campaign. For instance, since 50% of the properties are between the first and third quartiles, the campaign should produce material adequate to sell these properties.

6.3.2 Correlation

Correlation is a measure indicating how much two variables are associated with each other. Correlation is defined as:

$$\rho_{X,Y} = \frac{\text{cov}(X,Y)}{\sigma_X \sigma_y} = \frac{\sigma_{XY}}{\sigma_X \sigma_Y}, \tag{6.22}$$

for the entire population. For a sample, this is also known as the *Pearson correlation coefficient* (PCC) *r*, which shows the association between the variables. The PCC is defined as:

$$r = r_{X,Y} = \frac{s_{XY}}{s_X s_Y}, \tag{6.23}$$

where s_X is the sample standard deviation of X, and $s_{XY} = \text{cov}(X,Y)$ is the *sample covariance*. Generally, correlation is based on covariance. So covariance is the precursor of correlation or the "un-normalised" correlation. In statistics, *covariance* is defined as:

$$\text{Cov}[X,Y] = \mathbb{E}\left[(X - \mu_x)(Y - \mu_y)\right]. \tag{6.24}$$

Sample covariance is defined as:

$$\text{cov}(x,y) = \frac{\sum_i (x_i - \bar{x})(y_i - \bar{y})}{n - 1}. \tag{6.25}$$

This is abbreviated as $s_{xy} = \text{cov}(x,y)$.

For simple linear regression, the squared PCC is equivalent to the coefficient of determination: i.e. $r^2 = R^2$. Note that this is not generally true except for the simple linear regression.

The *coefficient of determination* is defined as:

$$R^2 = \frac{\sum_{i=1}^{n}(\hat{y}_i - \bar{y})^2}{\sum_{i=1}^{n}(y_i - \bar{y})^2} \tag{6.26}$$

where $\hat{y}_i$ is the predicted value from a simple linear regression model, $\bar{y}$ is the sample mean of the target variable and y_i is the target. That means that even without the linear regression prediction model, we are already in a position to give an accuracy statement about the quality of the model.

For instance, in the following example, we determine a simple linear regression model and its predictions y, abbreviated as yh. This is used to compute the R^2 value. Then we compare the R^2 value with the squared correlation r^2.

```
lr <- lm(H$Price~H$SqFt, H)  # Linear model
y <- H$Price; yh <- predict(lr); x <- H$SqFt
R2 = sum((yh-mean(y))^2)/sum((y-mean(y))^2)
R2; cor(y,x)^2
## [1] 0.3057894
## [1] 0.3057894
```

As we can see, the two measures are identical. We can say that 30.1% of the variation is explained by the model.

Let us return to the correlation. The correlation r summarises the relationship of two variables in a single value. For instance, the correlation between square foot and price cor(H$SqFt,H$Price) is 0.533. Now, it would be interesting to know whether this is good or bad. The correlation is always between minus one and plus one. Zero means there is no correlation according to the Pearson correlation formula. The value plus/minus one indicates a perfect correlation. For our example about homes, a positive value tells us that when the home is bigger, the sales price will higher. The interpretations of correlations is summarised in Table 6.4.

TABLE 6.4 Correlations and their meaning.

Range	Value of r interpretation
1	Perfect correlation.
(0, 1)	The two variables tend to increase or decrease together.
0	The two variables do not correlate at all.
(-1, 0)	One variable increases as the other decreases.
-1	Perfect negative (or inverse) correlation.

Often, the squared Pearson correlation coefficient is used (e.g. cor(H$SqFt,H$-Price = 0.31). Now the values must be between zero and one. As before, zero indicates no relationship between the variables, and one represents a perfect association. The following interpretations are often used in regard to variable associations (see Table 6.5).

TABLE 6.5 r^2 values and an interpretation of their associations.

Interval	Value of r^2 interpretation
[0.9, 1]	Very strong association
[0.8, 0.9)	Very strong association
[0.6, 0.8)	Moderate
[0.3, 0.6)	Weak
[0.1, 0.3)	Very weak
[0, 0.1)	No association

According to Table 6.5, the r^2 association between square foot and price is weak. As a manager, we interpret that a model predicting the price based on square footage has to be considered with care. There are other factors that may warrant a different price.

Figure 6.9 shows several visualisations of correlated normal distributed data. Correlation needs to be treated with caution. It may be possible that a very strong association was detected, but it was coincidental. The website www.tylervigen.com/spurious-correlations provides several examples such as the correlation between chicken consumption and crude oil imports, cheese consumption and doctorates awarded and more. On the other extreme, there might be a zero correlation when visual inspection clearly displays a correlation: for instance, a donut graph, square or any symmetric shape. Hence, it is recommended to visualise correlations. Figure 6.10 visualises the correlation between house prices and square footage.

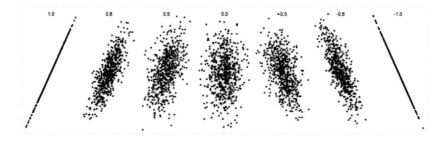

FIGURE 6.9 Normal distributed data with differing correlation coefficients.

```
ggplot(H,aes(x=SqFt,y=Price))+geom_point()
```

163

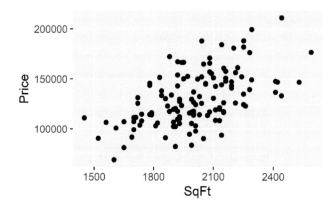

FIGURE 6.10 Correlation between square footage and price.

We can determine the correlations between all features. Returning to the business scenario, we determine the *correlation matrix*.

```
library(GGally)
ggpairs(H[,2:6])
```

The first row tells us the correlations to the target variable. The first column shows us the correlation plots. The diagonal represents the density distribution of the variable itself. Roughly speaking, this is a "continuous" histogram. The features bedrooms and bathrooms have similar correlations to the square footage feature. What if we could take all the observed information into account? Should we use all the other features? From a statistical standpoint, we should only use variables which are independent of each other: in practical terms, those that do not have a high inter-correlation with each other. This has the practical benefit of reducing the number of features. Some methods can do this automatically: e.g. LASSO via a regularisation term in its objective function. It would be interesting to discuss this in more detail, but it is beyond the scope of this book.

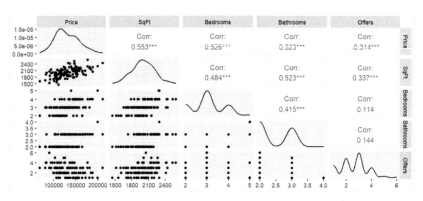

FIGURE 6.11 Correlation matrix for business scenario.

Generally, correlations help us quickly identify features relevant to our model. That means we begin building our model by selecting the feature with the highest correlation. In our business scenario, this was the feature SqFt.

6.4 Linear Regression

6.4.1 Simple Linear Regression

The simple linear regression model is given by:

$$\hat{y} = \beta_0 + \beta_1 x, \tag{6.27}$$

where β_0 is the intercept, and β_1 is the slope. A huge number of business applications use linear regression models; these are listed in Section 5.2.3 and supported with examples. Chapter 5 also showed how linear regressions are embedded in Data Analytics frameworks. Further, Section 5.2.2 discussed the business context using the house price example and provided an illustration of the errors. So we encourage the reader to revisit these sections.

We came across the simple linear regression in Chapter 3 (Business Intelligence) in the Analytics section (3.4.1), where we introduced it in the context of trend lines. We promised to show formulas for the simple linear regression. Surprisingly, the following formulas are difficult to find in the literature. Hence, I am providing the proof for them.

Our goal is to derive β_0 and β_1 such that the sum of squared errors is minimised. The sum of squared errors SS is given by:

$$SS = \sum_{i=1}^{n}(y_i - \hat{y}_i)^2 = \sum_{i=1}^{n}(y_i - \beta_o - \beta_1 x_i)^2 \tag{6.28}$$

Taking the partial derivatives of SS for (β_0, β_1) and setting them to zero allows us to find the optimal coefficients.

The partial derivative of SS for β_1 is

$$\frac{\partial SS}{\partial \beta_1} = -2\sum_{i=1}^{n}(y_i - \beta_o - \beta_1 x_i)x_i = 0, \tag{6.29}$$

which we set to zero to obtain the optimal coefficients. Similarly, the partial derivative of SS for β_0 is

$$\frac{\partial SS}{\partial \beta_0} = -2\sum_{i=1}^{n}(y_i - \beta_o - \beta_1 x_i)x_i = 0. \tag{6.30}$$

Now, we can solve the two simultaneous equations. Equation (6.11) can be simplified and transformed to express β_0:

$$\sum_{i=1}^{n} y_i = n\beta_0 - \beta_1 \sum_{i=1}^{n} x_i \Rightarrow \beta_0 = \bar{y} - \beta_1 \bar{x}$$

Equation (6.29) can be simplified and transformed to:

$$\sum_{i=1}^{n} x_i y_i = \beta_0 \sum_{i=1}^{n} x_i - \beta_1 \sum_{i=1}^{n} x_i^2$$

Substituting β_0 into the last equation gives

$$\sum_{i=1}^{n} x_i y_i = (\bar{y} - \beta_1 \bar{x}) n\bar{x} - \beta_1 \sum_{i=1}^{n} x_i^2$$

This can be written as:

$$\sum_{i=1}^{n} x_i y_i - \bar{y} n\bar{x} = \beta_1 \left(\sum_{i=1}^{n} x_i^2 - n\bar{x}^2 \right)$$

Hence, the derived formulas are:

$$\beta_0 = \bar{y} - \beta_1 \bar{x} \tag{6.31}$$

and

$$\beta_1 = \frac{\sum_{i=1}^{n} x_i y_i - \bar{x} \sum_{i=1}^{n} y_i}{\sum_{i=1}^{n} x_i^2 - n\bar{x}^2} \tag{6.32}$$

Here, $\bar{x} = \frac{1}{n} \sum_{i=1}^{n} x_i$ and $\bar{y} = \frac{1}{n} \sum_{i=1}^{n} y_i$ are the averages.

6.4.2 Multivariate Linear Regression

We can extend the previous simple linear regression model $\hat{y} = \beta_0 + \beta_1 x$, which has only one feature, to one with several features:

$$\hat{y} = \beta_0 + \beta_1 x_1 + \beta_2 x_2 + \cdots + \beta_n x_n \tag{6.33}$$

This formula can be simplified using vector notation. We define $\beta = [\beta_0 \, \beta_1 \, \beta_2 \cdots \beta_n]^T$ and $x = [x_0, x_1, \cdots x_n]^T$ (x_0 is set to value 1). Now, the linear regression model can be written as:

$$\hat{y} = \beta^T x \tag{6.34}$$

This model works for one record (one row) as input, assuming the coefficients β_i have been determined.

Two approaches to determining the model coefficients analytically are shown. Note, this section is optional. It assumes some familiarity with linear algebra (vectors, matrices, calculus).

Our objective is to minimise the error vector ε between the vectors y (observed values) and $\hat{y}$ (modelled values) because $y = \hat{y} + \varepsilon$. If you look at a 2D vector, it is obvious that the error is at a minimum when $\hat{y}$ and ε are orthogonal: i.e. $\hat{y} \perp \varepsilon$. Two vectors are orthogonal when their product is zero:

$$\hat{y} \perp \varepsilon \Rightarrow \hat{y}^{T}\varepsilon = 0.$$

(6.35)

The modelled (predicted) values are determined by $\hat{y} = X\beta$. The error is $\varepsilon = y - \hat{y} = y - X\beta$. Using these two formulas allows us to substitute $\hat{y}$ and ε:

$$\hat{y}^{T}\varepsilon = 0 \Rightarrow (X\beta)^{T}(y - X\beta) = 0$$

Applying the transposition, associative law and distributive law and realising that we can drop β^{T} gives us:

$$(X\beta)^{T}(y - X\beta) = \beta^{T}X^{T}(y - X\beta) = 0 \Rightarrow X^{T}y = (X^{T}X)\beta$$

Since $X^{T}X$ is a squared matrix, we can compute the inverse.

$$X^{T}y = (X^{T}X)\beta \Rightarrow (X^{T}X)^{-1}X^{T}y = (X^{T}X)^{-1}(X^{T}X)\beta$$

Hence, the prediction model coefficients are determined via

$$\beta = (X^{T}X)^{-1}X^{T}y$$

(6.36)

As a second approach (i.e. instead of using the exact mathematical method to find the coefficients for the linear regression model), it is possible to find them using the gradient descent method. That method's objective (aka cost function) is to minimise the MSE. We will revisit this method in the machine learning section. The gradient descent method requires feature scaling.

Now that we know how to obtain a linear regression model $y = \beta x$, we can return to its applications.

6.4.3 Applications, ML Parts and Statistics

We will apply the linear regression to two applications: house prices and geyser eruptions. Further, we will interlace the linear regression models with parts of the machine learning roadmap (see Section 5.3). We will consider the model evaluation and data split. Additionally, two more statistical topics, confidence intervals and prediction intervals, are introduced. These four topics are of general importance, relevant to all statistical and machine learning techniques.

Example 6.4.1 (House prices LR). Let us fit a regression line (i.e. a simple linear model, abbreviated lm) into the scatter plot we encountered when discussing correlations.

```
ggplot(H, aes(x=SqFt,y=Price)) + geom_point() + # Scatterplot
    geom_smooth(method = 'lm') # Linear regression
```

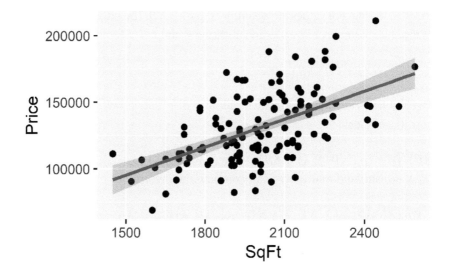

FIGURE 6.12 Linear regression for a business scenario.

The line represents the predicted home prices (aka response) given the variable square feet (aka predictor). We could use this line to identify homes which are below or above the modelled market prices. But please be aware that we are assuming that only the size of the property matters. The difference between predicted and observed value is known as *residual* (see Section 5.2.2 for a simple illustration). Since this model is a line, it must contain an intercept and a slope. The intercept and slope represent the coefficients β_0 and β_1 respectively. We determine the coefficients using Equation (6.4.2).

```
y = H$Price; x = H$SqFt; e = rep(1,nrow(H)) # one vector
X = cbind(e,x)
b = solve((t(X)%*%X)) %*% t(X) %*% y
t(b)
##              e           x
## [1,] -10091.13 70.22632
```

These coefficients could also have been derived using Equations (6.12) and (6.13). Although these formulas are nice didactically, in practice, you will use a function such as lm to obtain the linear regression model.

```
LR <- lm(Price ~ SqFt, data = H) # linear regression
c <- LR$coefficients; c
## (Intercept)              SqFt
## -10091.12991          70.22632
```

The slope tells us that each square foot increases the price of the property by \$70. Our model is $\hat{y} = \beta_0 + \beta_1 x \approx -10{,}091 + 70.23x$. For instance, if the real estate agency has a new property of 2,000 ft^2, then we can price it at $\hat{y} \approx -10{,}091 + 70.23 \times 2{,}000$ based on the square foot information only.

```
# predict(model,newdata = data.frame(SqFt=2000)) # general way
c[1]+ c[2]*2000
## (Intercept)
## 130361.5
```

Calculating the model values is also known as predicting the model values. We abbreviate the modelled (aka predicted) values with y and the observed values with y.

Let us now extend the model to accommodate more features.

```
y = H$Price; X = cbind(rep(1,nrow(H)),as.matrix(H[,3:6]))
b = solve((t(X)%*%X)) %*% t(X) %*% y; t(b)
##                    SqFt Bedrooms Bathrooms Offers
## [1,] -17347.38 61.83995 9319.753 12646.35 -13601.01
```

Note that sometimes there are duplicated records, which may exist on purpose (e.g. the same scenario was observed multiple times). In this case, a pseudo-inverse (generalised inverse) needs to be used: e.g. the Moore-Penrose inverse.

Example 6.4.2 (Old Faithful). We will now introduce a second application. Old Faithful is a geyser in Yellowstone National Park in Wyoming, United States.

Assume you have waited 80 minutes. How long will the eruption last? We will derive a model that predicts the duration of the geyser's eruption, depending on the waiting time.

FIGURE 6.13 Old Faithful geyser eruption.

This is followed by deriving a linear regression model for predictions. Then the quality of the model is discussed. Finally, the confidence and prediction intervals are introduced so that we can explain the certainty and range of the expected eruption time.

We introduce a linear regression model and determine its coefficients.

```
formula = eruptions ~ waiting #symbolic description of model
model = lm(formula, data=faithful) # fit a linear model
c = model$coefficients # coefficients(model) #an alternative
```

The coefficients are $\beta_0 = -1.874$ and $\beta_1 = -0.0756$. Let us use these coefficients. What is the eruption duration, given that we waited $w = 80$ minutes?

```
w = 80 #min waiting time
d = c[1] + c[2]*w; d
## (Intercept)
## 4.17622
```

We expect to observe an eruption lasting for 4.18 minutes (given 80 minutes waiting time).

Multiple predictions: Next, we predict the eruption times for waits of 40, 60, 80 and 100 minutes.

```
p = data.frame(waiting=c(40, 60,80,100))
predict(model,p)
##      1     2       3          4
## 1.151102 2.663661 4.176220 5.688779
```

Can you observe any systematic change? *Answer: every 20 minutes of waiting gives us an additional 1.51 minutes of eruption (see waiting coefficient β_1).* Now let us use this formula to derive the coefficients for the geyser prediction model.

Quality

In Section 6.2, we introduced several quality metrics. The objective when creating the linear regression model was to reduce the error between the modelled and observed prices.

Let us define y and determine y for the house prices one more time.

```
y <- H$Price # target (observed values)
f <- 'Price ~ SqFt + Bedrooms + Bathrooms + Offers' # formula
LR <- lm(f, data = H) # create LR model
yh <- predict(LR) # predicted values (modelled)
```

The MSE for the model is:

```
MSE <- function(y,yh){mean((y-yh)^2)}
MSE(y,yh)
## [1] 216189188
```

Often, the root MSE (RMSE) is used instead to make a statement about the quality of the model:

```
RMSE <- function(y,yh){sqrt(MSE(y,yh))}
RMSE(y,yh)
## [1] 14703.37
```

The MSE and RMSE are great for comparing models. To get a better feeling of the immediate quality, we use the MAPE.

```
MAPE <- function(y,yh){mean(abs((y4-yh)/y))*100}
MAPE(y,yh)
## [1] 9.367706
```

That means, on average, we observe an absolute deviation of 9.4%. This is probably a model the manager can work with in this area.

Often, we want to check the observed versus modelled values visually in a scatter plot.

```
qplot(y,yh, colour="red")+geom_abline(slope = 1)
```

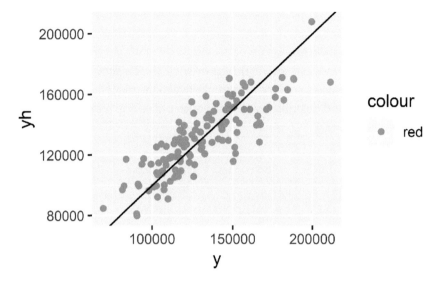

FIGURE 6.14 Observations versus predictions to assess quality.

By the way, this is one of the plots we used to introduce Section 6.2. Let us provide the MSE, RMSE and MAPE for the Old Faithful example. We will reuse the previously defined quality metrics.

```
y = faithful$eruptions
yh = predict(model)
MSE(y,yh); RMSE(y,yh); MAPE(y,yh)
## [1] 0.2447124
## [1] 0.4946842
## [1] 13.20326
```

Training and Test Data

It is common to divide data into training and test data. This gives reassurance that the fitted model will work for unseen data (simulated by the test data). The training data is used to train and learn the model. The test data "validates" the learned model. Please revisit Section 5.2.

Let us do a 70:30 data split: i.e. 70% of the data will be used for learning the model randomly, and the remaining 30% of the data will be used to test the accuracy of the model. We will make the split reproducible by fixing the seed of the random number with set.seed(1).

```
n = nrow(faithful)  # number of observations
ns = floor(.7*n)     # 70% of training data records
set.seed(1)             # set random generator (for reproducibility)
I = sample(1:n, ns) # sample of indexes
train = faithful[I,]  # training data (=70% of data)
test = faithful[-I,]  # test data (=30% of data)
```

Use the training data to learn the linear regression model and provide the RMSE for the training data.

```
lr <- lm (eruptions ~ waiting, data=train)

yh = predict(lr)
y = train$eruptions
rmse <- function(y,yh) {sqrt(mean((y-yh)^2))}
rmse(y,yh)
## [1] 0.4868275
```

Now compute the test RMSE for the model to see how well it performs for unseen data.

```
yh = predict(lr, newdata = test)
y  = test$eruptions rmse(y,yh)
## [1] 0.5140206
```

You should observe that the RMSE for the test data is higher than the RMSE for the training data.

Note a different seed will lead to a different accuracy. Hence, it would be better to repeat the splitting multiple times and use the average accuracy instead.

Confidence Interval

The confidence interval is defined by:

$$\left(\bar{x} - z\frac{\sigma}{\sqrt{n}}, \bar{x} + z\frac{\sigma}{\sqrt{n}} \right) \tag{6.34}$$

where z represents a factor that determines the range of the interval. The definition shows that the interval range is shorter when more observations are provided.

Determine the expected eruption time using many independent samples of 80 minutes of waiting. What is our 95% confidence interval of the expected eruption duration?

```
attach(faithful) # attach the data frame
my.lm = lm(eruptions ~ waiting)
w = data.frame(waiting=80)
predict(my.lm, w, interval = "confidence")
##   fit lwr upr
## 1 4.17622 4.104848 4.247592
```

Answer: the CI of the expected eruption time is [4.105, 4.248]

Prediction Interval

The prediction interval is defined as:

$$(\bar{x} - z\sigma, \bar{x} + z\sigma) \tag{6.35}$$

Comparing the confidence interval definition with this one, it can be observed that the interval is wider by $2\sqrt{n}$.

Which eruption time will we observe with 95% certainty when the waiting time for the eruption is 80 minutes?

```
predict(my.lm, w, interval = "predict")
##           fit         lwr           upr
## 1 4.17622 3.196089 5.156351
```

Answer: we will observe an eruption time between 3.2 and 5.2 minutes.

Overall, we expect the eruption to last for 4.18 minutes (with a 95% CI of [4.105, 4.248]), given a 80-minute waiting time. We predict with 95% certainty that the eruption will last between 3.2 and 5.2 minutes when the eruption occurs after 80 minutes of waiting.

6.5 Logistic Regression

We use the logistic regression model in the context of classification challenges.

Previously, we discussed the confusion matrix and provided three examples: insurance policies, fraud detection and advertisement effectiveness. The logistic regression is probably the most classic classification model. Later, we will discuss alternatives such as classification trees, neural networks and nearest neighbours.

One could wonder whether we could just use the linear regression for classifications. In Figure 6.15 (a), we added a linear regression and added a threshold line at 0.5.

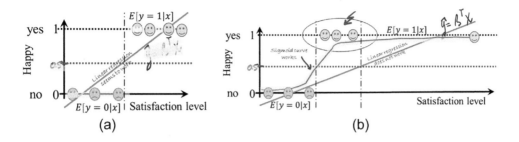

FIGURE 6.15 Classification with (a) linear regression, (b) Sigmoid curve (logistic regression).

That means that when the happiness level is below 0.5, the customers are classified as not happy and otherwise as happy. So it seems to work – at least in this instance. However, when one of the customers has a very high satisfaction level, the linear regression model in conjunction with the 0.5 threshold decision line fails (see Figure 6.15 (b)). However, fitting a sigmoid curve leads to the correct classification of happy and unhappy customers. This raises the question of how we can determine this curve? The *sigmoid function* (aka *logistic function*) is defined by

$$f(z) = \frac{1}{1+e^{-z}}$$
(6.36)

The function $f(z)$ is also abbreviated by $\sigma(z)$ and $\hat{p}$. It is in the range $[0, 1]$. The parameter z is equal to $\hat{\beta}^T X$. The function value $f(z)$ is converted to the discrete modelled value via $\hat{y} = [\hat{p} \geq 0.5]$:

$$\hat{y} = \begin{cases} 0 & \text{if } \hat{p} < 0.5, \\ 1 & \text{if } \hat{p} \geq 0.5. \end{cases}$$
(6.37)

The logistic regression model (including classification decision) is defined as:

$$\hat{y} = \left[\frac{1}{1+e^{-\beta^T x}} \geq 0.5 \right]$$
(6.38)

How can we learn the logistic regression model's parameters β from the target y and input X? With linear regression, we mentioned the use of the gradient descent method with the MSE as objective (cost) function. That means we aimed to minimise the mean squared error. For the logistic regression, we need to develop (find) another cost function $L(\beta)$ to be minimised:

$$L(\beta) = \frac{1}{m} \sum_{i=1}^{n} \text{cost}(y, f(z))$$
(6.39)

The natural logarithmic function can be used to amplify penalties for differing values. Hence, we propose the following cost function:

$$\text{cost}(y, f(z)) = \begin{cases} -\ln(f(z)) & \text{if } y = 1, \\ -\ln(1-f(z)) & \text{f } y = 0 \end{cases}$$
(6.40)

175

The two cases can be put in a single line using Iverson brackets:

$$\text{cost}(y, f(z)) = -\ln(f(z))[y = 1] - \ln(1 - f(z))[y = 0]$$

or using y directly:

$$\text{cost}(y, f(z)) = -\ln(f(z))y - \ln(1 - f(z))(1 - y)$$

This can be used with vector operations as well. Further, we can drop the factor $\frac{1}{m}$ from the objective function because it is a constant not influencing the minimisation algorithm. Hence, we can write:

$$L(\beta) = (y - 1)^T \ln(1 - f(z)) - y^T \ln(f(z)) \tag{6.41}$$

Generally, we prefer having a model with fewer features. This can be achieved by adding a *regularisation term*:

$$r_t = \frac{\lambda}{2n} \sum_{j=1}^{m} \beta_j^2 \tag{6.42}$$

to the cost function. As before, n represents the number of observations and m the number of features. λ is a number, chosen heuristically, to accommodate our wish to have fewer features. We can see that the regularisation term is at an optimum when all coefficients β_j^2 are zero. Obviously, this is counteracted by the "logarithmic" terms. The cost function with regularisation term is:

$$L(\beta) = (y - 1)^T \ln(1 - f(z)) - y^T \ln(f(z)) + \frac{\lambda}{2n} \sum_{j=1}^{m} \beta_j^2 \tag{6.43}$$

The *gradient descent algorithm* is very simple.

Algorithm 1: Gradient descent algorithm.

Require: step factor α; target y; features X; cost function L;

Ensure: Coefficients β

1: $\beta := 0$ ▷ initialise coefficients

2: **while** min $L(\beta)$ improves **do**

3:      **for** all β_j **do**

4:           concurrently update

5:           $\beta_j \leftarrow \beta_j - \alpha \dfrac{\partial}{\partial \beta_j} L(\beta)$ ▷ maximum flow along path

6:      **end for**

7: **end while**

The algorithm requires the input (features) and output (target) data. Further, the cost function and a step factor (aka learning factor) have to be provided. The step factor needs to be chosen such that it can converge (too large, it "oversteps"; too small, it gets "stuck" or it takes too long to converge). Here, we see that it is an advantage to normalise the features. This helps in finding an appropriate step factor. The cost function needs to be differentiable. Next, the algorithm runs as long as the cost function delivers lower values. The improvements are achieved by computing the first derivatives of the cost function and simultaneously updating all feature coefficients.

Figure 6.16 provides an example. It also illustrates that the algorithm can end up in local optima easily.

That means providing a cost function with one global minimum and no local optima helps.

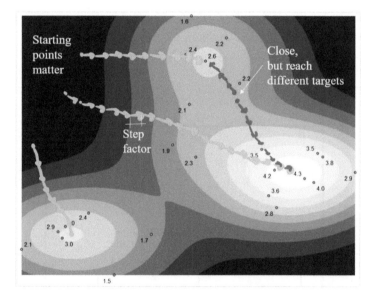

FIGURE 6.16 Gradient descent algorithm.

6.5.1 Multiple Classes – One versus All

Often, there are more than two classes. In this case, you divide the classes into one target class and group the other classes together. You repeat this for each class. The derived classifiers are used as an ensemble with majority vote. This procedure is called *one versus all* (OvA, aka one versus rest). This procedure allows us to use binary classifiers such as logistic regression, support vector machines and perceptron neural networks. Let us have a look at an example. Assume you have three classes A, B and C (Figure 6.17).

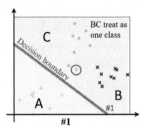 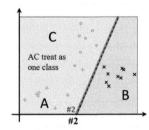 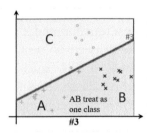

FIGURE 6.17 Multi classifier – one versus all.

This means you will create three classifiers: #1 for A versus BC, #2 for B versus AC and #3 for C versus AB. The classifiers are defined by their decision boundaries shown in green Figure 6.17. These boundaries can come from a logistic regression. Classifiers #2 and #3 work well (high confidence) for the provided points in class B and C. Classifier #1 covers all points from class C except one, so its confidence is lower. When a new point is provided, all three classifiers are run as an *ensemble* with its confidence deciding about a point's class. Figure 6.18 shows the ensemble ("combination") of the classifiers.

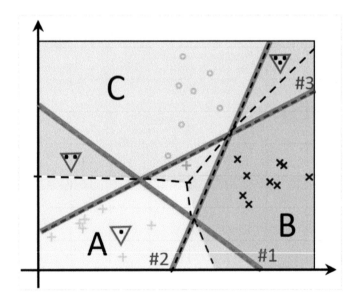

FIGURE 6.18 One-versus-all ensemble.

Let us have a look at three new points, shown as orange triangles with dots inside. The first point (triangle with one dot) is clearly identified as part of class A. The second point (triangle with two dots) is more interesting since it is between two decision boundaries. As it closer to class C, it is associated with it. Similarly, point three is associated with class C. Only one point is misclassified.

If there are many classes and there is a natural numeric order (e.g. a scale from one to one hundred), you may want to set the scale to a continuous one, do ordinary predictions, and round to the nearest class.

6.5.2 Old Faithful Example

Create a new feature long_eruptions for the Old Faithful dataset. Set long_eruptions to one if the eruption duration is more than three minutes and zero otherwise.

```
faithful$long_eruptions = (faithful$eruptions>3)*1
str(faithful)
## 'data.frame': 272 obs. of 3 variables:
## $ eruptions : num 3.6 1.8 3.33 2.28 4.53 . . .
## $ waiting   : num 79 54 74 62 85 55 88 85 51 85  . . .
## $ long_eruptions : num 1 0 1 0 1 0 1 1 0 1 . . .
```

Visualise the two classes.

```
ggplot(aes(x = waiting, y = eruptions,
  colour=factor(long_eruptions)),data = faithful) +
  geom_point(show.legend = FALSE, size=2)
```

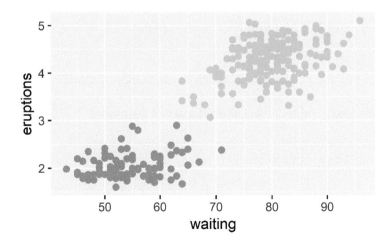

FIGURE 6.19 Old Faithful long and short eruptions.

Divide the data into training and test data using a 70:30 split.

```
n = nrow(faithful); set.seed(7); I = sample(1:n, .7*n);
train = faithful[I,];test = faithful[-I,];
```

We train the model using logistic regression.

```
logreg <- glm(long_eruptions ~ waiting, data = train,
              family = binomial)
logreg
##
## Call: glm(formula = long_eruptions ~ waiting, family . . .
##
## Coefficients:
## (Intercept)      waiting
## -42.4725         0.6456
##
## Degrees of Freedom: 189 Total (i.e. Null); 188, ' Residual
## Null Deviance:      245.4
## Residual Deviance: 19.07   AIC: 23.07
```

The output shows us the coefficients as with the linear regression.
Next, we predict the classes for the test data.

```
p = predict(logreg, newdata = test, type = "response")
cat('p=',p[1:8]) # show probabilities
## p= 0.9999959 0.9999994 0.9999922 0.9996237 0.9999851 . . .
yh = (p>.5)*1 # convert probability to 0 and 1
cat('yh=',yh[1:8]) # show predictions as binary values
## yh= 1 1 1 1 1 0 1 1
```

Now we determine and check the accuracy of the model.

```
y = test$long_eruptions
mean(y==yh)
## [1] 0.9878049
```

That means almost 99% of the eruption categories were identified correctly.
We can have a closer look at the quality using a confusion matrix.

```
y = test$long_eruptions
table(yh,y)
## y
## yh 0 1
## 0 30 0
## 1 1 51
```

That means only one observation was misclassified.

6.6 Summary

Descriptive statistics provide an overview of and insights into a business quickly, such as the number of assets and their average value. The correlations show us how much features depend on each other: e.g. the size, #bedrooms and #bathrooms explain the price variations. Linear regression prediction models are a powerful tool but cannot be used blindly: i.e. visual and data inspections need to be done before making decisions. Overall, statistical learning output created by data analysts can support managers to gain insights and make informed decisions. Modelling based on statistical learning methods is part of the CRISP-DM.

Linear regression is the "classic" and most used model. It is easy to interpret, easy to use and good for predictions. Quality measures give an idea about how good a model is. The (root) mean squared error is the standard measure for quality. Low bias and low variance are desired. High bias represents an underfitted model, and high variance reflects an overfitted model. Correlations are a measure to show how much business aspects (variables, features) are associated with the target or each other. This can assist in the building of efficient models.

Classifications are special predictions. Binary business outcomes can be modelled with logistic regression. Classification for multiple categories is achieved with the one-versus-all method.

Annotated Bibliography

Linear regression and logistic regression are introduced in a streamlined way:

1. Burkov, A. (2019). *The Hundred-Page Machine Learning Book*. Quebec City, Canada: Andriy Burkov.

Statistics are discussed in an entertaining but detailed way:

2. Field, A. P. (2021). *Discovering Statistics Using R and RStudio* (2nd ed.). London, UK: SAGE.

Related material is introduced from a managerial perspective:

3.   Jank, W. (2011). *Business Analytics for Managers*. New York: Springer.

A comprehensive but gentle introduction to statistical learning:

4.   James, G. et al. (2023). *An Introduction to Statistical Learning: With Applications in R*. 2nd ed. New York: Springer.

A detailed treatment of statistical learning:

5.   Hastie, T. et al. (2009). *The Elements of Statistical Learning: Data Mining, Inference, and Prediction* (2nd ed.). New York: Springer.

Chapter 8 contains a brief introduction to linear regression and additional details about the gradient descent algorithm. Chapter 9 gives a short overview of the logistic regression:

6.   Shah, C. (2020). *A Hands-on Introduction to Data Science*. Cambridge, UK: Cambridge University Press.

Python code and weighted regression is offered in Chapter 5:

7.   Watt, J. et al. (2020). *Machine Learning Refined: Foundations, Algorithms, and Applications*. Cambridge, UK: Cambridge University Press.

Resources

- Another Data Analytics tutorial: "Data Analytics Tutorial for Beginners – From Beginner to Pro in 10 Mins – DataFlair" (2019). Interesting tutorial: data-flair.training/blogs/data-analytics-tutorial/.

- Kaggle provides another logistic regression tutorial: www.kaggle.com/jeremyd/titanic-logistic-regression-in-r.

- The Titanic R library is yet another example using the Titanic dataset: rpubs.com/abhaypadda/logistic-regression-using-titanic-data.

- James, G. et al. (2023) is an excellent introduction to statistical learning. The corresponding website includes a lot of resources such as videos and the book itself: www.statlearning.com.

7. Supervised Machine Learning

7.1 Introduction

Machine learning (ML) is mainly concerned with identifying patterns in data in order to predict and classify. Previously, we used linear regression and logistic regression to achieve this. However, we heard about them in the context of statistical learning (SL) since they are widely used for inference about the population and hypotheses. Typically, SL relies on assumptions such as normality, homoscedasticity, independent variables and others, whereas ML often ignores these. We continue with supervised learning (i.e. the response is known) approaches. Please be sure you have done the statistical learning chapter. Particularly, we will look at tree-based methods such as the decision tree and random forest. Then we will look at a nearest neighbour approach.

This chapter works towards the following learning outcomes:

- Analyse and visualise data using a methodical analytical approach;
- Apply important data mining algorithms and techniques;
- Apply state-of-the-art methods and tools to build classification and predictive models.

DOI: 10.4324/9781003336099-10

7.2 Regression and Classification Trees

Decision tree models provide simple rules which are easy to interpret. They come in two "flavours": regression trees and classification trees. The former are used if the target is continuous, the latter when the target is categorical. Generally, decision tree (DT) algorithms derive models quickly from data. However, their accuracy is often lower than random forest, neural networks and other black-box algorithms. The resulting model tends to be easy to interpret. In this respect, it provides an advantage over black-box algorithms. Hence, they are applied in fields where an interpretation of the prediction is needed. For instance, the choice of a medical drug for a patient can be made via a decision tree. The tree's decision nodes identify essential patient characteristics. That means that, generally, decision tree models can be used to identify deciding features/ important input.

7.2.1 Regression Tree

A pure *regression tree* is one in which the target and all its features are continuous. A mixed regression tree is one in which the target is continuous, but one or more features are categorical. However, all types of regression tress have a continuous target variable. We will use the regression tree for predictions. The quality of models will be compared using the root mean squared error (RMSE) and the mean absolute percentage error (MAPE).

In the statistical learning tutorial, we introduced the Old Faithful dataset and predicted eruption times using linear regression. Now, we will do the prediction using the regression tree method.

We will begin by developing some basic understanding of the regression tree algorithm.

For simplicity, we will focus only on ten records from the original dataset: $I = (1, 2, 3, 4, 5, 6, 7, 8, 9, 10)$, $x = (63, 55, 90, 84, 73, 58, 76, 49, 48, 81)$ and $y = (2.367, 2.267, 4.417, 4.083, 4.067, 1.850, 3.883, 1.867, 1.867, 4.050)$.

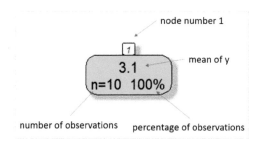

FIGURE 7.1 Root of a decision tree and explanation of its elements.

Here, I represents the indices, x the waiting time (in minutes) and y the eruption time (in minutes). This information will be summarised as the *root* node for the decision tree. Let us visualise the data.

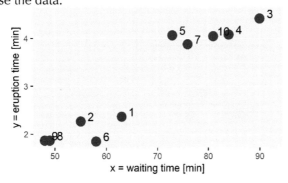

FIGURE 7.2 Sample of ten observations.

How would you split the data to minimise the MSE? Recall the mean squared error is:

$$MSE = \frac{1}{n}\sum_{k=1}^{n}(y_k - \hat{y}_k)^2,$$

where n is the number of observations, y_k is the observed value (response, output), $\hat{y}_k = \hat{f}(x_k)$ is the modelled value (prediction) and x_k is the input. Before using the MSE, try it intuitively – provide an x value and two y values. You probably made the split in a way that was similar to:

$$x_s = \frac{x_1 + x_5}{2} = \frac{63 + 73}{2} = 68,$$

i.e. $x_s = (x[1] + x[5])/2$.

Now we can use this to predict (approximate) the y values on the left c_1 and right side c_2:

$$c_1 = \frac{1}{5}(y_1 + y_2 + y_6 + y_8 + y_9) = 2.04$$

That means the MSE on the left side is:

$$MSE_{left} = \frac{1}{5}((y_1 - c_1)^2 + (y_2 - c_1)^2 + (y_6 - c_1)^2 + (y_8 - c_1)^2 + (y_9 - c_1)^2)$$

$$c_2 = \frac{1}{5}(y_5 + y_7 + y_{10} + y_4 + y_3) = 4.1$$

Similar to before we compute the MSE_{right}. Other splits will give a higher MSE. Let us visualise this additional information (Figure 7.3).

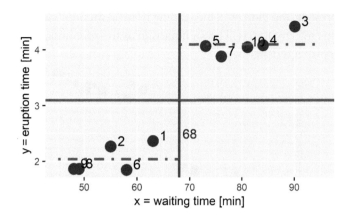

FIGURE 7.3 Build-up of decision tree: a first split.

A *decision stump* is a one-level decision tree. That means the root (internal node) is connected to the terminal nodes (known as *leaves*). The prediction is based on a single feature (also known as *1-rule*). How would you represent the information in Figure 7.3 as a decision stump?

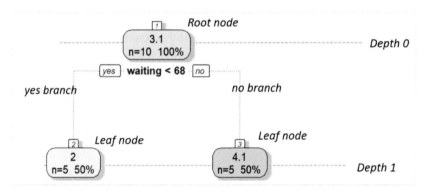

FIGURE 7.4 Decision tree stump.

Let's explain the graph (Figure 7.4). The numbers on the top of each node show the node numbers 1, 2 and 3. Let us consider node 1 (root node). If we take the average of all observations, we get $\bar{y} = 3.1$. This is the average eruption time taken from the $n = 10$ observations, which represent 100% of the data.

Underneath node 1 we have the 1-rule (decision, if condition). That means that if the wait time is less than 68 minutes, we follow the yes branch on the left; otherwise, we follow the no branch on the right. The yes branch takes us to node 2 (a leaf node). We can now read the node 2 information. If we waited less than 68 minutes, we predict that the eruption time is 2 minutes. This is based on $n = 5$ eruption time observations, which represent 50% of the data.

What is the eruption time if we waited 80 minutes? *Answer: 4.1 minutes.* Actually, any wait times longer than 68 minutes will lead to the same answer.

This uses the function rpart – **r**ecursive **p**artitioning **a**nd **r**egression **t**rees. It has a couple of rpart.control parameters, such as the minimum number of observations that must exist in a node in order for a split to be attempted (minsplit) and the maximum depth of the final tree (maxdepth). The root node is at depth zero.

We can further refine this tree by introducing a *level 2* decision tree. Can you split Figure 7.3 again? The "growing" of a tree requires a split leading to regions 1 (left) and 2 (right). This is a bit harder; looking at the left region, it is not obvious where to split. We need to test all possible splits and select the one that minimises the MSE. The rpart function helps us find these splits. We just have to increase the maxdepth by one level.

```
dt <- rpart (eruptions ~ waiting, D, minsplit=2, maxdepth=2)
fancyRpartPlot(dt,
    sub="Three split nodes - a level 2 regression tree.")
```

What is the expected eruption time when we waited 50, 60, 80, 65 or 100 minutes? Consider Figure 7.5 and 7.6 and compare it with the code output underneath.

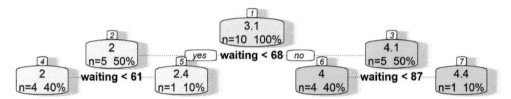

FIGURE 7.5 Decision tree at level 2.

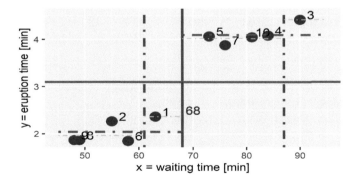

FIGURE 7.6 Decision tree approximating observations.

```
predict(dt, data.frame(waiting=c(50, 60, 80, 65, 100)))
##       1        2        3        4        5
## 1.96275 1.96275 4.02075 2.36700 4.41700
```

Reflect on how you obtained this tree. How many split points were created? Can you formulate this as an algorithm? Algorithm 2 shows a formulation for a regression algorithm.

Exercise 7.1 (DT for entire training data). We begin by learning a regression tree for the training data (e.g. 70% of the Old Faithful data). Then we evaluate the quality of the model by computing the MSE, RMSE and MAPE. Finally, we compare the results to those obtained using linear regression (Section 6.4.3).

```
set.seed(1); n=nrow(faithful); I=sample(n,.7*n);
train = faithful[I,]; test = faithful[-I,];

# Regression tree (default configuration)
dt <- rpart(eruptions ~ waiting, train)

# Quality measures
mse  <- function(y,yh) {mean((y-yh)^2)}
rmse <- function(y,yh) {sqrt(mse(y,yh))}
mape <- function(y,yh) {mean(abs((y-yh)/y))}
derr <- function(y,yh) {sprintf('MSE = %.3f, RMSE = %.3f,
    MAPE = %.2f%%\n',mse(y,yh),rmse(y,yh),100*mape(y,yh))}

# Evaluate DT
y  = test$eruptions
yh = predict(dt, newdata = test)
cat("Regression tree: ", derr(y,yh))
## Regression tree: MSE = 0.173, RMSE = 0.416, MAPE = 9.86%

# Compare with linear regression
lr <- lm(eruptions ~ waiting, train)
yh = predict(lr, newdata = test)
cat("linear regression: ", derr(y,yh))
## linear regression: MSE = 0.264, RMSE = 0.514, MAPE = 12.99%
```

Algorithm 2 Regression tree algorithm.

Require: Features X; target y;
Ensure: Feature identifiers and splitting points
1: **repeat**
2:      **for** j = 1 to #features **do** ◁ *Find best split for region*
3:          **for** k = 1 to #nodes **do** ◁ *Split feature j at s into two regions*
4:              $s = \dfrac{x_k + x_{k+1}}{2}$ ◁ *splitting point*
5:              R_1 = (a, s], R_2 = (s, b] ◁ *two regions*
6:              Get means c_1 and c_2 for the two regions
7:              **if** MSE R_1 + MSE R_2 smaller than before **then**
8:                  Set new best splitting point
9:              **end if**
10:         **end for**
11:         **if** Overall MSE is better than before **then**
12:             New best splitting point
13:         **end if**
14:     **end for**
15: **until** level or #leaf nodes are reached

We can see that the decision tree algorithm has a lower MSE. The corresponding decision tree using the default configuration (Figure 7.7) is surprisingly simple.

```
fancyRpartPlot (dt, sub="DT - default")
```

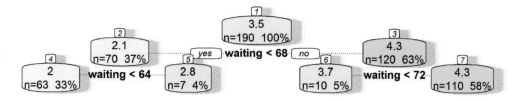

FIGURE 7.7 Decision tree with default configuration for Old Faithful training data.

Next, we would like to analyse a DT with several features. We will reuse our house price dataset but divide the price by one thousand for a better DT display. As before, we split the data into training and test data.

```
H <- read.csv('house-prices.csv'); H$Price <- H$Price/1000;
set.seed(7); n = nrow(H); I = sample(n, .7*n);# data split
```

We determine the regression tree with the default configuration and evaluate its quality.

```
dt <- rpart(Price ~., H[I,]) # default configuration
y = H$Price[-I]; yh = predict(dt, newdata = H[-I,])
cat ("Regression tree: ", derr(y,yh))
## Regression tree: MSE = 179.721, RMSE = 13.406, MAPE = 8.46%
```

This provides us with the complex decision tree shown in Figure 7.8. Pruning a decision tree reduces its complexity (bias); `printcp(dt)` displays **the complexity parameter (CP)** table, and `plotcp(dt)` gives a visual display (Figure 7.9) of it. This graph shows the relative errors. As we can see, the relative errors do not change much at a value of around 0.058. Hence, we will use this to prune the decision tree to reduce it to a size with four leaf nodes.

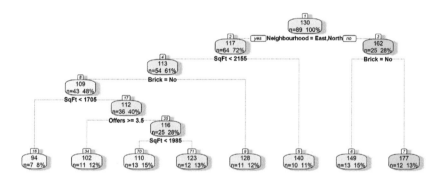

FIGURE 7.8 Complex decision tree.

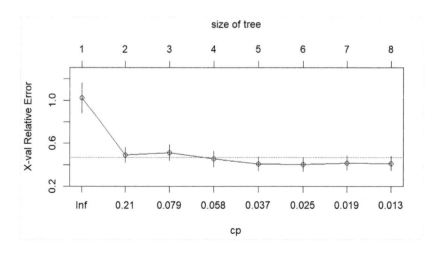

FIGURE 7.9 Complexity parameters.

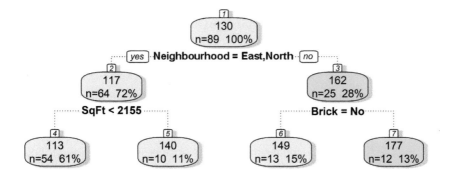

FIGURE 7.10 Complex decision tree pruned.

```
dtp <- prune(dt, cp=0.058)
fancyRpartPlot(dtp, sub="DT - pruned")
```

```
y = H$Price[-I]; yh = predict(dtp, newdata = H[-I,])
cat("Regression tree: ", derr(y,yh))
## Regression tree: MSE = 228.338, RMSE = 15.111, MAPE = 9.66%
```

The MAPE is 9.66% (tree size 4), which is a small increase from the previous 8.46% (tree size 8). This is also known as *post-pruning*.

Additionally, we could have done *pre-pruning*. Here, control parameters are provided as input to `rpart` such as `minbucket` (minimum number of observations in leaf node), `minsplit` (minimum number of observations for a split) and others.

7.2.2 Classification Trees

We will use the *Titanic dataset*, which is part of the titanic package. It has a training and test dataset. However, the test dataset does not have any target variable. Thus, we will only use the training dataset. Here, we will show how to use the *classification tree* method.

We begin by plotting a simple decision tree using `Survived ~ Sex` (Figure 7.11).

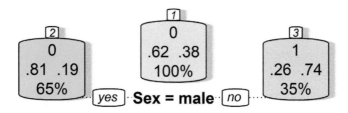

FIGURE 7.11 Basic decision tree for classifying survival.

```
dt <- rpart(Survived ~ Sex, data=titanic_train, method="class")
fancyRpartPlot(dt,sub="")
```

What is the meaning? The colour green means passengers have died, and blue means they survived. The root node (1) states that 62% of the passengers died. Hence, 38% survived. This agrees with the table we created earlier. Now there is the questions `Sex = male`. (Was the passenger male?) If the answer is yes, then we follow the left branch; otherwise, we follow the right one. Going to the left, we end up at the green node 2. That means males had an 81% chance of dying, and they constitute 65% of the data. So this tree is very easy to interpret.

What is the training accuracy of this tree?

```
yh = predict(dt,type="class"); y = titanic_train$Survived
mean(y == yh)
## [1] 0.7867565
```

As we can see, an accuracy of 78.7% was achieved.

Let us now get more factors into the tree. First, we will convert several fields to factors. Then we will set the age na fields to the average. The `Name` column will be dropped.

```
train = titanic_train; # simplify name
cols<-c("Survived","Pclass","Sex","Ticket","Cabin","Embarked")
train[cols] <- lapply(train[cols], factor) # transform
mv = mean(train$Age, na.rm =TRUE) # impute data
train$Age[is.na(train$Age)] <- mv;

# remove columns, e.g. train$Name = NULL
train=subset(train, select= -c(PassengerId,Name,Ticket,Cabin))
cat ("train: ",nrow(train),"rows"); head(train)
## train: 891 rows
## Survived Pclass Sex      Age    SibSp Parch Fare Emb.  . .
## 1        0      3 male    22.00000 1 0      7.2500     S
## 2        1      1 female 38.00000 1 0     71.2833     C
## 3        1      3 female 26.00000 0 0      7.9250     S
## 4        1      1 female 35.00000 1 0     53.1000     S
## 5        0      3 male    35.00000 0 0      8.0500     S
## 6        0      3 male    29.69912 0 0      8.4583     Q
```

Is the new training accuracy better using all factors?

As can be seen, the accuracy has improved by several percentage points to 83.3%. We visualise the new model in Figure 7.12.

Overfitting could lead to worse test accuracy. We will do pre-emptive pruning. Similar to the previous sub-section, the classification tree is pruned using `plotcp(dtc)` and a visual inspection. The complexity parameter (CP) 0.027 is found and used for pruning `prune(dtc, cp=0.027)`. This results in Figure 7.13. The training accuracy for this algorithm is 81.0%, which is only slightly worse, but the test accuracy should be better.

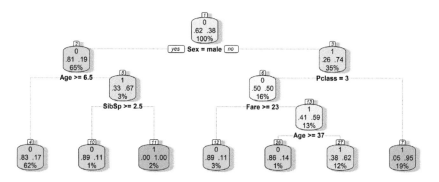

FIGURE 7.12 Classification model using several features.

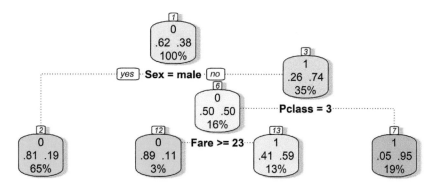

FIGURE 7.13 Classification model using several features.

7.3 Tree-Based Algorithms

7.3.1 Random Forest

Let us now use the *random forest* (RF) method. This method creates several decision trees by varying the number of features and the amount of data used. For a classification, these ensembles of trees make a majority vote of which group to choose for a given observation. For a prediction, the average of the ensemble trees' values is returned as a response.

The procedure is as follows:

- Take a sample from the training set;
- Take a subset of features;
- Grow trees to full extent;
- Predict new data using aggregation (majority vote for classification, average for regression).

The random forest function cannot deal with factors that have more than 53 categories, so we had to remove Ticket and Cabin from the input data.

```
#library(randomForest)
set.seed(7)  # for reproducibility
rf <- randomForest(Survived ~., data = train)
```

The training accuracy of this model is 83.1%, which agrees with the previously derived decision tree. Generally, the RF model should lead to equal or better results than the DT.

Example 7.3.1 (Classifications – Iris). The iris dataset is a collection of three flower types. We will use the iris dataset and divide it into test and train data.

```
n = nrow(iris); set.seed(1); I = sample(n, .7*n) # data split
train = iris[I,]; test = iris[-I,]
```

First, a classification tree is created, and its test accuracy is determined.

```
dt <- rpart(Species ~., data=train, method="class")
#fancyRpartPlot(dt)  # not much use too complex
yh <- predict(dt, type="class", newdata = test)
mean(yh == test$Species)
## [1] 0.9111111
```

A random forest model is learned, and its test accuracy and confusion matrix are given.

```
# library(randomForest)
set.seed(1)
rf <- randomForest(Species ~., data=train, importance=TRUE)
yh <- predict(rf,type="class", newdata = test)
mean(yh == test$Species)
## [1] 0.9555556
T (table(yh, test$Species))
##              yh
##               setosa versicolor virginica
## setosa            15          0         0
## versicolor         0         17         0
## virginica          0          2        11
```

We can see that the classifier only misplaced two observations.

7.3.2 Trees

There are several prominent decision tree algorithms, including:

- Chi-square automatic interaction detection (CHAID);
- ID3 algorithm (https://en.wikipedia.org/wiki/ID3_algorithm);
- C4.5 algorithm;
- C5.0 algorithm;
- Learning of top-down induction of decision (DT learning).

Chi-square automatic interaction detection (CHAID) is a decision tree algorithm. It works for predictions and classifications. Moreover, it detects the interaction between features. The dominant features are found using chi-square tests. C4.5 uses gain ratio to identify the essential features.

7.4 Nearest Neighbours Classifier

The *k-nearest neighbours* (kNN) classifier takes the *k* nearest points (from an arbitrary point to the input) and assigns the most likely class. The concept of the 3NN is illustrated in Figure 7.14.

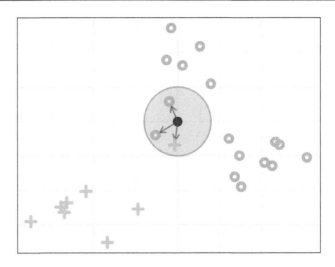

FIGURE 7.14 The kNN concept for $k = 1$, $k = 3$ and $k = 15$.

The *Euclidean distances* from an arbitrary point (x_0, y_0) (red dot or point under examination) to the input features x and y are computed:

$$d = \sqrt{(x - x_0)^2 + (y - y_0)^2} \tag{7.1}$$

That means that each point has an associated distance. The three closest points are selected. These are called the *neighbours* of x_0 and define the *neighbourhood* of x_0. In our example, the neighbours are x_3, x_{18} and x_{21}, and the neighbourhood is {3, 18, 21}. Each neighbour has an associated target class yi. The neighbourhood is used to determine the class. In this example, we have the blue-cross and orange-circle classes. There are two orange points and one blue point. Hence, the red point is assigned to the orange class. A bit more formally:

$$P[Y = j \mid X = x_0] = \frac{1}{k} \sum_{i \in N_0} I(y_i = j), \tag{7.2}$$

where j is the target class, x_0 is the point under examination, k is the number of neighbours, N_0 is the neighbourhood, i is a point identifier in the neighbourhood and I is the indicator function. I returns one when the target class y_i is equal to j; otherwise, I returns zero. In the previous example, we computed the probability of x_0 being in the orange class (o) via:

$$P[Y = o \mid X = x_0] = \frac{1}{3}\left(I(y_3 = o) + I(y_{18} = o) + I(y_{21} = o)\right) = \frac{1}{3}(0 + 1 + 1) = \frac{2}{3}$$

If the probability is greater than 0.5, it is assigned to the class. An issue arises when the probability is exactly 0.5, which happens when k is an even number. Some kNN implementations assign the class value randomly, which leads to a ragged decision boundary. Let us look at the choice of k. In the previous example, there are 24 observations. We could attempt 24 different k values. However, small classes become dominated by larger ones. In our example, once $k > 15$, the class boundary disappears. Hence, the kNN algorithms discriminate against the minority class when k grows. This can be countered by balancing the training data.

Figure 7.15 shows the kNN algorithm for $k \in \{1, 3, 15\}$.

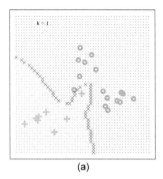
(a)

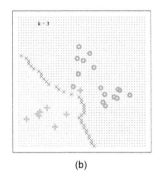
(b)

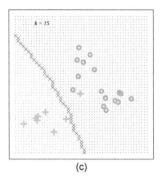
(c)

FIGURE 7.15 Influence of k on the decision boundary for the nearest neighbours for (a) $k = 1$, (b) $k = 3$ and (c) $k = 15$.

The smallest $k = 1$ shows a very flexible class boundary. Our initial conceptual example was based on $k = 3$, which shows a simpler decision boundary while $k = 15$ provides an almost linear boundary, which is the simplest of all. The question arises: Which k should we use?

Dividing the data into training and test data allows us to determine the optimal k heuristically. The corresponding optimum is known as the *Bayes classifier optimum*.

Create a kNN classifier and determine its test accuracy.

```
# library (class)
knn.cf=knn(train[,1:4],test[,1:4],train$Species, k=3,prob=TRUE)
table(knn.cf, test$Species)
##
## knn.cf      setosa versicolor virginica
## setosa          15          0         0
## versicolor       0         17         1
## virginica        0          0        12
mean(knn.cf == test$Species)
## [1] 0.9777778
```

7.5 Summary

Supervised learning has many applications, such as detecting credit card default, determining salary, classifying images and predicting the stock market. A decision tree is a heuristic with an interpretable solution model. Decision trees are divided into regression trees and classification trees. The underlying logic of the regression tree was introduced with great care. Pruning and complexity parameters were applied to an example. Classification trees were evaluated. A random forest is a combination of decision trees. Classifications can be done using the k-nearest neighbours method. Overall, this chapter illustrated the usage of a few machine learning techniques.

Annotated Bibliography

Section 3.3 introduces decision tree learning with the example of the ID3 algorithm:

1. Burkov, A. (2019). *The Hundred-Page Machine Learning Book*. Quebec City, Canada: Andriy Burkov.

Decision trees are discussed in Section 6.2 using a human resource example:

2. Jank, W. (2011). *Business Analytics for Managers*. New York: Springer.

Tree-based methods are introduced in Chapter 8:

3. James, G. et al. (2013). *An Introduction to Statistical Learning* (2nd ed.). New York: Springer.

A detailed technical treatment of trees, boosting trees and random forests is provided:

4. Hastie, T. et al. (2009). *The Elements of Statistical Learning: Data Mining, Inference, and Prediction* (2nd ed.). New York: Springer.

Two sections (9.5 and 9.6) provide an idea about tree algorithms:

5. Shah, C. (2020). *A Hands-on Introduction to Data Science*. Cambridge, UK: Cambridge University Press.

Chapter 14 is dedicated to tree-based learners:

6. Watt, J. et al. (2020). *Machine Learning Refined: Foundations, Algorithms, and Applications*. Cambridge, UK: Cambridge University Press.

Resources

- Trevor Stephens – Titanic an excellent tutorial, which provided several inspirations for this one: trevorstephens.com/kaggle-titanic-tutorial/r-part-2-the-gender-class-mode;

- On Kaggle, Jeremy's notebook about the Titanic provides code that uses the logistic regression: www.kaggle.com/code/jeremyd/titanic-logistic-regression-in-r.

8. Unsupervised Machine Learning

8.1 Introduction

In this chapter, unsupervised learning will be introduced. In contrast to supervised learning, no target variable is available to guide the learning via quality measures.

The most prominent unsupervised learning application is clustering. There are a few clustering algorithms. Often used is the k-means algorithm. Hierarchical clustering comes in two main flavours: bottom up (agglomerative clustering) and top down (divisive clustering).

However, there are other essential unsupervised machine learning applications such as anomaly detection, dimensionality reduction (e.g. PCA), self-organising maps (SOM) and expectation maximisation (EM). There are also neural networks autoencoder, neural deep belief networks and generative adversarial networks (GANs).

This chapter works towards the following learning outcome:

- Analysing and visualising data using a methodical analytical approach.

DOI: 10.4324/9781003336099-11

8.2 *K-Means* Clustering

The *k-means* algorithm is a popular heuristic which finds k clusters by minimising the distance between observation and cluster centre.

8.2.1 *Application*

As a first application we will use the *k-means* algorithm to distinguish different types of iris-flowers. Irises are purple flowers. We will consider the following species: setosa, virginica and versicolor.

| Setosa | Versicolor | Virginica |

FIGURE 8.1 Illustration of three types of iris species.

We will use the R built-in dataset, which is based on Edgar Anderson's work, which was popularised by Fisher (1936).

First, the structure of the data is considered.

```
#data(iris); head(iris); summary(iris);
str(iris)
## 'data.frame': 150 obs. of 5 variables:
## $ Sepal.Length: num 5.1 4.9 4.7 4.6 5 5.4 4.6 5. . .
## $ Sepal.Width: num 3.5 3 3.2 3.1 3.6 3.9 3.4 3.4. . .
## $ Petal.Length: num 1.4 1.4 1.3 1.5 1.4 1.7 1.4 1.5. . .
## $ Petal.Width: num 0.2 0.2 0.2 0.2 0.2 0.4 0.3 0.2
## $ Species: Factor w/ 3 levels "setosa","versicolor": 1. . .
```

As we can see, the species is already within the dataset, which defeats the purpose of clustering. However, pretend that we want to define three different species automatically. The species defined originally are compared to the ones suggested by the clustering algorithm.

Let us visualise the cluster using the petal's length and width (Figure 8.2).

```
ggplot(iris, aes(Petal.Length, Petal.Width, color = Species))+
  geom_point()+ theme(legend.position = c(.18,.73))
```

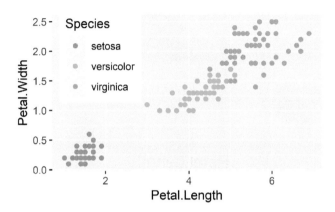

FIGURE 8.2 Scatter plot of petal data for iris flowers.

The cluster on the left seems to be straightforward to identify. The top ones are slightly more difficult to distinguish. Nevertheless, we keep on using petal length and width and ignore the sepal (green cover for petals) variables. The *k*-means function is used to form three clusters. We start the algorithm's core 30 times by setting nstart=30 (i.e. the initial centres of the clusters are placed 30 times randomly). How well do they fit the given species classification?

```
set.seed(7)
cm <- kmeans(iris[, 3:4], 3, nstart = 30)
t(table(cm$cluster, iris$Species))
##
##                1     2     3
## setosa         0    50     0
## versicolor     2     0    48
## virginica     46     0     4
```

We see that the setosa cluster is perfectly matched, and 96% of the versicolor species are identified, as are 92% of the virginica species. A visualisation of these clusters can be achieved easily (Figure 8.3).

```
library(factoextra)
fviz_cluster(cm, data = iris[, 3:4],
             palette = c("#FFCC99", "#0066CC", "#606060"),
             geom = "point",ggtheme = theme_bw())
```

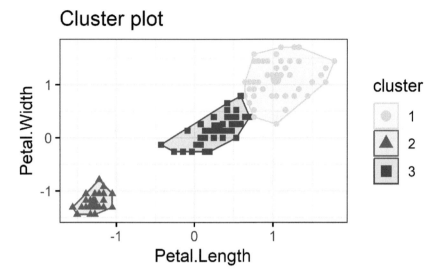

FIGURE 8.3 Clusters of *k*-means clusters.

It is interesting that using all four features leads to worse results.

```
set.seed(7)
cm <- kmeans(iris[, 1:4], 3, nstart = 30)
t(table(cm$cluster, iris$Species))
##
##                1     2     3
## setosa         0     0     50
## versicolor     48    2     0
## virginica      14    36    0
```

In the previous dataset, the target (response) was known, but we pretended not to know it. Generally, if there is a categorical response variable (i.e. classes are pre-defined), a supervised classification algorithm is used. If the target is unknown, then similar objects are grouped together.

8.2.2 *Concept and Algorithm*

Figure 8.4 shows the end result of a *k*-means algorithm with 23 observations and three clusters.

Cluster one has $h_1 = 7$ points, cluster two C_2 has $h_2 = 9$ observations and $h_3 = 7$ nodes. The objective of the *k*-means algorithm is to minimise the distance between the cluster centre and its nodes for all k clusters. The most popular distance is the *Euclidean distance,* which is also known as l_2 norm (aka *Frobenius norm*):

$$\|d\|_2 = \sqrt{d_1^2 + d_2^2 + \cdots + d_m^2} = \sqrt{\sum_{k=1}^{m} d_k^2} \tag{8.1}$$

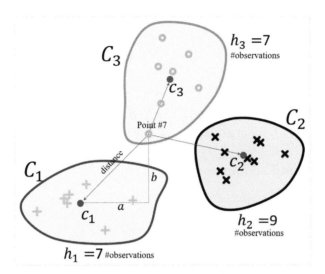

FIGURE 8.4 *K*-means concept.

In Figure 8.4, there are $m = 2$ features. The distance for point 7 is computed by obtaining $a = d_1 = x_{71} - c_{11}$ and $a = d_1 = x_{72} - c_{12}$, where c_{ij} represents the centroid for cluster i and its feature j.

There are several more norms. The Manhattan norm (aka l_1 norm or *taxicab* norm) is defined by

$$\|d\|_1 = |d_1| + |d_2| + \cdots + |d_m| = \sum_{k=1}^{m} |d_k|. \tag{8.2}$$

Generally, the *l*p norm is obtained by

$$\|d\|_p = \left(\sum_{k=1}^{m} |d_k|^p \right)^{1/p} \tag{8.3}$$

Other distances used are the maximum $\max_k d_k$, *Levenshtein distance* (between character sequences), *Mahalanobis distance* (between a point and a distribution) and *Hamming distance* (between strings of equal length), to mention just a few.

Understanding the algorithm allows us to fine-tune it or adapt it to cover our particular needs. The algorithm requires as input a set of data points $F = (f_{ij})$ (numerical features) and the number of clusters k. It will return a cluster assignment I and the corresponding centroids C. The algorithm is shown here:

Algorithm 1 k-means.

Require: data points $F = (f_{ij}) \in \mathbb{R}^{n \times m}$; number of clusters k
Ensure: cluster assignment $I \in K^n$, centroids $C \in \mathbb{R}^{k \times m}$
1: **for** r in R **do** $\triangleright multiple\ starts$
2:    $J \in U(1,n)^k$ $\triangleright random\ node\ indices$
3:    $C := F_J$ $\triangleright centroids$
4:    **repeat**
5:        $D_k := \|F - eC_k\|$, $k \in K$ $\triangleright distance\ to\ centroid$
6:        $I_i := \arg\min D^{(i)}$, $i \in N$ $\triangleright assign\ cluster\ index$
7:        $C_{k:} := \frac{1}{h}\sum F_{I=k,:}$, $k \in K$ $\triangleright update\ centroid$
8:    **until** no improvement
9: **end for**

The procedure will do multiple starts to avoid local optima. We begin by randomly selecting k points as potential centroids. Then the distances from all points to all the centroids are computed. For this example, the distance to the first centroid $D_1 = \|F - eC_1\|$ is calculated, where e is a one vector; so are D_2 and D_3. Then we decide, for each point, which cluster is closest. This new (updated) assignment of clusters allows us to update the centroids' locations. Once there is no improvement in the total minimal distance, the algorithm stops.

8.3 Hierarchical Clustering

We will consider an agglomerative (bottom-up) approach. The procedure for bottom-up hierarchical clustering begins by considering each observation (aka record, individual, point) and forming a singleton cluster. In order to combine two clusters (e.g. G and H), we need to define a (dis)similarity measure [inverse distance] $d(G, H)$, such as the Euclidean distance. Since clusters usually consist of several elements, there are a variety of options to link them. The most prominent linkages are:

- Single $- min_{g \in G, h \in H} d(g,h)$, nearest neighbour, leads to "loose" clusters;
- Complete $- max_{g \in G, h \in H} d(g,h)$, furthest neighbour, leads to "compact" clusters;

- Average – weighted versus unweighted, leads to "medium compact" clusters;
- Centroid $\|c_G - c_H\|^2$, leads to less variance between clusters;
- Ward $\dfrac{\|G\|\|H\|}{\|G \cup H\|} \|c_G - c_H\|^2$, distance between mean vectors of G and H, minimum increase of sum of squares, leads to less variance within clusters.

We will cluster the iris petal data using complete linkage hierarchically. First, scale the data by mean and standard deviation. Then determine all distances between all observations.

```
hc = iris[, 3:4] %>% scale %>% dist %>% hclust()
hc
##
## Cluster method    : complete
## Distance          : euclidean
## Number of objects: 150
```

The output tells us that the complete clustering method and Euclidean distance were applied to 150 objects.

We can determine the top three clusters and compare them to the actual species.

```
I = cutree (hc, 3)
t(table(I, iris$Species))
##          I
##                     1     2     3
## setosa             50     0     0
## versicolor          0    25    25
## virginica           0    50     0
```

We see that the setosa class is identified in the same way. However, versicolor and virginica are identified differently from the original classification. The problem is that we used the complete linkage, which was inappropriate in this case.

We can visualise the modelled clusters.

```
X = iris[, 3:4];
qplot(X[,1],X[,2],geom   =   "point",   color=as.factor(I))+
xlab(TeX("petal length $x_1$"))+
ylab(TeX("petal width,
  $x_2$"))+
theme(legend.position = "none")
```

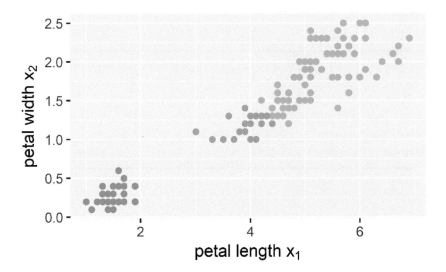

FIGURE 8.5 Iris petal length and width.

8.3.1 Dendrogram

A small sample (30 observations) is used to gain more insight into dendrograms and their linkages. We begin by defining a function that prepares our dendrogram for plotting.

```
ppdend <- function(D, method="average", nb_clusters=3){
   return(D %>% scale %>% dist %>% hclust(method = method) %>%

      as.dendrogram %>%   set("branches_k_color", k=nb_clusters) %>%
      set("branches_lwd", .6) %>% set("labels_colors") %>%
      set("labels_cex", c(.6,.6)) %>%   set("leaves_pch", 19) %>%
      set("leaves_col", c("blue", "purple")))
}
```

```
set.seed(1); I = sample(1:150, 30);
X = iris[I, 3:4];
par(mfrow =c(2,3), mar = c(1, 1, 1, 1))
plot (ppdend(X,"single"),main="single")
plot (ppdend(X,"complete"),main="complete")
plot (ppdend(X,"average"),main="average")
plot (ppdend(X,"centroid"),main="centroid")
plot (ppdend(X,"ward.D"),main="ward.D")
plot (ppdend(X,"ward.D2"),main="ward.D2")
```

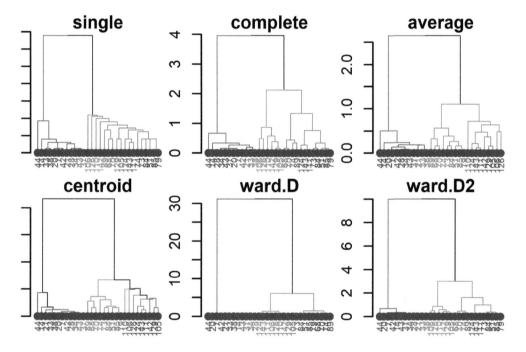

FIGURE 8.6 Dendrograms and their linkages.

Let us have a look at a few more dendrogram visualisations.

```
dend <- ppdend(X)
p1<-ggplot(as.ggdend(dend)) # as ggplot
p2<-ggplot(as.ggdend(dend), labels = FALSE) +
scale_y_reverse(expand = c(0.2, 0)) +
 coord_polar(theta="x") # as polar coordinate plot
gridExtra::grid.arrange(p1,p2,nrow=1)
```

Divisive clustering – The procedure begins with a single cluster containing all data points. Then the clusters are divide into "child" clusters recursively. For instance, use the *k*-means algorithm repeatedly or see Macnaughton-Smith (1965) for one of the first approaches, Gersho and Gray (1992) in the context of signal compression and Kaufman and Rousseeuw (2009) for alternatives. Hastie et al. (2009, p. 526) state that divisive clustering "has not been well studied".

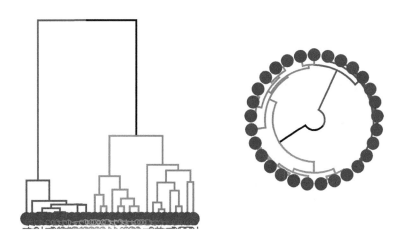

FIGURE 8.7 Alternative dendrograms.

8.4 Self-Organising Maps

Self-organising map (SOM), also known as a *Kohonen map* (Kohonen, 1990), is a machine learning technique used for clustering. It groups similar objects together and maps them on a two-dimensional surface. It is motivated by the sensory processing of the brain. That means hearing, seeing and other input are processed in dedicated brain sections and linked together. SOM can be used for supervised and unsupervised machine learning. Here, we will focus on the unsupervised approach.

General usage: grouping of similar objects, reducing dimensionality, feature detection.

Applications: Grouping of documents, customer segmentation, crime levels, economic well-being, military spending etc.

Let the data consist of n observations (*objects*) with m features. The aim is to create a predetermined number of clusters (*groups*) and arrange them on a grid such that similar groups are close to each other. A *group* (aka *prototype*) is represented by a single vector (m-dimensional), which is associated to a *cell* on the grid. Each point $x_{i:}$ is assigned to the closest group. The colon in $x_{i:}$ indicates that it is a row vector: i.e. an observation rather than an input/feature vector. An assigned point is placed randomly (usually via Gaussian distribution) into a cell. The point-to-group association is similar to the assignment step in the k-means algorithm. Again, the Euclidean distance can be used for this purpose. The closest prototype is known as the *best matching unit* (BMU). The prototypes are arranged on a grid G, which is square or rectangular. The grid points are represented by spheres or hexagons. Often, the number of prototypes n_p is a squared number. Let $G = (g_{ab})$ represent that grid, where g_{ab} is the weight for cell (a, b). The cells are spheres or hexagons with radius r. Let us have a look at a typical SOM visualisation (Figure 8.w8).

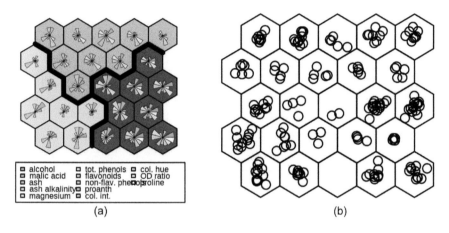

(a)   (b)

FIGURE 8.8 SOM clusters of wines.

The dataset `wines` ("Wine" 1991) is used, which contains $m = 13$ attributes. Three types of wines (Barbera, Barolo and Grignolino) are related to these attributes. In the visualisations in Figure 8.8, we see a 5 × 5 grid. This implies that 25 groups (prototypes) are created. Similar prototypes are located next to each other. The cells on the left show the contributions of the features (aka codes). A reliability check of each cell is obtained by observing the count of observations assigned to each cell (right visual in Figure 8.8).

The learning of the prototypes is done via the following steps.

1. Initialise prototypes p_k (e.g. by sampling them from the given input).

2. Determine BMU with coordinates (a^*, b^*) for a randomly chosen x_t as explained earlier, where t is an iteration variable.

3. Update weights of surrounding prototypes. The coordinates of the prototypes and Euclidean distance $\left(d = \sqrt{(a - a^*)^2 + (b - b^*)^2} \right)$ are used to adjust the learning rate $\delta = \Delta(t, d)$ and update the prototypes:

$$p_k \leftarrow p_k + \delta(x_{t:} - p_k)$$

The learning rate function is defined:

$$\Delta(t,d) = \alpha(t)\exp\frac{-d^2}{2\beta(t)^2},$$

where $\alpha(t) = \alpha_0\exp\frac{-t}{\tau_\alpha}$ and $\beta(t) = \beta_0\exp\frac{-t}{\tau_\beta}$. These "dumping by factors" resemble physics annealing concepts, but their benefits are questionable.

4. Repeat previous steps until convergence.

SOM offers interesting visualisations for large feature spaces: i.e. when the data is high dimensional. SOM compresses the n observations into k prototypes with weights.

Let us look at the iris dataset for a few examples. The dataset has $n = 150$ observations, four features and one output. We will use the SOM algorithm as unsupervised ML technique. The kohonen R-library is documented by Wehrens and Buydens (2007), who are the creators of this library. We will create an almost trivial example to build up our confidence in the algorithm's output.

```
library(kohonen)
df <- iris[,c(3,4)]; D <- as.matrix(df) set.seed(7)
sg <- kohonen::somgrid(xdim = 3, ydim = 1, topo = "hexagonal")
sm <- som(D, sg, rlen = 100, keep.data =TRUE, dist.fcts
        ="euclidean")
```

Only petal length and width are used as inputs. We want to extract three clusters. A minimalistic SOM is created consisting of three prototypes (groups). A 1 × 3 grid will be used. The command getCodes (sm) returns the prototypes illustrated in Figure 8.9 as red crosses. These points are nicely located in the centres of the clusters; sm$unit. classif captures the association of the observations to the groups. This allows us to colour code the observations. As we see in Figure 8.9, only a few observations deviate from the original classifications.

Let us use the same dataset again, but this time with all four features. We drop column five because that's the existing class specification. Because the Euclidean distance was used, prior scaling of the input features is required. We create a hexagonal 4 × 4 grid. Basically, this is an empty model template. That means we will learn the 16 prototypes and fill the grid with a learning algorithm.

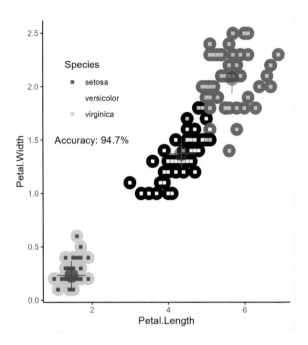

FIGURE 8.9 SOM for clustering.

```
library(kohonen)
D  <-scale(as.matrix(iris[,-5]))
sg <-kohonen::somgrid(xdim = 4, ydim = 4, topo = "hexagonal")
sm <-som(D,sg,rlen=500,keep.data=TRUE,dist.fcts= "euclidean")
```

This is equivalent to compressing the 150 observations to 16 units. The learning algorithm `som` requires the input data and grid as input. We specify the "run length" `rlen`, which means 150 observations are seen 500 times by the algorithm (final $t = 150 \times 500$). The training progress is shown in the figure that follows. We keep the data in the output sg. The distance function used is the Euclidean distance, but other distance functions (see previous section) can be used. This function returns the learned prototypes `sm$codes`, the input data points associated to the cells (prototypes) in `sm$unit.classif`. The n distances between $x_{i:}$ and p_k are returned in `distances`.

Since we created 16 prototypes, we will cluster them using the k-means algorithm. The code's cell mapping is shown in Figure 8.10, including the clusters as background colour.

```
clust <- kmeans(sm$codes[[1]], 3)
plot(sm, type="codes",
     bgcol=rainbow(9)[clust$cluster],main="")
add.cluster.boundaries(sm, clust$cluster)
```

The visual on the left of Figure 8.10 explains the codes (features) behind the grouping, which has to be considered in conjunction with the frequency (count) of the observations behind each cell. We observe that the count for the cells on the bottom right (visual in the middle) is high (20–25). This represents one cluster. In the three cells next to it, there are no observations, which provides a natural separation. The red cells on the right have similarities identified by the codes mainly dominated by the petal characteristics. The suggested classification agrees with the Setosa class but suggests a different division for the other two classes. Interestingly, omitting the sepal features leads to a classification similar to the original one.

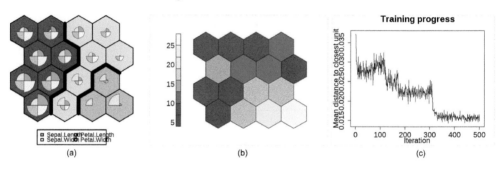

FIGURE 8.10 Self-organising map: (a) clusters and code contributions, (b) count visualisations and (c) training progress.

Further reading: Hastie et al. (2009, 2, s. 14.4, pp. 528ff) discuss self-organising maps (SOM) in more detail. Wilmott (2022) dedicates Chapter 8 to SOM. Wikipedia (2023b) provides a good overview of SOM. There is an entire book detailing this method by its creator (Kohonen, 2012).

SOM link well to *principle component analysis* (PCA), which is a kind of compression [dimension reduction]. James et al. (2013, 112, s. 6.3, pp. 228ff and s. 10.2, pp. 374ff) discuss PCA under the banner of dimension reduction and provide an overview of the PCA concept and transition to principle components regression (PCR).

8.5 Expectation Maximisation

Expectation maximisation (EM) is a probabilistic learning method. It is used as a clustering approach. One of its advantages is that it can deal with incomplete data. In 2008, it was identified as one of the top ten machine learning algorithms (Wu et al., 2008). Often, it is assumed that data consists of normal distributions, and a corresponding EM algorithm is used. This specific EM implementation is also known as a *Gaussian mixture model* (GMM). We will introduce the GMM for two clusters here, which can be extended easily to multiple clusters. For a discussion of the general EM algorithm, we refer the interested reader to Hastie et al. (2009). First, we will show the usage of an already implemented EM algorithm in the R library mclust. The following data is used for demonstration purposes.

```
ggplot(iris,aes(x=Petal.Length))+
geom_histogram(bins = 30, fill="red")
```

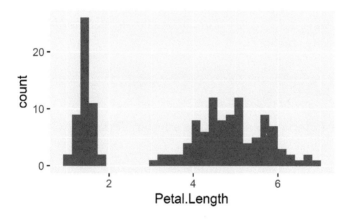

FIGURE 8.11 Histogram of the petal length of iris flowers.

First, we run the model with the default parameters. How many cluster have been identified?

```
library(mclust)
em = Mclust(iris$Petal.Width, verbose = FALSE)
table(em$classification, iris$Species)
##
## setosa versicolor virginica
##    1      48          0         0
##    2       2         50        50
```

Answer: two with 48 and 102 nodes. The command `summary(em)` reveals that the Gaussian mixture model was used.

Now we let the EM algorithm find three clusters with G=3. How well do the clusters agree with the defined species?

```
em3 <- Mclust(iris[,3:4], G = 3, verbose = FALSE)
table (em3$classification, iris$Species)
##
##         setosa versicolor virginica
##   1       50        0          0
##   2        0       48          2
##   3        0        2         48
```

Answer: the first cluster agrees perfectly. The second and third have five flowers identified differently.

A quick reminder: *Gaussian distribution* (aka *normal distribution*) is defined by its probability density function:

$$f\left(x,\mu,\sigma^2\right) = \frac{1}{\sigma\sqrt{2\pi}} e^{-\frac{1}{2}\left(\frac{x-\mu}{\sigma}\right)^2} \tag{8.4}$$

where μ is the expectation, and σ is the standard deviation (variance σ^2). When $\mu = 0$ and $\sigma = 1$, we call

$$f(x) = \frac{e^{-x^2/2}}{\sqrt{2\pi}} \tag{8.5}$$

the *standard normal distribution*.

The mixture EM algorithm can be implemented fairly easily. We will do this to determine two clusters. That means we assume that the data is based on a mixture of two normal distributions f_1 and f_2:

$$g(x) = \alpha_1 f_1\left(x,\mu_1,\sigma_1^2\right) + \alpha_2 f_2\left(x,\mu_2,\sigma_2^2\right) \tag{8.6}$$

where $P(\delta = 1) = \alpha_1$ with $\delta \in \{0, 1\}$ and $\alpha_1 + \alpha_2 = 1$. That means that, given x, we have to find the parameters $\mu_1, \sigma_1^2, \mu_2, \sigma_2^2$ and the mixture weight α_1.

Traditionally, we would find the maximum likelihood estimator (MLE) of the independent data points applied to g(x). The joint density function is given by $\Pi_{i=1}^n g(x_i)$. The product can be converted into sums using the logarithm, giving us the log likelihood:

$$L(x) = \sum_{i=1}^{n} \log\left(g(x_i)\right) \tag{8.7}$$

It is difficult to solve this directly. Hence, we use the EM algorithm.

Step 1: We **initialise** μ_1 and μ_2 randomly by selecting two points from the data. The variances are initialised by setting them to half the sample variance $s^2/2$. The mixture weight is set to $\alpha_k = 0.5$. We could also run the k-means algorithm since it determines centroids (i.e. the sample means as estimates for μ_k). The sample variances for each cluster represent the initial σ_i estimates, and the weight $\alpha_k = \dfrac{n_k}{n}$ is the proportion n of observations per cluster.

Step 2: Expectation. Here, we compute the *responsibilities* $r_{i1} = \alpha_1 f_1(x_i)/s$ and $r_{i2} = \alpha_2 f_2(x_i)/s$, where $s = f_1(x_i) + f_2(x_i)$. The responsibilities are used to decide in which class a point falls. If $r_{i1} = r_{i2}$, then point x_i belongs to class 1; otherwise, it's class 2.

Step 3: Maximise. This step updates mean μ_k, variance σ_k^2 and weight α:

$$\mu_k = \frac{\sum_{i=1}^{n} r_{ik} x_i}{\sum_{i=1}^{n} r_{ik}}$$

$$\sigma_k^2 = \frac{\sum_{i=1}^{n} r_{ik} (x_i - \mu_k)^2}{\sum_{i=1}^{n} r_{ik}}$$

$$\alpha_k = \frac{1}{n} \sum_{i=1}^{n} r_{ik}$$

This description is represented as R code here:

```
myEM <-function(x, eps=1E-2, max_iter=20){
  # Step 1: Initialize mu, s2
  mu <- sample(x,2) # choose centroids randomly
  v  <- var(x)/2 # a s2 estimate
  s2 <- c(v, v) # squared standard deviation
  a  <- t(c(1,1))*.5 # mixture probability

  converged = FALSE; mu_o=mu; s2_o=s2; k=1;
  while(!converged){
    # Step 2: Expectation Step
    n <- length(x)
    P <- matrix(NA, nrow = n, ncol = 2)
    for (i in 1:n) {
      P[i, 1] <- dnorm(x[i], mu[1], sqrt(s2[1]))
```

```
      P[i, 2] <- dnorm(x[i], mu[2], sqrt(s2[2]))
    }
    R <- (rep(1,n)%*%a)*P # responsibility
    R <- R/rowSums(R)

    #Step 3: Maximisation Step - update mu, s2 and a
    mu[1] <- sum(R[, 1] * x)/sum(R[,1])
    mu[2] <- sum(R[, 2] * x)/sum(R[,2])
    s2[1] <- sum(R[, 1] * (x - mu[1])^2)/sum(R[,1])
    s2[2] <- sum(R[, 2] * (x - mu[2])^2)/sum(R[,2])
    a     <- t(colMeans(R))

    #Step 4: Repeat Steps 2 and 3 until convergence
    if (sum(abs(mu-mu_o))<eps & sum(abs(s2-s2_o))<eps){
      converged=TRUE
    } else {mu_o=mu; s2_o=s2}
    if (k>max_iter){break} else {k<-k+1}

  }

  return(list(mean=mu,variance=s2,alpha=a))

}
```

It is easy to adjust this code for multiple mixtures. Multiple features can be accommodated by replacing dnorm with a multivariate Gaussian function and reconsidering the maximisation step.

Applying the iris data x<-iris$Petal.Length to the code myEM(x) leads to similar results. Figure 8.12 shows the algorithm at three stages.

The first stage is just after initialisation. We are showing the petal length and its frequency distribution (green histogram). The vertical orange and light-blue lines are the initial random means, and the horizontal dashed lines represent two standard deviations to the left and right. The initial standard deviations are quite large. After the third iteration, the means have move to the distribution centres the variances have reduced. Additionally, f_1 and f_2 for the data points have been scaled and overlaid. One can see the shapes of normal distributions as expected. The red dots and lines show the scaled responsibility r_1. The EM algorithm converges after five iterations. The orange dots approximate the shape of the histogram very well.

Further Reading: Hastie et al. (2009, s. 8.5, p. 272) introduce the EM using a mixture model, and they provide the general EM algorithm. Further, they give the EM as an maximisation-maximisation procedure. Shah (2020, s. 10.4, p. 299) introduces EM using a coin model. He uses R code and discusses the quality of the model using AIC and BIC. Brunton and Kutz (2022, s. 5.5, p. 186) introduce EM via mixture models. Wu

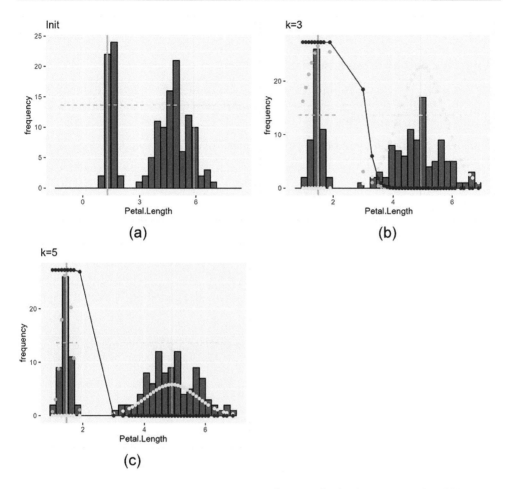

FIGURE 8.12 Expectation maximisation at (a) initialisation, (b) third iteration and (c) fifth iteration.

et al. (2008) identify EM as one of the top ten machine learning algorithms. A mixture model is introduced.

8.6 Summary

Unsupervised learners were introduced. Primarily, we use them for clustering. We began with the k-means algorithm and revealed its inner workings. This is an efficient algorithm, which works well for many real-world applications. Then we dived into hierarchical clustering and viewed many ways of linking observations. Self-organising maps allowed us to learn more about underlying groups (codes). Finally, we used expectation maximisation with Gaussian mixtures, which are suitable for clustering, especially when the data is normally distributed.

Annotated Bibliography

A nice introduction to expectation maximisation:

1. Brunton, S. L. and Nathan Kutz, J. (2022). *Data-Driven Science and Engineering: Machine Learning, Dynamical Systems, and Control*. Cambridge, UK: Cambridge University Press.

Contains a good discussion of PCA in the context of dimension reduction:

2. James, G. et al. (2013). *An Introduction to Statistical Learning*. 2nd ed. New York: Springer.

An EM procedure, SOM details and much more are provided:

3. Hastie, T. et al. (2009). *The Elements of Statistical Learning: Data Mining, Inference, and Prediction*. 2nd ed. New York: Springer.

A dedicated book to SOM by its creator:

4. Kohonen, T. (2012). *Self-Organizing Maps*. 3rd ed. Heidelberg, Germany: Springer.

Includes a simple EM introduction:

5. Shah, C. (2020). *A Hands-on Introduction to Data Science*. Cambridge, UK: Cambridge University Press.

Resources

- EM by Fong Chun Chan (Accessed: 30 January 2024) provides a detailed R implementation with some back ground: tinyheero.github.io/2016/01/03/gmm-em.html.

- SOM by Inayatus (Accessed: 30 January 2024) an introduction to SOM with R code: rpubs.com/AlgoritmaAcademy/som.

- The Ultimate Guide to Self-Organizing Maps (SOMs) by Super-DataScience Team (Accessed: 30 January 2024): superdatascience.com/blogs/the-ultimate-guide-to-self-organizing-maps-soms.

FOUR

Artificial Intelligence

AI goes beyond supervised and unsupervised learning by covering topics such as optimisations, reasoning under uncertainty and games.

9. Artificial Intelligence

9.1 Introduction

Artificial intelligence (AI) is concerned with:

- Enabling computers to "think";
- Creating machines that are "intelligent";
- Enabling computers to perceive, reason and act;
- Synthesising intelligent behaviour in artefacts.

Previously, we looked at statistical and machine learning. Learning is an essential area of AI. But this is only one part; it also includes problem solving (e.g. optimisations), planning, communicating, acting and reasoning.

Two more learning methods are considered in this chapter: artificial neural networks (ANN) and support vector machines (SVM). ANN, particularly deep NN, have gained a lot of popularity lately, due to their success in image classifications and speech recognition. SVM have been among the top machine learning algorithms because of their good quality metrics.

Problem solving is often achieved using optimisations. An exact approach using a mathematical program shows the efficiency of formulating and solving business

DOI: 10.4324/9781003336099-13

challenges. A brute-force approach will give a general idea about the search space. Meta heuristics are mentioned, one of them being the genetic algorithm (GA). The GA will be discussed in more detail.

Most games (e.g. chess) make use of AI. One of the most popular techniques is the minimax algorithm, which provides the best way forward in a game of rational players.

An introduction to Bayesian belief networks (BBN) will give a first impression about reasoning under uncertainty.

9.1.1 AI Applications

AI examples: A normal day begins with your smartphone waking you up. You may greet Alexa or your Google's smart speaker by saying, "Good morning". Your AI kicks in, activating its speech recognition and retrieves weather information and tailored news. The weather forecast was created by an AI algorithm using computer simulations of atmospheric physics or deep generative network (Heaven, 2021). The customised news was compiled by learning your preferences. Happy with all this information, you prepare to travel to work. You check Google Maps and find the best route to work, including the estimated duration. Route optimisations are based on shortest path algorithms, which is an optimisation and so a typical AI technique. If you are using a smart car such as a Tesla, its AI might not only use the SatNav but may also be in self-drive mode to get you safely to work. Once back at home, you may want to stream movies. You could use Netflix or Prime Video's AI suggestions for this.

Here are some examples from daily life and more.

- Alexa, Siri, Bixby and Google's smart speaker with its speech recognition;
- Navigation and travel: Google Maps finds the best route;
- Weather forecasts are based on AI;
- Netflix and Prime Video recommend movies for you;
- Google Translate assists you when you are on holiday;
- Image editing when you take a photo with your smartphone;
- Smart cars like Teslas can drive and learn from each other;
- Social media: Facebook adverts, LinkedIn likely connections;
- Video games: NPCs use AI;
- Adverts on your Google Search;
- Recommendations and pricing for your Amazon shopping or e-commerce in general;
- Banking and finance: fraud detection/protection;
- Customer service bots;
- Security: camera to recognise people approaching your home;

- Healthcare;
- E-mail spam filters.

9.1.2 Classic AI Areas

Traditional AI areas are shown in Figure 9.1.

Much Data Analytics and Data Science literature gives priority to the AI topic **learning**, which includes supervised and unsupervised learning. We discussed this in previous chapters, and we will continue in this chapter. We have briefly touched on probabilistic models such as the expectation maximisation algorithm. We have not discussed reinforcement learning. Reinforcement learning rewards (or punishes) actions of an agent. Hence, the agent learns to maximise its rewards. For instance, it can be used to learn to play a video game. Wilmott (2022) provides a gentle introduction to this topic and Heitzinger (2022) discusses this topic in great detail. This is the most popular topic currently.

Problem solving has found its way into AI from the Operational Research discipline. Today, problem solving is also known as Prescriptive Analytics. Its most important tool are optimisations. We will introduce optimisations with a simple example. The machine learning algorithms also follow optimisations (e.g. minimise error), but the problem-solving algorithms are far better suited for optimal decision making. They strive to find the best possible answer (global optimum: e.g. optimal route from A to B). However, due to complexity, one has to fall back on local searches. AI for games such as chess makes use of adversarial searches. We will talk about this later. Often, when optimising, we assume the correctness of the given data.

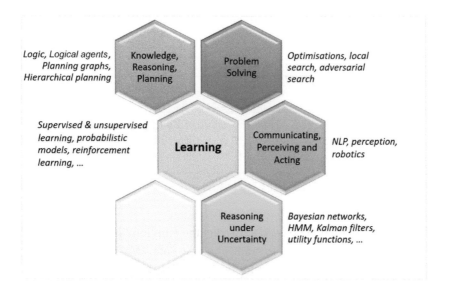

FIGURE 9.1 Classic AI areas.

Reasoning under uncertainty occurs often in the real world and accommodates for the lack of confidence in the given data. It utilises probability concepts to allow informed decision making. Bayesian networks, hidden Markov models (HMM), Kalman filters and utility functions are examples of this area.

Communicating, perceiving and acting are also traditional AI areas. Natural Language Processing is one of its most prominent topics. We will introduce the growing ChatGPT engine, which helps in the writing and coding processes. We will point the interested reader to relevant NLP R libraries. Robotics are frequently used in the industry. We will briefly touch on this topic.

The AI topic area **knowledge, reasoning and planning** comprises topics such as logic (i.e. simple rules and implications), logical agents (agents based on logic), planning graphs and hierarchical planning.

9.2 Learning – ANN and SVM

This section introduces artificial neural networks (ANN) and support vector machines (SVM).

9.2.1 Recap

In order to compare ANN and SVM, we will quickly recap parts of statistical learning (see Section 6.4). Feel free to skip this sub-section.

We need two accuracy measures: root mean squared error (RMSE) and mean absolute percentage error (MAPE). The function `disp.err` will display these measures.

```
#cat('\14'); rm(list=ls());graphics.off(); # for RStudio
rmse     <- function(y,yh) {sqrt(mean((y-yh)^2))}
mape     <- function(y,yh) {mean(abs((y-yh)/y))}
disp.err <- function(y,yh) {cat sprintf("MAPE: %.1f%%,
RMSE: %.2f\n", mape(y, yh)*100, rmse(y, yh)))}
```

The dataset faithful will be used to predict the eruption time given the waiting time. As usual, we divide the data into train and test data. We create sample indices for approximately 70% of the Old Faithful data used for training purposes. For reproducibility, the random number generator is initialised with seed 7. We will need the test response repeatedly; hence, we save it as *y*.

```
D = faithful; n = nrow(D)
set.seed(7);  I = sample(n,.7*n)
train = D[I,]; test = D[-I,]
y = test$eruptions
```

Linear model

The linear model and its evaluation are provided here.

```
flm = lm(eruptions ~ waiting, data = train)
yh = predict(flm, newdata = test) ### Test-accuracy
disp.err(y, yh)
## MAPE: 14.5%, RMSE: 0.52
```

Figure 9.2 visualises the eruption time (in minutes) for the predictions and observations over the waiting time (in minutes) for the entire dataset.

```
ggplot(faithful, aes(waiting,eruptions)) + geom_point() +
    geom_point(data=data.frame(waiting = faithful$waiting,
        eruptions = predict(flm, newdata = faithful)),
            colour="purple")
```

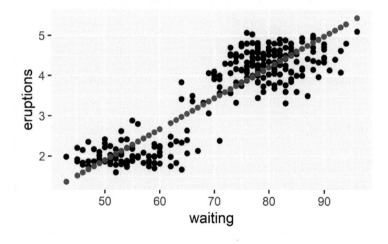

FIGURE 9.2 Modelled linear regression values.

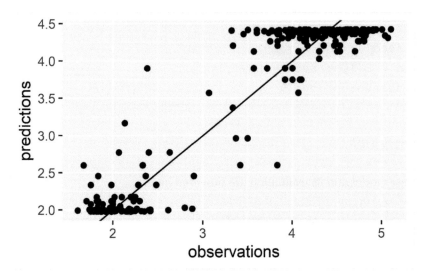

FIGURE 9.3 Observations versus prediction quality.

This graph reveals that there are apparently two types of eruption times: short ones, which last about 2 minutes, and long ones of about 4.4 minutes. Further, the graph reveals that waiting times must have been rounded because many dots are "stacked up".

Another typical visualisation to observe the quality of the model is to plot predictions versus observations.

```
observations = faithful$eruptions;
predictions = predict(flm, newdata = faithful)
qplot(observations, predictions)+geom_abline(slope = 1)
```

For an optimal model, all points have to lie on the diagonal.

9.2.2 ANN Model

Artificial neural networks (ANNs) are inspired by the human brain. It is estimated that the human brain contains 10^{11} neurons. A *neuron* receives input signals from other neurons via so-called dentrites. These signals are aggregated in the soma, which sends its signal to another *neuron* via an axon, which fires once the soma reaches a certain potential (called *activation function*). This motivates the creation of artificial neurons. Figure 9.3 shows the concept of the biological neuron and an artificial neuron representation.

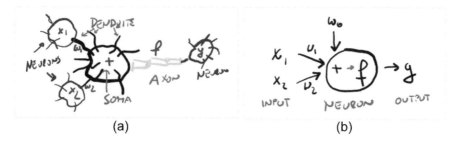

FIGURE 9.4 Neuron (a) biological components and (b) mathematical model schematic.

The mathematical formula for this simple neuron is $y = f(w_0 + w_1x_1 + w_2x_2)$. Here, f is the activation function leading to the output of the neuron. This is also known as the "firing" of the neuron. The simplest activation function is the linear function or identity function. This simplifies the previous example to $y = w_0 + w_1x_1 + w_2x_2$.

Typical examples of activation functions are the (standard) logistic function $1/(1 + e^{-x})$ (soft step), tangent hyperbolicus tanh x, soft-plus $\log(1 + e^x)$, rectified linear unit (ReLU) $[x > 0]x$ and binary step $[x > 0]$, linear x. Pragati Baheti discusses activation functions in her blog (2024).

Single-layer ANN

We will create a neural network with one hidden layer that contains three neurons. The ANN requires the library neuralnet. Other interesting neural network libraries are nnet, gamlss and RSNNS.

Let us build a neural network with three hidden layers to predict eruption times for given wait times of 40, 60, 80 and 100 minutes.

```
library(neuralnet)
ann = neuralnet (eruptions ~ waiting,
        data = train,
        hidden = 3,
        linear.output = TRUE)
### Usage
predict(ann, data.frame(waiting=c(40, 60,80,100)))
##            [,1]
## [1,] 1.975541
## [2,] 2.171599
## [3,] 4.386380
## [4,] 4.416602
```

That means if we wait 80 minutes, the expected eruption time will be 4.39 minutes. What is the test accuracy (MAPE, RMSE) for this model?

```
yh = predict(ann, newdata = test)
derr(y, yh)
## MAPE: 9.419826 %, RMSE: 0.3672063
```

That means this ANN MAPE is approximately 5% better than the linear regression. The neural network is trained (learned) by default by minimising the sum of squared errors. This is equivalent to minimising the root mean squared error (RMSE). In theory, any differentiable function can be used. In case of classification problems, it is better to use a loss function cross-entropy (CE) or a cost function best on the logistic function.

The ANN can be visualised using the common plot command.

```
plot(ann)
```

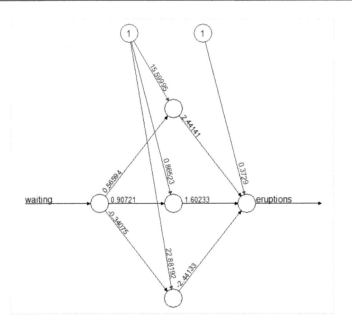

FIGURE 9.5 Artificial neural network model.

Figure 9.5 shows the input layer (waiting – actually only one neuron), the hidden layer with three neurons and the output layer (eruptions – just one neuron). The result of the output layer is also known as *hypothesis*. The blue nodes are the *bias units*.

For instance, assume the waiting time is a_{11} = 2 minutes. Hence, the first neuron in the hidden layer a_{21} gets as input $15.6 + 0.566a_{11} = w_{10}a_{10} + w_{11}a_{11}$. Then the activation function "fires". By default. neuralnet uses the logistic function as activation function f and offers the tangent hyperbolicus. This feeds into the output neuron, which has the same activation function. Hence, the eruption time is $a_{31} = f\left(\sum_{i=1}^{4} w_{2i}a_{2i}\right)$.

The library `NeuralNetTools` allows another way to plot ANNs using `plot-net(ann)`. There is a blog (beckmw.wordpress.com/2013/11/14/visualizing-neural-networks-in-r-update, Accessed 30 January 2024) discussing visualisation of neural networks.

Figure 9.6 visualises the eruption time (in minutes) for the predictions and observations over the waiting time (in minutes) for the entire dataset. However, the neural network model ann is used.

```
ggplot (faithful, aes(waiting,eruptions)) + geom_point() +
    geom_point(data=data.frame(waiting = faithful$waiting,
        eruptions = predict(ann, newdata = faithful)),
        colour="blue")
```

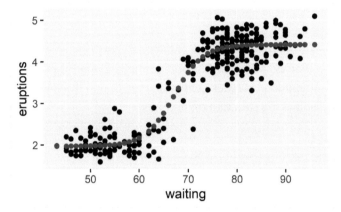

FIGURE 9.6 Neural network model approximating the eruptions.

The figure seems to better fit the data. It goes through the middle of the two clusters. The quality is illustrated in Figure 9.7.

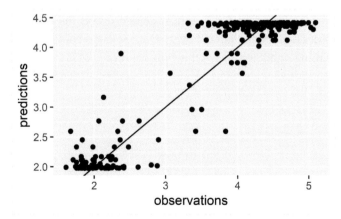

FIGURE 9.7 Observed versus ANN model values (predictions).

It can be seen that there is a systematic error at prediction times 2.0 and 4.4 minutes.

Two-layer ANN

Now we will create an ANN with two hidden layers. The first hidden layer contains three neurons and the second one four neurons.

```
set.seed(7)
ann21 = neuralnet (eruptions ~ waiting,
                    data = train,
                    hidden = c(3,4))
yh = predict(ann21, newdata = test)
derr(y, yh)
## MAPE: 9.757795 %, RMSE: 0.3813751
```

We observe that the algorithm's running time is longer (it may not even converge, depending on the random number generator's seed), and the RMSE has not improved. The following displays the structure of the ANN.

```
plot(ann21)
```

It is believed that more layers are more beneficial than more neurons in a layer due to the repeated application of the activation function. So an NN with one layer and three neurons should be worse than a NN with three layers and one neuron. In the previous example, the RMSE are similar – 0.367 versus 0.371. In general, one cannot state that a more complex neural network is better. Furthermore, the quality of the NN depends on the learning algorithm.

There are several algorithms that can be used to learn the weights for the neural network. The default algorithm for neuralnet is the resilient back-propagation algorithm with weight backtracking rprop+. The most classic one is the *back-propagation* algorithm, which is documented in almost every Data Science book. Here, it is important to find a good learning rate. Please, see this blog for more details.

```
set.seed (7); #cat('\014')
ann.bp = neuralnet (eruptions ~ waiting,
                     data = train,
                     hidden = c(3,4),
                     algorithm = "backprop",
                     learningrate=1E-3)
yh = predict(ann.bp, newdata = test)
derr(y, yh)
## MAPE: 40.17317 %, RMSE: 1.155791
```

We observe that for this particular example, the errors are significantly higher, and a reduced learning rate (e.g. 1E-6) leads to convergence of the algorithm.

There are several basic questions regarding the design of NNs. How many layers should be used? How many neurons should be within a layer? The number of neurons in the input and output layers must equal the number of associated input and output variables. Neural networks only require hidden layers when they need to be separated non-linearly. Let us assume we are using the ANN for a non-linear classification problem with two input variables and one output variable. That means we can visualise the problem on a two-dimensional plane. If the decision boundaries can be approximated by two lines, then two neurons are required in the first hidden layer. If we need four lines to approximate the decision boundary, then we need four neurons in the first hidden layer plus two neurons in the second layer. This should give an idea of how to construct NNs for these kinds of challenges. It becomes more interesting with more input and output variables, but this is beyond the scope of this introductory ANN section.

9.2.3 Support Vector Machines (SVM)

A *support vector machine* (SVM) is a supervised ML technique for classification and prediction. One of its benefits is that tuning of meta parameters is often not required. Furthermore, it can be used for linear and non-linear data.

Let us begin with two simple examples illustrating a linear and radial kernel.

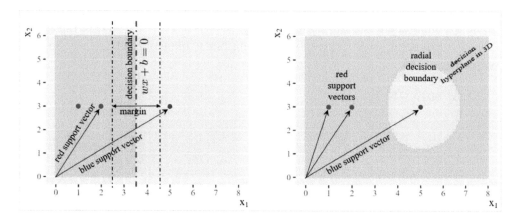

FIGURE 9.8 SVM with two kernels.

We have placed two observations ((2,3),(1,3)) on the right into class Red and one observation (5,3) into class Blue. This data returns a red and blue support vector. These are vectors that are used to obtain the decision border (a line in 2D or a hyperplane in higher dimensions) aka a boundary. It may be better to reserve the word *boundary* to integrate the margin. Generally, a linear hyperplane (e.g. line) is defined via $wx + b = 0$, where $w = (w_1, w_2, \cdots, w_n)$ (to avoid applying the transpose, we will assume that w is a row vector) are the weights of the hyperplane, and b is the intercept. We will explain shortly how the hyperplane and support vectors are related. Instead of finding a linear decision boundary, we could have found a non-linear one using a radial basis function $\exp(\gamma \|x - x_i\|)$, where γ is Gaussian kernel width, x_i are the observations and x the classification line points. The non-linear data can even be circular or entangled as illustrated in Figure 9.9.

Here, we used SVM classifiers with radial kernels and visualised the resulting decision boundaries.

The Figure 9.9 shows a linear kernel example, which we will use to explain the concept of the linear support vector classifier.

The objective is to find a hyperplane that separates the classes in the "best" way. Here, "best" refers to the line which maximises the margins. The margins are defined by identifying the data points from both classes which are closest to the decision boundary. These data points are called support vectors. In this example, we see that it is possible to draw a line to separate the red and blue observations without misclassifying any data points x_i. This means we can find hard margins; otherwise, soft margins have to suffice. How can we define the objective function? In Figure 9.10, the decision boundary splits the space into two regions defined by $wx_i + b < 0$ for the red points and $wx_i + b > 0$ for the blue points. That means a point from the orange region inserted into $wx_i + b$ returns a negative value. This motivates the choice of the associated class value to be $y_i = -1$. On the other side of the hyperplane, a positive value $wx_i + b$ is returned. Hence, we set the numerical value $y_i = +1$ for blue observations. Furthermore, we want to set the margins to be two units apart. The two corresponding regions are $wx_i + b < -1$ and $wx_i + b > +1$. The two inequalities can be combined (using our y_i numerical class definition) and written as:

$$(wx_i + b)y_i - 1 > 0 \tag{9.1}$$

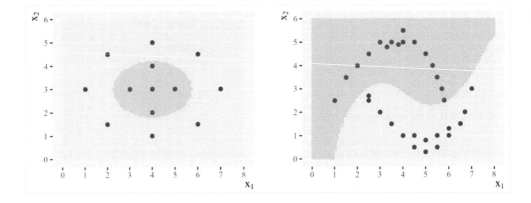

FIGURE 9.9 SVM patterns.

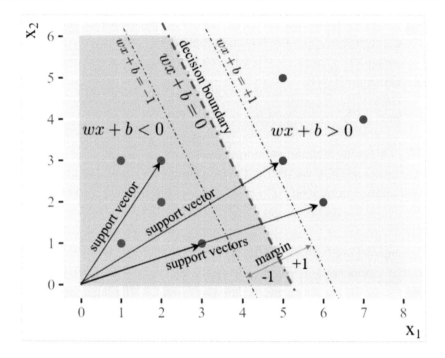

FIGURE 9.10 SVM simple concept.

The margin difference of two "opposite" vectors (e.g. x_1 amd x_2) on the margin lines is:

$$wx_1 + b - 1 - wx_2 - b - 1 = 0 \Rightarrow w(x_1 - x_2) = 2. \tag{9.2}$$

The inner product rule provides the distances $w(x_1 - x_2) = \|w\|\|x_1 - x_2\|$. In the 1990s, SVMs were enhanced by the kernel trick and soft margins (Cortes and Vapnik, 1995). The distance between x_1 and x_2 is:

$$\|x_1 - x_2\| = \frac{2}{\|w\|}, \tag{9.3}$$

which we would like to maximise. The dual to this is the minimisation of the inverse $\frac{1}{2}\|w\|$. This allows us to formulate the hard margin SVM classifier optimisations as:

$$\min\|w\| \text{ subject to} : (wx_i + b)y_i \geq 1, i \in \{1, 2, \cdots n\}. \tag{9.4}$$

Quadratic programming allows a more efficient way of solving this mathematical program but requires us to change the optimisation formulation to:

$$\min\|w\|^2 \text{ subject to} : (wx_i + b)y_i - 1 \geq 0, i \in \{1, 2, \cdots n\}. \tag{9.5}$$

If the classes overlap, the objective (cost) function needs to be relaxed. This is known as a soft-margin approach. It is commonly achieved with the *hinge loss function* $H(x_i, y_i) = \max(0, 1 - y_i(w_x - i - b))$, which is related to the logistic regression. The soft margin SVM is:

$$\min C \|w\|^2 + \frac{1}{n} \sum_{i=1}^{n} H(x_i, y_i) \text{ subject to} : (wx_i + b)y_i - 1 \geq 0, \ i \in \{1, 2, \cdots n\}, \tag{9.6}$$

where C is a tuning (regularisation/penalisation) parameter. This type of SVM is called C-classification. If we restrict C to the range [0, 1], the SVM type is known as ½-classification (pronounced *nu*), which is related to the ratio of the training error and support vectors. Another common type is one-classification, which is used for outlier detection.

To summarise, we have shown the conceptual framework of the SVM classifier. We showed that support vectors are used to define the margins and decision boundaries. SVM kernels can be used for various different scenarios. The linear and radial kernels were emphasised. Three types of SVM classifiers were mentioned, and the C-classification type was discussed in detail. Next, we will show SVM in the context of regressions.

Support Vector Regression

The idea of SVR is to create a decision boundary (including the margin) such that most data points are covered. As in the classification approach, the objective is to minimise $\frac{1}{2}ww^T$. This time, we keep the real y_i value. The objective is subject to keeping the distance of the observations below ε: i.e.

$$|y_i - (wx_i + b)| \leq \varepsilon \tag{9.7}$$

This type of SVM is known as e-SVM or, more precisely, epsilon-insensitive SVM regression. This is similar to the hard margins of SV classifications. Soft margins deal with each individual observation. For additional flexibility, lower and upper margins are considered separately.

$$y_i - (wx_i + b) \leq \varepsilon + \alpha_i \qquad (wx_i + b) - y_i \leq \varepsilon + \beta_i \tag{9.8}$$

These individual margins need to be minimised. Thus, a new loss function is required:

$$L = \frac{1}{2}ww^T + C \sum_{i=1}^{n} (\alpha_i + \beta_i), \tag{9.9}$$

where C is a penalty factor. As with the support vector classifications, other kernels, such as the Gaussian and polynomial ones, can be used instead of the linear kernel. We observe that we are not attempting to reduce the MSE but rather the errors around the hyperplane. This makes SVR more robust against outliers.

Example 9.1 (Prediction of eruption time). As an example, we predict the eruption time (in minutes) for the geyser Old Faithful, given the waiting time (min). This is a regression model. Hence, we create a support vector regression model. The library e1071 has these optimisations for SVM classifications and regressions implemented within the method svm. Calling svm with the default configurations returns the learned model.

```
n = nrow(faithful); ns = floor(.7*n); # sample size
set.seed(7); I = sample(1:n,ns); # random indices
train = faithful[I,]; test = faithful[-I,]; y = test$eruptions;

sm = svm (eruptions ~ waiting, data = train)
sm # default model

## ...
## Parameters      :
##        SVM-Type  : eps-regression
## SVM-Kernel       : radial
##          cost    : 1
##          gamma   : 1
##        epsilon   : 0.1
##
## Number of Support Vectors: 141
```

As we can see, the SVM-type is an e-regression ($\varepsilon = 0.1$) with a radial kernel ($\gamma = 1$). Out of the 190 observations, 141 were used as support vectors.

The test quality metrics MAPE and RMSE are:

```
yh = predict(sm, newdata = test)
derr(y, yh)
## MAPE: 9.323547 %, RMSE: 0.3676319
```

This outperforms the linear model lm (eruptions ~ waiting, data = train), which has MAPE: 14.50% and a RMSE of 0.51. If we'd use a linear kernel for the SVM, a similar MAPE of 14.57% is obtained.

Visualise the model predictions for the entire dataset.

```
ggplot(faithful, aes(waiting,eruptions)) + geom_point() +
    geom_point(data=data.frame(waiting = faithful$waiting,
        eruptions = predict(sm, newdata = faithful)),
            colour="red")
```

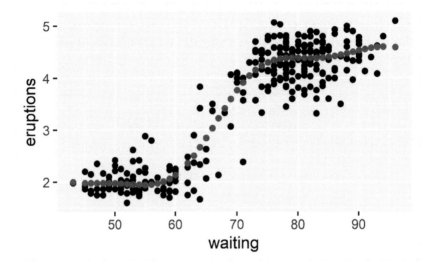

As an SVM classification example, we will consider the iris data, which contains three flower species. Since the data is almost balanced, we will use accuracy as the quality metric. (Otherwise, balanced accuracy is recommended; see Section 6.2 for details.)

```
# Split into training and test data
n = nrow(iris); ns = floor(.7*n); set.seed(7); I = sample(n,ns);
train = iris[I,]; test = iris[-I,]; y = test$Species;
# SVM
sm = svm(Species ~., data = train)
sm
##
## Parameters:
##       SVM-Type : C-classification
## SVM-Kernel    : radial
##           cost : 1
##
## Number of Support Vectors: 46
```

The learned SVM model is a C-classification type with a radial kernel and uses 46 support vectors.

```
# Accuracy functions
pacc <- function(y,yh) {
   cm = table(y, yh); A = sum(diag(cm))/sum(cm);
   cat(sprintf("Accuracy: %.1f%%", A*100))
}
accuracy <- function(model, data){
   y = data[,ncol(data)] # last column contains target
   yh = predict(model, newdata = data)
   pacc(y,yh)
}
accuracy(sm, test)
## Accuracy: 93.3%
```

The SVM classifies the data with 93.3% accuracy. The multinomial logistic regression `multinom(Species ~., data=train, trace=FALSE)` achieves the same accuracy. The same accuracy is achieved using just the petals' dimensions using the previous SVM. Figure 9.11 provides a visualisation of the decision boundaries.

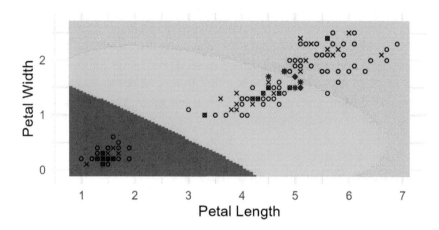

FIGURE 9.11 SVM Iris borders.

The training data is shown via circles, test data as x and misclassifications with a dark red cross. Using a linear kernel with all features increases the accuracy to 97.8%.

Further reading: Wilmott (2022) introduces neural networks in Chapter 10. He discusses the topological and mathematical structure. Several activation functions are provided. Forward and backward propagation algorithms are explained. Autoencoder and recurrent neural networks are mentioned. James et al. (2013) discuss neural networks in their deep learning chapter. They introduce single- and multi-layer, convolutional and recurrent neural networks. The backpropagation algorithm is explained in addition to regularisation, dropout learning and network tuning. It includes R code. Watt et al. (2020) provide the models and mathematical formulations for single- and multi-layer networks, including a description of several activation functions. Python code shows the creation of a neural network from scratch. The appendix discusses reverse mode automatic differentiation, which includes backpropagation as a special case. Hastie et al. (2009) introduce the single-layer neural network and its backpropagation algorithm. Brunton and Kutz (2022) introduce the single- and multi-layer NN in a compact way supported by Matlab and Python code. Activation functions are given in a concise way. Backpropagation explanation reveals mathematical details. Of all the texts, it has the most details about deep convolutional NNs, recurrent NNs and autoencoders and shows the diversity of NNs. Additionally, it applies NNs to dynamical systems.

Shah (2020) s. 9.9 briefly introduces the underlying theory of SVMs for classifications and provides a prediction example in R. Brunton and Kutz (2022) s. 5.7 explain linear and non-linear SVMs. They discuss kernel methods for SVMs. A Python/Matlab example is provided. Watt et al. (2020) s. 6.5 introduce SVMs via the margin perceptron and the softmax cost function. They discuss soft and hard margins, entropy and quality metrics. Wilmott (2022) gives a gentle derivation of the objective function. James et al. (2013) dedicate Chapter 9 to SVMs. The mathematical program for the maximal margin classifier is provided. The reader is made aware of the difference between SV classifiers and SVMs. The case of more than two classes is discussed. The relationship with the logistic regression is explained. Their lab section includes information about cost, scaling and tuning. It also provides ROC plots. Burkov (2019) gives a concise, intuitive introduction to SVM in Sections 1.3 and 3.4. The book by Vapnik (2000) is one of the most comprehensive exts amongst the previous ones.

9.3 Problem Solving – GA and SA

A fleet of vehicles needs to deliver goods to customers in such a way that the total delivery time is minimised. These kind of challenges are knowns as *vehicle routing problems* (VRP). If there is only one vehicle, it is called the *travelling salesman problem* (TSP). In the TSP, a salesman has to visit n towns but is allowed to visit each one only once. There are many more challenges relevant for industry, such as the facility location problem, dynamic lot sizing and production mix. These kinds of problems are more in the domain of Operational Analytics rather than Data Analytics. However, the underlying methods are used to solve Data Analytics challenges such as insurance policy buyer classification or customer segmentation.

We will begin with an example and the make the reader aware of the methods typically found in this field.

9.3.1 Knapsack Problem

A knapsack with a weight restriction $\hat{w}$ has to be packed with items. Each item i has a weight and a value v_i.

The objective is to maximise the total value by deciding whether to pack or not pack an item x_i: i.e. $x_i \in \{0,1\}$

$$\max_{x} \left\{ \sum_{i=1}^{n} v_i x_i : \sum_{i=1}^{n} w_i x_i \leq \hat{w} \right\} \tag{9.10}$$

By the way, this is the same as $\max_x \left\{ vx : wx \leq \hat{w} \right\}$ in vector notation.

Let us assume $v = \begin{bmatrix} 6 & 5 & 8 & 9 & 6 & 7 & 3 \end{bmatrix}$, $w = \begin{bmatrix} 2 & 3 & 6 & 7 & 5 & 9 & 4 \end{bmatrix}$ and $\hat{w} = 9$. What items should be packed?

We begin by defining the data.

```
v  = c(6, 5, 8, 9, 6, 7, 3) # values
w  = c(2, 3, 6, 7, 5, 9, 4) # weights
wh = 9 # weight limit (including values)
n  = length(v) # number of elements (required later)
```

Warmup. Let x be decision vector for which items have to be packed. Define x such that items 1 and 3 are packed. What is the value and weight of packing items 1 and 3? Use the dot product.

```
x = c(1,0,1,0,0,0,0)
v %*% x # value
##      [,1]
## [1,] 14
w %*% x # weight
##      [,1]
## [1,] 8
```

Is this a feasible solution? Is it an optimal solution? This depends on whether the solution value can be increased without violating the weight constraint.

9.3.2 Brute Force

Write a function that finds the optimal solution using a *brute force* approach. That means all configurations (here, packing options) are tested, and all feasible solutions are evaluated. (Note: You may want to do a few preparation exercises first – see the following.)

```
# Brute force (maximise value)
knapsackBF <- function(v, w, wh) {
    n = length(v); best.v = -Inf;
        for (nb in (0:2^7-1)) {
            x = as.integer (intToBits(nb)) [1:n]
            if (w %*% x <= wh) {# then weight constraint ok
                if (v %*% x > best.v) {# then new best value
                    best.v = v %*% x
                    sol = x
                    cat('New solution:', x,"» value:", best.v,"\n")
            }
        }
    }
    cat("Best solution value:", best.v, "\nusing x = ", sol, "\n")
return (sol)
}
x = knapsackBF(v, w, wh)
## New solution: 0 0 0 0 0 0 0 » value: 0
## New solution: 1 0 0 0 0 0 0 » value: 6
## New solution: 1 1 0 0 0 0 0 » value: 11
## New solution: 1 0 1 0 0 0 0 » value: 14
## New solution: 1 0 0 1 0 0 0 » value: 15
## Best solution value: 15
## using x = 1 0 0 1 0 0 0
```

That means items 1 and 4 need to be packed (use which(x==1)). These items have a value of 15 = v %*% x (individual values are 6 and 9 = v[sol==1]) with weights 2 and 7.

Exercise 9.1 (Combinations). If you have four items, how many combinations are there to pack them? $2^4 = 16$ represents four objects as binary numbers and all potential states. $1 + 4 + 6 + 4 + 1$ is motivated by the binomial distribution $(a + b)^n$.

Exercise 9.2 (Converting integers and bits). Convert the number 6 into bits using int-ToBits() and then convert the bits back into integers using the following two functions.

```
bits = intToBits(6)
as.integer(bits)
## [1] 0 1 1 0 0 0 0 0 0 0 0 0 0 0 0 0 0 0 0 0 0 0 0 0 ...
```

How do you convert this binary number into a decimal number? This is achieved using the following calculation: $0 * 2^0 + 1 * s2^1 + 1 * 2^2 + 0 * 2^3 + \ldots$.

9.3.3 Genetic Algorithm

We will use a genetic algorithm with a binary chromosome algorithm (rbga.bin) to solve the knapsack problem. The algorithm is part of the genalg library.

The algorithm requires an evaluation function which contains the constraints and objective function. Note that rbga.bin only minimises: i.e. we need to invert the objective to maximise.

Your task is to write the evaluation function evalFun for the knapsack problem. Assume that v, w and $\hat{w}$ are known in the global environment and x is the input. Return $-v \cdot x$ if the weight is less than $\hat{w}$, otherwise $+\infty$. Test the function with $x = \begin{bmatrix} 1 & 1 & 0 & 0 & 0 & 0 & 0 \end{bmatrix}$. Is the solution feasible? If yes, what is the solution value?

```
evalFun <- function(x) {
    if (w %*% x <= wh) {# then weight constraint ok
      return (-(v %*% x)) # invert value to maximise
    } else {return(+INF)}
}
evalFun(c(1,1,0,0,0,0,0)) # test
##         [,1]
## [1,] -11
```

Answer: The solution is feasible, and the solution value is -11.

Now let us call the GA using most of the default parameter settings. What is the best solution and its value?

```
myGA <- rbga.bin(evalFunc = evalFun, size = n)
# Best solution
best.v = -min(myGA$best) # best solution value for
    iteration
idx = which.min(myGA$evaluations) # index of individual
sol = myGA$population[idx,] # best found solution
cat("Best solution value:", best.v, "\nusing x = ", sol,  "\n")
## Best solution value: 15
## using x = 1 0 0 1 0 0 0
```

Answer: The best found solution (in this case, it is also the best solution) is $x = \begin{bmatrix} 1 & 0 & 0 & 1 & 0 & 0 & 0 \end{bmatrix}$, with solution value 15.

What default parameters are shown using the summary function on myGA?

```
cat(summary(myGA))
## GA Settings
## Type                    = binary chromosome
## Population size         = 200
## Number of Generations   = 100
## Elitism                 = 40
## Mutation Chance         = 0.125
##
## Search Domain
## Var 1 = [,]
## Var 0 = [,]
##
## GA Results
## Best Solution: 1 0 0 1 0 0 0
```

Answer: Population size, number of generations, elitism and mutation chance.

Change the mutation chance (mutationChance) to $\frac{1}{n}$, population size (pop-Size) to 20 and the number of iterations (iters) to 40.

Did the algorithm still return the same solution? Did the algorithm find the solution faster?

```
myGA <- rbga.bin(evalFunc = evalFun, size = n,
                 mutationChance = 1/n, popSize = 20, iters
                 = 40)
best.v = -min(myGA$best);
sol = myGA$population[which.min(myGA$evaluations),]
cat("Best solution value:", best.v, "\nusing x = ", sol,"\n")
## Best solution value: 15
## using x = 1 0 0 1 0 0 0
```

Answer: The same solution was found, and the algorithm ran faster. Note: Results may vary because of different random number generation.

9.3.4 Methods Overview

Optimisations can be divided into three categories: heuristics, meta heuristics and exact approaches (Table 9.1). Most optimisations try to minimise or maximise an objective function subject to some constraints. For instance, minimise the travel distance subject to each

TABLE 9.1 Optimisation approaches.

Heuristics	Meta heuristics	Exact approaches
Greedy algorithms	Simulated annealing (SA)	Linear programs (LP)
Local searches (LS)	Genetic algorithms (GA)	Integer programs (IP)
Multi-start LS	Tabu-search (TS)	Combinatorial optimisation
	Ant-algorithm	Semi-definite programming

customer being visited exactly once. Occasionally, optimisations try to find a solution for a target value.

Heuristics are algorithms that find good solutions. Their runtimes are usually fast. However, sometimes they only return local optima. Greedy heuristics are extremely fast and improve in direction of greatest gain. Note that a greedy algorithm can become an exact approach once it's proven that it reaches the global optima (e.g. Dijkstra algorithm). Local search algorithms have an initial solution as the starting point in the search space. They check their neighbourhood (i.e. an area of surrounding solutions) and, based on their findings, proceed to search for the best solution. Multi-start local searches try to overcome the risk of getting stuck in a local optima.

Meta heuristics are usually based on heuristics but tend to integrate mechanisms to escape local optima and guarantee optimal solutions if the runtime is long enough (i.e. converge to the global optimum). We have discussed the usage of the genetic algorithm before. It has some similarities with the multi-start local search. However, it is inspired by nature – more specifically, the growth of populations. Let us look at an example in which we want to find the minimum.

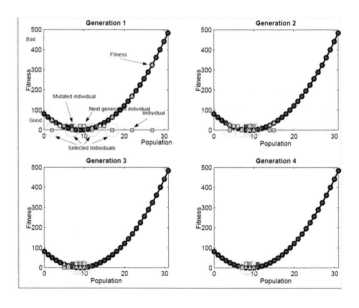

FIGURE 9.12 GA concept.

We begin with a random initial population (green squares). This population consists of individuals (solutions) to the problem. Each individual has a fitness (solution value). Now the fittest individuals (parents) are selected (green circles) to create the next generation of individuals (i.e. children). The children are created via a crossover operation to the parents. (Usually, a child comes from two parents). In order to escape local optima, a mutation (minor random change) to the children happens. These children form the next generation. The process continues until a global optimum is found or – more often – a runtime limit has been reached.

Simulated annealing is a meta heuristic used for optimisation problems. Simulated annealing is inspired from physics by freezing materials. It is based on random movements in the search space but directed to the global optima. Please explore the TSP blog and the related Github repository (github.com/toddwschneider/shiny-salesman, Accessed 30 January 2024).

Exact approaches find the optimal solution. A mathematical program is formulated (see the knapsack problem), and a solver engine returns the solution for it. That means once the problem is formulated, a solution is obtained. For linear programs, the simplex method (part of a solver engine) finds the exact solution. Linear programme means the decision variables are all real valued. Often, the decision variables are binary or integers, as in the knapsack, VRP and TSP problems. Then the challenge is called an integer programme. Combinatorial and semi-definite programming also fall into the class of exact approaches. The MathProg solver on Smartana.org includes several examples to get you started with formulating optimisation problems. Please see Examples » Basic Optimisations » Knapsack to find the mathematical program to solve the knapsack problem exactly.

9.4 Games – Minimax

9.4.1 Chess

Chess is a prominent testing environment for AI approaches. It has been used by famous people like Alan Turing, Claude Shannon and John van Neumann, just to mention a few, and is considered an intellectual game. Gary Kasparov supported the development and "scientific experiment" of computer chess engines. Before 1997, he had several encounters, decisively winning against them (e.g. 1995). In 1997, the unthinkable happened: the "machine", Deep Blue, won against the reigning world chess champion Gary Kasparov. The organisation and suspicious activities during this event may dent this achievement. However, from this point forward, the strength of the machines continued rising. Currently, chess engines are far beyond the strength of human chess players (including world champions), and we are starting to experience a new era of humans learning from machines. In my opinion, there are few notable achievements. Mathew Lai's paper demonstrates that deep reinforcement learning can be used to create a strong chess engine (Lai, 2015). A summary by arXiv (2020) popularised his work. Soon after this, he began working for Google. Three years later (March 2018) Google's AlphaGo won against Lee Sedol, the reigning world champion in Go (computationally a more challenging game than chess). The general structure of the new algorithm allowed its adaptation to AlphaZero. AlphaZero beat the best chess program up to this point, Stockfish in 2019, but the conditions may not have been fair. In March 2023, Stockfish 15 was ranked as the best chess engine with 3533 Elos on CCRL 40/15 (rapid chess). On SSDF, Leela Chess Zero is ranked as number one with 3575 Elos, followed by Stockfish with 3574 Elos in classical chess. In comparison, the strongest current player – Magnus Carlsen – has 2,852 classic Elos and 2,839 rapid Elos. On Chess.com, about 700 players have more than 2,500 Elos, and the mode is at 500 Elos with 2.7 million players.

In 2006, I implemented a chess program for fun. I called it "Greedy Edi" and uploaded it to Matlab Central (Garn, 2023). It was used for simple robot experiments and got mentioned in an AI book (Jones, 2008). In 2021, I created a virtual reality version of it (Garn, 2021). In 2023, I adapted Greedy Edi to Smart Edi by integrating the Stockfish engine. Hence, Smart Edi is the strongest chess program because it uses the highest-rated chess engine. There are usually two parts to a chess program: the user interface and the engine. How did I start developing Greedy Edi? Step 1: I began by displaying the board and pieces. Step 2: Moving a piece. I added the logic for moving the pieces (Figure 9.13). The black knight has eight possible fields it can reach. These are identified by x and y coordinates.

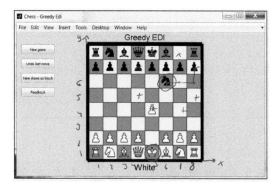

FIGURE 9.13 Chess – Greedy Edi knight.

The Matlab code snipped shows a function returning a matrix of the possible fields.

```
function T = toFields(position)
% determines all possibles fields witin the board

M = [[2 1 -1 -2 -2 -1 1 2]',[1 2 2 1 -1 -2 -2 -1]'];
e = ones(8,1);
D = e*position + M;
I = sum((D > 0 & D < 9),2)==2 ; % only fields within the board
T = D(I,:);
```

FIGURE 9.14 Chess – Greedy Edi knight – Matlab.

It hard codes the eight moving patterns: i.e. two fields to the right and one up. This is added to the current knight's position and limited to the board. Another function takes care of more intrinsic details such as whether the field is occupied by another piece. The most interesting challenge occurs from check constraints. That means that, by moving the piece, would the king be exposed to a check. Step 3: Evaluation of the board. The simplest way is to assign a value to each piece. Traditionally, the pawn is used as a unit. The knight and bishop are assigned the value of three pawns. The rook gets five pawns, the queen nine pawns and the king four pawns. At the same time, the king has "infinite" value because capturing the king ends the game. A simple evaluation function just adds up all the piece values on the board. A slightly better evaluation function (originally proposed by Turing) includes the mobility of the pieces (i.e. number of possible fields. Step 4: Determine the best move. This is where the chess engine kicks in. This could be as simple as determining the ply (a half move) that returns the maximum value from all possible plies. However, the most prominent algorithm is the one introduced in the next section: the minimax algorithm with alpha-beta pruning. Step 5: Continue with Step 2 until game is over. Obviously, this is a rough simplification.

The library `rchess` has the class Chess, which contains several useful methods (`names(chess)`) such as `plot` (display board), `pgn` (a chess notation) and `in-check` function. Let us begin with white's move (first ply) - pawn to e4.

```
library(rchess)
chess <- Chess$new()
chess$move("e4")
plot(chess)
```

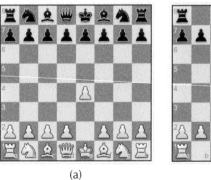 

(a)   (b)

FIGURE 9.15 Chess (a) first ply is pawn to e4; (b) several more moves.

Let us do a few more moves to demonstrate how to select between two figures.

```
chess$move("c5") # Black's ply
chess$move("Nf3")$move("e6");
chess$move("Na3")$move("Nc6")
chess$move("Nc4")$move("Nf6")
chess$move("Nce5") # how to select from two figures
plot(chess)
```

These moves are displayed in Figure 9.15 (b).

Now, we could use our `minimax` algorithm if we had an evaluation function. A simple evaluation function is to count the material; `chess$get()` returns the colour and figure type. However, we will immediately jump to one of (if not the) most popular chess engine in the world, **Stockfish.**

We will replicate these moves in Stockfish and let Stockfish find a move.

```
library(stockfish)
engine <- fish$new()
engine$uci()
#engine$isready() # should return true
moves = "moves e2e4 c7c5 g1f3 e7e6
                b1a3 b8c6 a3c4 g8f6 c4e5"
engine$position(type="startpos", position=moves)
response = engine$go()
engine$quit()
cat(response)
## info depth 21 seldepth 27 multipv 1 score cp 169 nodes
## 3581127 nps 1763233 hashfull 946 tbhits 0 time 2031 pv
## c6e5 f3e5 d8c7 e5g4 f6e4 . . . f1b5 c8d7 b5d7 d8d7 f3d4
```

It finds black's move Nxe5 (i.e. the night on c6 beats the pawn on e5) and anticipates white's next move Nxe5 (and gives the anticipated main line).

Let me introduce a simple "initial" function (`getPly`: i.e. it needs a bit more work) that converts between `rchess` and stockfish notation. This allows us to plot `Stockfish's` response.

```
getPly <- function(response){ # in rchess notation
  ply  = str_extract(response,'[a-h][1-8][a-h][1-8]')
  from = substr(ply,1,2); to = substr(ply,3,4);
  fig  = toupper(chess$get(from)$type)
  hit  = !is.null(chess$get(to)$type)
```

```
    if (fig ==   'P' && !hit) fig = "";
    if (hit) {mv = paste0(fig, 'x', to)
      } else {mv = paste0(fig, to)}
    return(mv)
  }
mv = getPly(response)
chess$move(mv)
plot(chess)
```

FIGURE 9.16 Chess engine move.

This code linked with an interactive board returns an almost unbeatable chess programme. Stockfish uses the Universal Chess Interface, which enables it to communicate with any user interface. Please find Stockfish's source code on GitHub, which includes more details about the UCI options available and the source code. The source code reveals the evaluation function and how the best move is found. However, we will create our own chess engine now using the most popular algorithm for this.

9.4.2 Minimax Algorithm

We will implement the minimax algorithm and integrate $\alpha - \beta$ pruning into it.

Our objective is to create a simple example to test our implementation of the minimax algorithm. We assume a simplified chess game. White has two options to make a move. Similarly, black has two options to respond. Once the game tree reaches depth 3, all positions are evaluated. Figure 9.17 shows the minimax example, which we will reproduce.

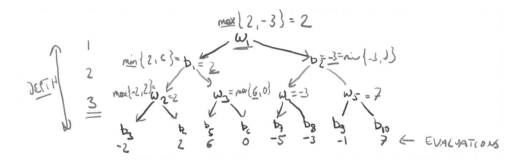

FIGURE 9.17 Minimax example.

Each node name in this example represents a *position* (state). At the beginning, we are in position w_1. From this state, we have two potential plies (usually in chess there are about twenty plies on average) to end up in position b_1 or b_2. The algorithm we propose will go down the game tree to depth 3 and return the evaluation from the leaf node (bottom). The most trivial case is when the game tree has only one position: i.e. the root node is also the leaf node, and the depth is zero. In this case, the position is evaluated. So we will write a recursive function which returns from its recursion when it reaches depth zero. In our example, we start the minimax algorithm with depth 3 at w_1. Then, we call minimax again with b_1 reducing depth to 2, and again with w_2 with depth 1, and again with b_3 and depth 0. Now position b_3 is evaluated, returning the value -2, and w_2 has a second branch (ply) leading to b_4 and returning the value 2. The best move for white in position w_2 is max{-2, 2} = 2. The recursion returns one level up to b_1. Minimax iterates through all potential plies, and the next one is w_3. Again, recursively, we reach b_5 and b_6, returning the values 0 and 6 to state w_3, allowing us to evaluate state 3, giving us the choice between 6 and 0. Since white maximises its gain, 6 is chosen. Now black has the opposite objective to minimise its losses. Hence, at b_1, it has to decide whether to transition from b_1 to w_2 or to w_3. Since min$\{w_2, w_3\}$ is 2, black will transition to w_2. So far, the discovered line in reverse order is $b_4 \leftarrow w_2 \leftarrow b_1$ as main line. Now the sub-tree starting with b_2 gets analysed the same way, evaluating to -3. The root node's evaluation uses max$\{b_1, b_2\}$, returning the value 2 as best choice. Hence, the anticipated main line is $w_1 \rightarrow b_1 \rightarrow w_2 \rightarrow b_4$ with an evaluated gain of 2 (e.g. in chess, two pawns).

This will be implemented in R. Functions for the positions, node evaluations and game-over state are hard coded for now but can be easily replaced for a more realistic game.

```
getPositions <- function(pos){
switch (pos,
    'w1'= c('b1', 'b2'),      'b1'= c('w2', 'w3' ),
    'b2'= c('w4', 'w5' ),     'w2'= c('b3', 'b4' ),
    'w3'= c('b5', 'b6' ),     'w4'= c('b7', 'b8' ),
    'w5'= c('b9', 'b10'))
```

```
} cat("Positions resulting from b1: ", getPositions('b1'),
     "\n") # test
## Positions resulting from b1: w2 w3
gameOver <- function (pos) {
 return(FALSE) # always returns FALSE (template code)
}
evaluate <- function(pos) {
 switch(pos,
    'b3' = -2, 'b4'  = 2,  'b5' = 6,  'b6'  = 0,
    'b7' = -5, 'b8'  = -3, 'b9' = -1, 'b10' = 7)
}
cat("Value of position b3 is ", evaluate('b3'), "\n",)
## Value of position b3 is -2
```

Next, we will implement the minimax algorithm explained earlier.

```
minimax <- function(pos='w1', depth = 1, player = TRUE){
  if (depth == 0 || gameOver(pos)) {
    return (evaluate (pos))
  }
  if (player) {# white
    eval.max = -Inf;
    for (p in getPositions(pos)){
      eval.p = minimax(p, depth-1, FALSE)
      eval.max = max(eval.max, eval.p)
    }
    return (eval.max)
  } else {# player black
    eval.min = +Inf;
    for (p in getPositions(pos)){
      eval.p = minimax(p, depth-1, TRUE)
      eval.min = min(eval.min, eval.p)
    }
    return (eval.min)
  }
}
cat("Position evaluation (depth 3): ", minimax(depth = 3),"\n")
## Position evaluation (depth 3): 2
```

This algorithm is universal and can be used for any challenge that involves two players (or competing rational agents). The disadvantage of this algorithm is the growth of the tree.

$\alpha - \beta$ *Pruning*

Pruning branches of the tree which are irrelevant can significantly reduce the required analysis, saving memory and time. We achieve this by remembering the evaluations for both players. Branches are not analysed when α and β identify that no better evaluation can be found.

```
minimaxab <- function(pos='w1', depth = 1, player = TRUE,
                      alpha = -Inf, beta = +Inf){
  if (depth == 0 || gameOver(pos)) {return (evaluate(pos))}
  if (player) {
    eval.max = -Inf;
    for (p in getPositions(pos)){
      eval.p = minimaxab(p, depth-1, FALSE, alpha, beta)
      eval.max = max(eval.max, eval.p)
      alpha = max(alpha, eval.p)
      if (beta <= alpha) {break}
    }
    return (eval.max)
  } else {
    eval.min = +Inf;
    for (p in getPositions(pos)){
      eval.p = minimaxab(p, depth-1, TRUE, alpha, beta)
      eval.min = min(eval.min, eval.p)
    }
    beta = min(beta, eval.p)
    if (beta <= alpha) {break}
    return (eval.min)
  }
}
minimaxab(depth = 3, alpha = -Inf, beta = +Inf) ### Test fun.
## [1] 2
```

Exercise 9.3 (Recursive functions). Write a recursive function that computes factorial powers facPow for positive integers. (Note this function exists as factorial.) Test the function for $n = 5$.

$$n! = n(n-1)!, 0! = 1, n > 1$$

```
facPow <- function(n){
  if (n==0) return(1) else return (n * facPow (n-1))
}
facPow (5)
## [1] 120
```

Exercise 9.4 (Fibonacci numbers). Next implement the Fibonacci numbers as recursive function (see Section 4.3.2 or smartana.org).

Exercise 9.5 (Tic-Tac-Toe). Please explore this Tic-Tac-Toe blog (r-bloggers.com/2017/06/tic-tac-toe-part-3-the-minimax-algorithm, Accessed 30 January 2024).

9.5 Reasoning Under Uncertainty – BBN

Reasoning under uncertainty occurs often in the real world and accommodates for the lack of confidence in the given data. It utilises probability concepts to allow informed decision making. Bayesian networks, hidden Markov models (HMM), Kalman filters and utility functions are examples of this area.

In this section, we will focus on reasoning under uncertainty with *Bayesian belief networks* (BBN). BBN are based on probability theory. We will assume the reader has a basic understanding of probability theory. If not, please read Chapter 6 in Garn (2018). A more comprehensive text is Ross (2020). Some of the material that follows can also be found in my book (Garn, 2018).

Fundamental to BBN are conditional probabilities.

Definition 9.5.1 (conditional probability). The *conditional probability* $P(E|F)$ is defined as the ratio of the *joint probability* $P(EF)$ and the marginal probability $P(f)$:

$$P(E \mid F) := \frac{P(EF)}{P(F)} \tag{9.11}$$

We state this as the probability that event E occurs ("enters"), given that F has occurred "first".

If the conditional probability is known, then the *joint probability* can be obtained via:

$$P(EF) = P(E \mid F)P(F) \tag{9.12}$$

Let us spend another moment to observe a very interesting relationship between joint and conditional probabilities. First, we notice that $P(EF) = P(FE)$. This allows us to state:

$$P(E \mid F)P(F) = P(EF) = P(F \mid E)P(E) \tag{9.13}$$

That means that suddenly, we can go "backwards" in the probability tree. $P(E \mid F)$ is the *posterior* probability as before, but $P(F \mid E)$ becomes the *prior* probability. This can be used in "updating" probabilities without the knowledge of joint probabilities.

Generally, this relationship is known as the *Bayes rule*, in honour of Thomas Bayes, who is credited with its discovery:

$$P(E \mid F) = \frac{P(F \mid E)P(E)}{P(F)} \tag{9.14}$$

The Bayes rule allows the introduction of a simple Bayesian network (Figure 9.18), which is a more "compressed" form of probability trees.

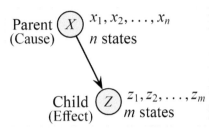

FIGURE 9.18 Simple Bayesian network.

Bayesian networks are built on conditional probability tables. Bayesian networks have multiple applications; the most popular are in health, bioinformatics and military decision making. There are several classic examples (test instances) such as Asia (health), burglar alarm and wet grass, which can be found in the online repository bn-learn.com/bnrepository. Figure 9.19 shows the conditional probability tables of the wet grass example.

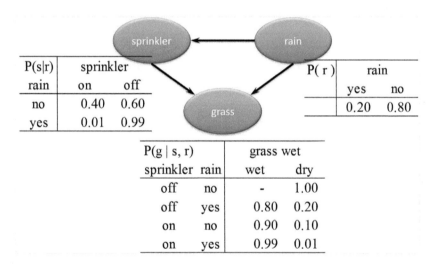

FIGURE 9.19 Bayesian network – wet grass example with conditional probabilities.

For instance, the likelihood that it has not rained is $P(r = yes) = 0.8$. There is a $P(s = on|r = no) = 0.4$ probability that it has not rained and that the sprinkler was on. This value was given to us in the CPT in Figure 9.19. If it rained, there is the slight chance $P(s = on|r = yes) = 0.01$ that the sprinkler was on. What was the likelihood of the sprinkler being on? Sprinkler on & no rain + sprinkler on & rain = $P(s = on|r) = P(s = on|r = yes)P(r = yes) + P(s = on|r = no)P(r = no) = .4 \times .8 + .01 \times .2 = .32 + .002 = .322$. Hence, the likelihood that the sprinkler was on is 32.2%. This is shown in Figure 9.20.

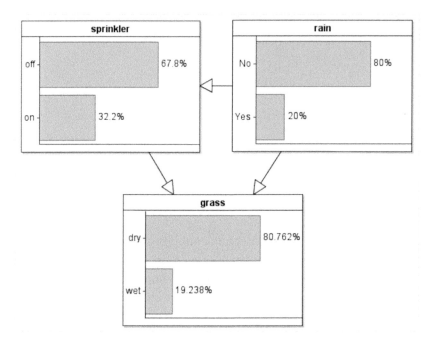

FIGURE 9.20 Bayesian network in Agena Risk – wet grass example showing effect probabilities.

Assume there is evidence that it rained: i.e. the rain probability changes to 100%. What is the probability of the sprinkler having been on? 1%. This can be read directly from the CPT or computed as before.

Now, more interesting, assume that we observed that the grass is wet. This is hard evidence: i.e. $P(g = wet \,|\, s, r) = 1$. What is the probability that it rained? 83.4%. The likelihood that the sprinkler was on is only 17.7%.

That means we can update the rain probabilities. If we know for sure the sprinkler was on, then the likelihood that it did not rain reduces to 99.3%. This example shows us that even in a simple scenario, we can get several insights.

Obviously, there are far more interesting applications of Bayesian networks. One of their main applications is in the health sector. They are also used in bioinformatics. Military decision making also makes use of these networks. Louvieris et al. (2010) as well as Garn and Louvieris (2015) give more details about this kind of applications.

Further applications

For instance, what is the likelihood of a military search operation succeeding? Assume soldiers are missing in Afghanistan. A search operation is initiated. Apache helicopters are scanning three areas. What are the chances of finding the missing soldiers? This is a typical probability application.

An example of a business application can be the choice of location that has the greatest chance to maximise success, such as a business specialising in bicycles that wants to decide on the best location for their stores to maximise profit.

In marketing, probability theory can be used to estimate the impact of an advertising campaign. For instance, a new e-book company has to decide on its marketing channels. The company explores the impact of web, radio and TV, which are subject to uncertainty. Taking the related costs into account, a decision has to be made.

Questions like these are the ones we attempt to quantify in order to help us in make a qualified decision.

The theory of Bayesian network comprises continuous (e.g. normal) distribution and discrete probabilities. It is concerned with parameter learning (probabilities, CPTs, distributions) and structure learning (graph: nodes and arcs).

Industry provides multiple professional tools such as Agena Risk, BayesiaLab, Hugin and many more – see Kevin Murphy's graphical model software list. In programming languages, Bayesian network libraries are available as well. For instance, in Matlab, Kevin Murphy's toolbox can be used. In R, the package bnlearn can be used.

We will introduce the subject in R using a survey about transportation usage. Five factors will be considered with regard to which mode of travel is used.

- Travel (T): The transportation mode preference for *car*, *train* or *other* usage;
- Occupation (O): The type of employment: employed (*emp*) or a self-employed (*self*);
- Residence (R): Size of the city (*small* or *big*) an individual lives in;
- Education (E): High school (*high*) or university degree (*uni*) completed;
- Age (A): *Young* if the person is below 30 years, *adult* for a person between 30 and 60 years and *old* for people above 60;
- Sex (S): The gender of a person – male (*M*) or female (*F*).

Defining the Network

We begin by defining the network.

```
p_load(bnlearn, Rgraphviz)
dag = model2network("[A][S][E|A:S][O|E][R|E][T|O:R] ")
fmt = list (nodes=nodes(dag), fill="orange",
            arcs = arcs(dag), col="black",lwd=3)
par(mar=c(1,1,1,1))
gh <- graphviz.plot(dag, layout = "dot", highlight=fmt)
```

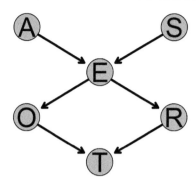

FIGURE 9.21 Defining a Bayesian belief network (BBN).

We can control the layout (e.g. left to right), nodes and edges of this graph.

```
gh <- layoutGraph(gh,
    attrs=list(graph=list(rankdir="LR")))
nodeRenderInfo(gh)$fill[]="orange";
    edgeRenderInfo(gh)$lwd[]=3
nodeRenderInfo(gh)$shape["T"]= "rectangle"
nodeRenderInfo(gh)$fill["E"]="lightblue"
par(mar=c(1,1,1,1))
renderGraph(gh)
```

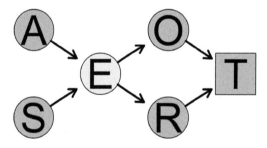

FIGURE 9.22 Alternative layout for Bayesian belief network (BBN).

The graphical structure suggest that education (E) depends on age (A) and sex (S). Next, we consider the network's arc (E, O), which consists of the education node E and the occupation node O. This suggests that O depends on E only. Similarly, the residence (R) depends merely on education. Finally, the travel mode depends on occupation and residence. We used the word *depend* in the context of conditional probability.

States and probabilities

We define the states and probabilities and display all conditional probability tables (CPTs).

```
A.lv <- c("young", "adult", "old"); S.lv <- c("M", "F")
E.lv <- c("high", "uni")
O.lv <- c("emp", "self"); R.lv <- c("small", "big")
T.lv <- c("car", "train", "other")

A.prob <- array(c(0.3,0.5,0.2),
  dim=3, dimnames=list(A =  A.lv))
S.prob <- array(c(0.6,0.4),
  dim=2, dimnames=list(S = S.lv))
E.prob <- array(c(0.75,0.25,0.72,0.28,0.88,0.12,
                  0.64,0.36,0.70,0.30,0.90,0.10),
  dim=c(2,3,2), dimnames = list(E = E.lv, A = A.lv, S =S.lv))
O.prob <- array(c(0.96,0.04,0.92,0.08), dim = c(2,2),
                  dimnames = list(O = O.lv, E = E.lv))
R.prob <- array(c(0.25,0.75,0.2,0.8), dim = c(2,2),
                  dimnames = list(R = R.lv, E = E.lv))
T.prob <- array(c(0.48,0.42,0.10,0.56,0.36,0.08,
                  0.58,0.24,0.18,0.70,0.21,0.09),
  dim=c(3,2,2), dimnames = list(T = T.lv, O = O.lv, R =R.lv))
cpt <- list(A = A.prob, S = S.prob, E = E.prob,
            O = O.prob, R = R.prob, T = T.prob)
cpt$E
##, , S = M
##
##       A
## E    young adult    old
## high 0.75   0.72   0.88
## uni  0.25   0.28   0.12
##
##, , S = F
##
##       A
## E    young adult old
## high 0.64    0.7 0.9
## uni  0.36    0.3 0.1
```

Applying the BBN

Let us say we would like to know which mode of transportation is used by a young female with a university education who is self-employed and lives in a big city.

```
bbn = custom.fit(dag, cpt)
newdata = data.frame(A = factor("young",levels = A.lv),
S = factor("F",levels = S.lv),E = factor("uni",levels =
    E.lv),
O = factor("self",levels =
    O.lv),R=factor("big",levels=R.lv))
predict(bbn, node = "T", data = newdata)
## [1] car
## Levels: car train other
```

First, we need to link the network structure with the probabilities using the custom. fit function. Then the evidence is used. The BBN predicts that the individual will use a car as transportation mode.

Now let us assume there is evidence the educational background is high school and look at some corresponding probabilities $P(S = M, T = car|E = high)$, $P(S = F, T = car|E = high)$, and $P(A = adult, T = car|E = high)$.

```
set.seed(7);
a=cpquery(bbn,event=(S=="M") & (T=="car"), evidence= (E=="high"))
b=cpquery(bbn,event=(S=="F") & (T=="car"), evidence=(E=="high"))
c=cpquery(bbn,event=(A=="adult") & (T=="car"),evidence=(E=="high"))
d=cpquery(bbn,event = (T == "car"),evidence =
(A=="young") & (S=="F") & (E=="uni") & (O=="self") & (R=="big"))
cat(sprintf("a=%.3f, b=%.3f, c=%.3f,d=%.3f",a,b,c,d))
## a=0.354, b=0.213, c=0.267, d=0.778
```

The first three probabilities indicate that the event of using a car with being male, female or an adult is low, given the evidence of a high school degree. The last probability $P(T = car|A = young, S = F, E = uni, O = sel f, R = big) = .632$ indicates a likely use of a car given the evidence.

An interactive environment can be found using the library `BayesianNetwork` and the function `BayesianNetwork()`.

Further reading: The transportation survey example can also be found on the bnlearn. com website and in Ness (2019). Scutari (2010) is the paper introducing the bnlearn package. The Rgraphviz package is due to Hansen et al. (2022). The website ("bnlearn – Bayesian network structure learning" 2023) provides more details about the bnlearn package, Bayesian networks and related literature. Ness's (2019) lecture notes give a tutorial on Bayesian networks with many details. Nielsen and Jensen (2013) is an easy-to-read introduction to Bayesian networks.

9.6 Summary

A comprehensive introduction to artificial intelligence was provided. It identified the important areas and related techniques. Awareness of the amount of daily exposure to AI was triggered. The fundamentals of artificial neural networks (ANNs) were introduced. Several examples of ANNs were given. Support vector machines (SVMs) were established with great care for classification challenges. This included definitions of support vectors and kernels.

We proceeded by showing its applicability for regression problems. The AI domain of problem solving using genetic algorithms was entered. This allowed the formulation of a mathematical program and solving it with a meta heuristic, thereby exposing the inner workings of the genetic algorithm. An overview of problem-solving methods was provided.

We discussed chess in the context of AI in the area of games. Here, we showed how to use existing R libraries to utilise the strongest chess engine (Stockfish). Further, the minimax algorithm was presented to create a rudimentary chess engine, thereby establishing the benefits of recursive programming.

Finally, the AI domain of reasoning under uncertainty was initiated via Bayesian belief networks.

Annotated Bibliography

We have been generous with further reading advice throughout the chapter. Here, we will just select a few key texts.

A comprehensive and classic book about artificial intelligence:

1. Russell, S. and Norvig, P. (2020). *Artificial Intelligence: A Modern Approach (Pearson Series in Artificial Intelligence)*. London: Pearson.

An easy-to-read introduction to Bayesian belief networks:

2. Nielsen, T. D. and Jensen, F. V. (2013). *Bayesian Networks and Decision Graphs. Information Science and Statistics*. New York: Springer.

Provides a useful chapter about support vector machines, amongst others:

3. James, G. et al. (2023). *An Introduction to Statistical Learning.* Vol. 112 (2nd ed.). Springer.

One of the better ANN introductions can be found in:

4. Brunton, S. L. and Nathan Kutz, J. (2022). *Data-Driven Science and Engineering: Machine Learning, Dynamical Systems, and Control* (2nd ed.). Cambridge, England: Cambridge University Press.

Resources

- An excellent chart of neural networks by Fjodor van Veen and Stefan Leijnen: asimovinstitute.org/neural-network-zoo.
- Learn by marketing, learnbymarketing.com/tutorials/neural-networks-in-r-tutorial, offers another neural network R tutorial.
- A discussion about hidden layers/neurons to use in ANN can be found at: towardsdatascience.com/beginners-ask-how-many-hidden-layers-neurons-to-use-in-artificial-neural-networks-51466afa0d3e.
- Daily life AI examples: beebom.com/examples-of-artificial-intelligence.

The final part lists references to books and articles. It contains an index of essential terms.

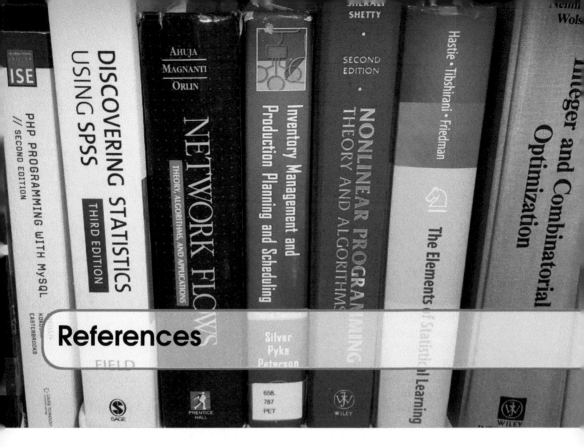

References

Adam, F. and Pomerol, J.-C. (2008). Developing practical decision support tools using dashboards of information. In: *Handbook on Decision Support Systems 2: Variations*. Ed. by Burstein, F. and Holsapple, C. W. Berlin, Germany: Springer, pp. 175–193.

arXiv (2020). Deep learning machine teaches itself chess in 72 hours, plays at international master level. *MIT Technology Review*.

Baheti, P. Activation Functions in Neural Networks [12 Types & Use Cases] (Accessed 30 January 2024).

Beaulieu, A. (2020). *Learning SQL: Generate, Manipulate, and Retrieve Data* (3rd ed.). Farnham: O'Reilly. https://www.amazon.co.uk/Learning-SQL-Generate-Manipulate-Retrieve/dp/1492057614.

Brauer, C. (2020). *A-Very-Short-Introduction-to-R*. [Online]. https://github.com/ClaudiaBrauer/A-very-short-introduction-to-R (Accessed 23 October 2020).

Brunton, S. L. and Nathan Kutz, J. (2022). *Data-Driven Science and Engineering: Machine Learning, Dynamical Systems, and Control*. Cambridge University Press.

Burkov, A. (2019). *The Hundred-Page Machine Learning Book*. Vol. 1. Quebec City, Canada: Andriy Burkov.

Chapman, P. et al. (2000). *CRISP-DM 1.0: Step-by-Step Data Mining Guide*. SPSS Inc., pp. 1–73.

Chawla, N. V. et al. (2002). SMOTE: Synthetic minority over-sampling technique. *Journal of Artificial Intelligence Research* 16, 321–357.

Codd, E. F. (1970). A relational model of data for large shared data banks. *Communications of the ACM* 13 (6), 377–387.

Cortes, C. and Vapnik, V. (1995). Support-vector networks. *Machine Learning* 20, 273–297.

263

Data Analytics Tutorial for Beginners – From Beginner to Pro in 10 Mins *DataFlair* (2019). [Online]. https://data-flair.training/blogs/data-analytics-tutorial (Accessed 20 October 2020).

Data protection and your business. https://www.gov.uk/data-protection-your-business (Accessed 30 January 2024).

DB-Engines Ranking (2023). [Online]. https://db-engines.com/en/ranking (Accessed 17 June 2023).

De Boer, M. (2023). *Install an On-Premises Data Gateway.* [Online]. https://learn.microsoft.com/en-us/data-integration/gateway/service-gateway-install (Accessed 15 December 2023).

Debarros, A. (2022). *Practical SQL A Beginner's Guide to Storytelling with Data* (2nd ed.). San Francisco, CA: No Starch Press.

Debuse, J. C. W. et al. (1999). A methodology for knowledge discovery: A KDD roadmap. In: *SYS Technical Report (SYS-C99-01)*. School of Computing Sciences, University of East Anglia.

Debuse, J. C. W. et al. (2001). Building the KDD roadmap: A methodology for knowledge discovery. In: *Industrial Knowledge Management: A Micro-level Approach*. New York: Springer, pp. 179–196.

Deckler, G. and Powell, B. (2021). *Microsoft Power BI Cookbook* (2nd ed.). Birmingham, England: Packt Publishing.

Deckler, G. and Powell, B. (2022). *Mastering Microsoft Power BI* (2nd ed.). Birmingham, England: Packt Publishing.

Diebold, F. X. (2007). *Elements of Forecasting* (4th ed.). Mason, OH: Thomson South-Western.

Du, H. (2010) *Data Mining Techniques and Applications: An Introduction*. Andover, England: Cengage Learning.

Fayyad, U. et al. (1996). The KDD process for extracting useful knowledge from volumes of data. *Communications of the ACM* 39 (11), 27–34.

Field, A. P. (2021). *Discovering Statistics Using R and Rstudio* (2nd ed.). London: SAGE.

Fisher, R. A. (1936). The use of multiple measurements in taxonomic problems. *Annals of Eugenics* 7 (2), 179–188.

Garn, W. (2018). *Introduction to Management Science: Modelling, Optimisation and Probability*. London, UK: Smartana Ltd.

Garn, W. (2021). *Chess by Wolfgang Garn.* [Online]. https://www.youtube.com/watch?v=KJ_RMxSvlx8 (Accessed 12 December 2023).

Garn, W. (2023). *Chess with "Greedy Edi".* [Online]. https://uk.mathworks.com/matlabcentral/fileexchange/25775-chess-with-greedy-edi (Accessed 12 December 2023).

Garn, W. and Aitken, J. (2015). Splitting Hybrid Make-to-Order and Make-to-Stock Demand Profiles. arXiv: 1504.03594 [stat.ME].

Garn, W. and Louvieris, P. (2015). Conditional Probability Generation Methods for High Reliability Effects-Based Decision Making. arXiv: 1512.08553 [cs.AI].

Gersho, A. and Gray, R. M. (1992). *Vector Quantization and Signal Compression*. Vol. 159. New York, NY: Springer Science & Business Media.

Hansen, K. D. et al. (2022). Rgraphviz: Provides Plotting Capabilities for R Graph Objects. R package version 2.42.0.

Hastie, T. et al. (2009). *The Elements of Statistical Learning: Data Mining, Inference, and Prediction*. 2nd ed. New York: Springer.

Heaven, W. D. (2021). DeepMind's AI predicts almost exactly when and where it's going to rain. *MIT Technology Review*.

Heitzinger, C. (2022). *Algorithms with JULIA: Optimization, Machine Learning, and Differential Equations Using the JULIA Language*. Cham, Switzerland: Springer Nature.

Jain, R. (1991). *The Art of Computer Systems Performance Analysis: Techniques for Experimental Design, Measurement, Simulation, and Modeling*. Hoboken, NJ: Wiley.

James, G. et al. (2023). *An Introduction to Statistical Learning* (2nd ed.). New York: Springer.

Jank, W. (2011). *Business Analytics for Managers*. New York: Springer.

Jones, M. T. (2008). *Artificial Intelligence: A Systems Approach*. Hingham, MA: Infinity Science Press.

Kaufman, L. and Rousseeuw, P. J. (2009). *Finding Groups in Data: An Introduction to Cluster Analysis*. Hoboken, NJ: John Wiley & Sons.

Kaur, J. (2022). *Cognitive Analytics Tools and Its Applications | A Quick Guide*. [Online]. www.xenonstack.com/insights/what-is-cognitive-analytics

Klopfenstein, D. (2023). *Power Query M Formula Language*. [Online]. https://learn.microsoft.com/en-us/powerquery-m (Accessed 13 December 2023).

Knaflic, C. N. (2015). *Storytelling with Data: A Data Visualization Guide for Business Professionals*. Hoboken, NJ: John Wiley & Sons.

Knight, D. et al. (2022). *Microsoft Power BI Quick Start Guide*. Birmingham, England: Packt Publishing.

Kohonen, T. (1990). The self-organizing map. *Proceedings of the IEEE* 78 (9), 1464–1480.

Kohonen, T. (2012). *Self-Organizing Maps* (3rd ed.). Heidelberg, Germany: Springer.

Lai, M. (2015). Giraffe: Using Deep Reinforcement Learning to Play Chess. arXiv: 1509.01549 [cs.AI].

Louvieris, P. et al. (2010). Assessing critical success factors for military decision support. *Expert Systems with Applications* 37 (12), 8229–8241.

Macnaughton-Smith, P. N. M. (1965). *Some Statistical and Other Numerical Techniques for Classifying Individuals*. London, Great Britain.

Martínez-Plumed, F. et al. (2019). CRISP-DM twenty years later: From data mining processes to data science trajectories. *IEEE Transactions on Knowledge and Data Engineering* 33 (8), 3048–3061.

Minewiskan (2023a). *Data Analysis Expressions (DAX)*. [Online]. https://learn.microsoft.com/en-us/dax (Accessed 13 December 2023).

Minewiskan (2023b). *DAX Text Functions*. [Online]. https://learn.microsoft.com/en-us/dax/text-functions-dax (Accessed 13 December 2023).

Mixson, E. (2021). 5 Things to know about data curation. *AI, Data & Analytics Network*. www.aidataanalytics.network/data-science-ai/articles/5-things-to-know-about-data-curation.

ML.NET (2023). *Power BI Uses Key Influencers Using ML.NET | . NET*. [Online]. https://dotnet.microsoft.com/en-us/platform/customers/power-bi (Accessed 13 December 2023).

Ness, R. (2019). *Lecture Notes for Causality in Machine Learning*. Boston, MA: Northeastern University Khoury College. https://bookdown.org/robertness/causalml/docs.

Ness, R. (2024). *Causal AI*. New York, NY: Manning Publications.

Nielsen, T. D. and Jensen, F. V. (2013). *Bayesian Networks and Decision Graphs. Information Science and Statistics*. New York: Springer. https://books.google.co.uk/books?id=cWLaBwAAQBAJ.

Nivard, M. (2023). GPTStudio. [Online] https://github.com/MichelNivard/GPTstudio (Accessed 26 February 2024).

Provost, F. and Fawcett, T. (2013). *Data Science for Business: What You Need to Know About Data Mining and Data-Analytic Thinking*. CA: O'Reilly Media.

Ross, S. M. (2020). *Introduction to probability and statistics for engineers and scientists*. 6th ed. Oxford, England: Academic press.

Russell, S. and Norvig, P. (2020). *Artificial Intelligence: A Modern Approach (Pearson Series in Artificial Intelligence)*. London, England: Pearson. www.amazon.com/Artificial-Intelligence-A-Modern-Approach/dp/0134610997.

Scutari, M. (2010). Learning Bayesian networks with the bnlearn R package. *Journal of Statistical Software* 35 (3), 1–22. doi: 10.18637/jss.v035.i03.

Shah, C. (2020). *A Hands-on Introduction to Data Science*. Cambridge, England: Cambridge University Press.

Shalev-Shwartz, S. and Zhang, T. (2013). Stochastic dual coordinate ascent methods for regularized loss minimization. *Journal of Machine Learning Research* 14 (1).

Shields, W. (2019). *SQL QuickStart Guide: The Simplified Beginner's Guide to Managing, Analyzing, and Manipulating Data With SQL*. ClydeBank Media LLC. https://www.amazon.co.uk/SQL-QuickStart-Guide-Simplified-Manipulating/dp/1945051752.

SQL Tutorial (2023). [Online] https://www.w3schools.com/sql/default.asp (Accessed 16 June 2023).

SuperAnnotate (2021). *Data Curation: Your ML Success Formula*. [Online]. www.superannotate.com/blog/data-curation-in-machine-learning (Accessed 22 June 2023).

Vapnik, V. (2000). *The Nature of Statistical Learning Theory* (2nd ed.). New York, NY: Springer Science + Business Media.

Watt, J. et al. (2020). *Machine Learning Refined: Foundations, Algorithms, and Applications*. Cambridge University Press.

Wehrens, R. and Buydens, L. M. C. (2007). Self-and super-organizing maps in R: The Kohonen package. *Journal of Statistical Software* 21 (5), 1–19. doi: 10.18637/jss.v021.i05.

Wikipedia (2023a). *Golden Ratio*. [Online]. https://en.wikipedia.org/wiki/Golden_ratio (Accessed 13 December 2023).

Wikipedia (2023b). *Self-Organizing Map*. [Online]. https://en.wikipedia.org/wiki/Self-organizing_map (Accessed 6 March 2023).

Wilmott, P. (2020). *Machine Learning: An Applied Mathematics Introduction*. Stone, England: Panda Ohana Publishing.

Wu, X. et al. (2008). Top 10 algorithms in data mining. *Knowledge and Information Systems* 14, 1–37.

Index

For Product Safety Concerns and Information please contact our EU representative GPSR@taylorandfrancis.com Taylor & Francis Verlag GmbH, Kaufingerstraße 24, 80331 München, Germany

T - #0189 - 230425 - C282 - 246/174/13 - PB - 9781032372624 - Matt Lamination